McGraw Hill Education create™

Course   Accounting Ethics

Professor   Dave Scott

Krannert School of Management
Purdue University

 create™

http://create.mheducation.com

ISBN-10: 1307191142   ISBN-13: 9781307191141

Contents

Credits

Chapter

1

Ethical Reasoning: Implications for Accounting

Learning Objectives

After studying Chapter 1, you should be able to:

LO 1-1   Explain how integrity enables a CPA to withstand pressures and avoid subordination of judgment.

LO 1-2   Discuss the relationship between one's values and ethics, and legal obligations.

LO 1-3   Describe how the pillars of character support ethical decision making.

LO 1-4   Differentiate between moral philosophies and their effect on ethical reasoning in accounting.

LO 1-5   Explain the concept of the public interest in accounting.

LO 1-6   Discuss the Principles section of the AICPA Code of Professional Conduct.

LO 1-7   Apply the IMA Statement of Ethical and Professional Practice to a case study.

Ethics Reflection

Penn State Child Abuse Scandal: A Culture of Indifference

What motivates an otherwise ethical person to do the wrong thing when faced with an ethical dilemma? Why does a good person act wrongly in a particular situation? These are the ethical questions that arise from the Penn State scandal. Football head coach Joe Paterno and administrators at Penn State University looked the other way and failed to act on irrefutable evidence that former assistant coach Jerry Sandusky had molested young boys, an offense for which Sandusky currently is serving a 30- to 60-year sentence. According to the independent report by Louis Freeh that investigated the sexual abuse, the top administrators at Penn State and Joe Paterno sheltered a child predator harming children for over a decade by concealing Sandusky's activities from the board of trustees, the university community, and authorities. They exposed the first abused child to additional harm by alerting Sandusky, who was the only one who knew the child's identity, of what assistant coach Mike McQueary saw in the shower on the night of February 9, 2001.[1] McQueary testified at the June 2012 trial of Sandusky that he observed the abuse[2] and informed Paterno, who reported the incident to his superiors but did not confront Sandusky or report the incident to the board of trustees or the police.[3]

Reasons for Unethical Actions

The report gives the following explanations for the failure of university leaders to take action:

- The desire to avoid the bad publicity
- The failure of the university's board of trustees to have reporting mechanisms in place to ensure disclosure of major risks
- A president who discouraged discussion and dissent
- A lack of awareness of the Clery Act, which requires colleges and universities participating in federal financial aid programs to keep and disclose information about crimes committed on and near their campuses
- A lack of whistleblower policies and protections
- A culture of reverence for the football program that was ingrained at all levels of the campus community

Explanations for Unethical Actions

Former Penn State president Graham Spanier, who was fired by the board of trustees in November 2011, is quoted as discussing in an interview with Jeffrey Toobin of the *New Yorker* about how the university worked that "honesty, integrity, and always doing what was in the *best interests of the university* [italics added] was how everyone agreed to operate and . . . we've always operated as a family. Our personal and social and professional lives were all very intertwined."[4]

A culture that fosters organizational interests to the exclusion of others explains what happened at Penn State, and it happens in other organizations as well, such as Enron and WorldCom. The culture of an organization should be built on ethical values such as honesty, integrity, responsibility, and accountability. While Penn State may have claimed to follow such principles, the reality was that its actions did not match these behavioral norms.

Postscript

The Penn State case just does not seem to go away. Here is a list of actions subsequent to the initial case:

- As of the summer 2015, at least seven civil cases as well as criminal complaints against three former Penn State administrators have been pending.
- In January 2015, the National Collegiate Athletic Association (NCAA) agreed to restore 111 of former head coach Joe Paterno's wins between 1998–2011, making Paterno once again the winningest coach in major college football.
- The Paterno family brought a lawsuit to contest the consent decree's statement that the head coach covered for Sandusky to protect the school's football program.
- The statue of Paterno that was tore down will be replaced by a projected $300,000 life-sized bronze sculpture downtown, about two miles from the original site, after Pennsylvanians overwhelmingly voted to support the school putting the statue out again by a margin of 59 to 25.

Ethical Blind Spots

Leaders of organizations who may be successful at what they do and see themselves as ethical and moral still cultivate a collection of what Max Bazerman and Ann Trebrunsel call *blind spots*.[5] Blind spots are the gaps between who you want to be and the person you actually are. In other words, most of us want to do the right thing—to act ethically—but internal and external pressures get in the way.

As you read this chapter, think about the following questions: (1) What would you have done if you had been in Joe Paterno's position, and why? (2) Which ethical reasoning methods can help me to make ethical decisions in accounting? (3) What are my ethical obligations to the public?

Have the courage to say no. Have the courage to face the truth. Do the right thing because it is right. These are the magic keys to living your life with integrity.

W. Clement Stone (1902–2002)

This quote by William Clement Stone, a businessman, philanthropist, and self-help book author, underscores the importance of integrity in decision making. Notice that the quote addresses integrity in one's personal life. That is because one has to act with integrity when making personal decisions in order to be best equipped to act with integrity on a professional level. Integrity, indeed all of ethics, is not a spigot that can be turned on or off depending on one's whims or whether the matter at hand is personal or professional. As the ancient Greeks knew, we learn how to be ethical by practicing and exercising those virtues that enable us to lead a life of excellence.

Joe Paterno and other university leaders did not act with integrity. They let external considerations of reputation and image dictate their internal actions. Ironically, the very factor—reputation—that they guarded so closely was the first to be brought down by the disclosure of a cover-up in the sex scandal case.

In accounting, internal accountants and auditors may be pressured by superiors to manipulate financial results. The external auditors may have to deal with pressures imposed on them by clients to put the best face on the financial statements regardless of whether they conform to generally accepted accounting principles (GAAP). It is the ethical value of integrity that provides the moral courage to resist the temptation to stand by silently while a company misstates its financial statement amounts.

Integrity: The Basis of Accounting

LO 1-1
Explain how integrity enables a CPA to withstand pressures and avoid subordination of judgment.

According to Mintz (1995), "Integrity is a fundamental trait of character that enables a CPA to withstand client and competitive pressures that might otherwise lead to the subordination of judgment."[6] A person of integrity will act out of moral principle and not expediency. That person will do what is right, even if it means the loss of a job or client. In accounting, the public interest (i.e., investors and creditors) always must be placed ahead of one's own self-interest or the interests of others, including a supervisor or client.

Integrity means that a person acts on principle—a conviction that there is a right way to act when faced with an ethical dilemma. For example, assume that your tax client fails to inform you about an amount of earned income for the year, and you confront the client on this issue. The client tells you not to record it and reminds you that there is no W-2 or 1099 form to document the earnings. The client adds that you will not get to audit the company's financial statements anymore if you do not adhere to the client's wishes. Would you decide to "go along to get along"? If you are a person of integrity, you should not allow the client to dictate how the tax rules will be applied in the client's situation. You are the professional and know the tax regulations best, and you have an ethical obligation to report taxes in accordance with the law. If you go along with the client and the Internal Revenue Service (IRS) investigates and sanctions you for failing to follow the IRS Tax Code, then you may suffer irreparable harm to your reputation. An important point is that a professional must never let loyalty to a client cloud good judgment and ethical decision making.

Worldcom: Cynthia Cooper: Hero and Role Model

Cynthia Cooper's experience at WorldCom illustrates how the internal audit function should work and how a person of integrity can put a stop to financial fraud. It all unraveled in April and May 2002 when Gene Morse, an auditor at WorldCom, couldn't find any documentation to support a claim of $500 million in computer expenses. Morse approached Cooper, the company's director of internal auditing and Morse's boss, who instructed Morse to "keep going." A series of obscure tips led Morse and Cooper to suspect that WorldCom was cooking the books. Cooper formed an investigation team to determine whether their hunch was right.

In its initial investigation, the team discovered $3.8 billion of misallocated expenses and phony accounting entries.[7] Cooper approached the chief financial officer (CFO), Scott Sullivan, but was dissatisfied with his explanations. The chief executive officer (CEO) of the company, Bernie Ebbers, had already resigned under pressure from WorldCom's board of directors, so Cooper went to the audit committee. The committee interviewed Sullivan about the accounting issues and did not get a satisfactory answer. Still, the committee was reluctant to take any action. Cooper persisted anyway. Eventually, one member of the audit committee told her to approach the outside auditors to get their take on the matter. Cooper gathered additional evidence of fraud, and ultimately KPMG, the firm that had replaced Arthur Andersen—the auditors during the fraud—supported Cooper. Sullivan was asked to resign, refused to do so, and was fired.[8]

One tragic result of the fraud and cover-up at WorldCom is the case of Betty Vinson. It is not unusual for someone who is genuinely a good person to get caught up in fraud. Vinson, a former WorldCom mid-level accounting manager, went along with the fraud because her superiors told her to do so. She was convinced that it would be a one-time action. It rarely works that way, however, because once a company starts to engage in accounting fraud, it feels compelled to continue the charade into the future to keep up the appearance that each period's results are as good as or better than prior periods. The key to maintaining one's integrity and ethical perspective is not to take the first step down the proverbial *ethical slippery slope.*

Vinson pleaded guilty in October 2002 to participating in the financial fraud at the company. She was sentenced to five months in prison and five months of house arrest. Vinson represents the typical "pawn" in a financial fraud: an accountant who had no interest or desire to commit fraud but got caught up in it when Sullivan, her boss, instructed her to make improper accounting entries. The rationalization by Sullivan that the company had to "make the numbers appear better than they really were" did nothing to ease her guilty conscience. Judge Barbara Jones, who sentenced Vinson, commented that "Ms. Vinson was among the least culpable members of the conspiracy at WorldCom. . . . Still, had Vinson refused to do what she was asked, it's possible this conspiracy might have been nipped in the bud."[9]

Accounting students should reflect on what they would do if they faced a situation similar to the one that led Vinson to do something that was out of character. Once she agreed to go along with making improper entries, it was difficult to turn back. The company could have threatened to disclose her role in the original fraud and cover-up if Vinson then acted on her beliefs. From an ethical (and practical) perspective it is much better to just do the right thing from the very beginning, so that you can't be blackmailed or intimidated later.

Vinson became involved in the fraud because she had feared losing her job, her benefits, and the means to provide for her family. She must live with the consequences of her actions for the rest of her life. On the other hand, Cynthia Cooper, on her own initiative, ordered the internal investigation that led to the discovery of the $11 billion fraud at WorldCom. Cooper did all the right things to bring the fraud out in the open. Cooper received the Accounting Exemplar Award in 2004 given by the American Accounting Association and was inducted into the American Institute of Certified Public Accountants (AICPA) Hall of Fame in 2005.

Cooper truly is a positive role model. She discusses the foundation of her ethics that she developed as a youngster because of her mother's influence in her book *Extraordinary Circumstances: The Journey of a Corporate Whistleblower.* Cooper says: "Fight the good fight. Don't ever allow yourself to be intimidated. . . . Think about the consequences of your actions. I've seen too many people ruin their lives."[10]

Religious and Philosophical Foundations of Ethics

Virtually all the world's great religions contain in their religious texts some version of the Golden Rule: "Do unto others as you would wish them to do unto you." In other words, we should treat others the way we would want to be treated. This is the basic ethic that guides all religions. If we believe honesty is important, then we should be honest with others and expect the same in return. One result of this ethic is the concept that every person shares certain inherent human rights, which will be discussed later in this chapter. Exhibit 1.1 provides some examples of the universality of the Golden Rule in world religions provided by the character education organization Teaching Values.[11]

EXHIBIT 1.1   The Universality of the Golden Rule in the World Religions

Religion	Expression of the Golden Rule	Citation
Christianity	All things whatsoever ye would that men should do to you, Do ye so to them; for this is the law and the prophets.	Matthew 7:1
Confucianism	Do not do to others what you would not like yourself. Then there will be no resentment against you, either in the family or in the state.	Analects 12:2
Buddhism	Hurt not others in ways that you yourself would find hurtful.	Uda–navarga 5,1
Hinduism	This is the sum of duty, do naught onto others what you would not have them do unto you.	Mahabharata 5, 1517
Islam	No one of you is a believer until he desires for his brother that which he desires for himself.	Sunnah
Judaism	What is hateful to you, do not do to your fellowman. This is the entire Law; all the rest is commentary.	Talmud, Shabbat 3id
Taoism	Regard your neighbor's gain as your gain, and your neighbor's loss as your own loss.	Tai Shang Kan Yin P'ien
Zoroastrianism	That nature alone is good which refrains from doing to another whatsoever is not good for itself.	Dadisten-I-dinik, 94, 5

Integrity is the key to carrying out the Golden Rule. A person of integrity acts with truthfulness, courage, sincerity, and honesty. Integrity means to have the courage to stand by your principles even in the face of pressure to bow to the demands of others. As previously mentioned, integrity has particular importance for certified public accountants (CPAs), who often are pressured by their employers and clients to give in to their demands. The ethical responsibility of a CPA in these instances is to adhere to the ethics of the accounting profession and not to subordinate professional judgment to the judgment of others. Integrity encompasses the whole of the person, and it is the foundational virtue of the ancient Greek philosophy of virtue.

The origins of Western philosophy trace back to the ancient Greeks, including Socrates, Plato, and Aristotle. The ancient Greek philosophy of virtue deals with questions such as: What is the best sort of life for human beings to live? Greek thinkers saw the attainment of a good life as the *telos,* the end or goal of human existence. For most Greek philosophers, the end is *eudaimonia,* which is usually translated as "happiness." However, the Greeks thought that the end goal of happiness meant much more than just experiencing pleasure or satisfaction. The ultimate goal of happiness was to attain some objectively good status, the life of excellence. The Greek word for excellence is *arete,* the customary translation of which is "virtue." Thus for the Greeks, "excellences" or "virtues" were the qualities that made a life admirable or excellent. They did not restrict their thinking to characteristics we regard as moral virtues, such as courage, justice, and temperance, but included others we think of as nonmoral, such as wisdom.[12]

Modern philosophies have been posited as ways to living an ethical life. Unlike virtue theory that relies on both the characteristics of a decision and the person making that decision, these philosophies rely more on methods of ethical reasoning, and they, too, can be used to facilitate ethical decision making. We review these philosophies later in the chapter.

What Is Ethics?

> ## LO 1-2
> Discuss the relationship between one's values and ethics, and legal obligations.

The term *ethics* is derived from the Greek word *ethikos,* which itself is derived from the Greek word *ethos,* meaning "custom" or "character." Morals are from the Latin word *moralis,* meaning "customs," with the Latin word *mores* being defined as "manners, morals, character."

In philosophy, ethical behavior is that which is "good." The Western tradition of ethics is sometimes called "moral philosophy." The field of ethics or moral philosophy involves developing, defending, and recommending concepts of right and wrong behavior. These concepts do not change as one's desires and motivations change. They are not relative to the situation. They are immutable.

In a general sense, ethics (or moral philosophy) addresses fundamental questions such as: How should I live my life? That question leads to others, such as: What sort of person should I strive to be? What values are important? What standards or principles should I live by?[13] There are various ways to define the concept of ethics. The simplest may be to say that ethics deals with "right" and "wrong." However, it is difficult to judge what may be right or wrong in a particular situation without some frame of reference.

In addition, the ethical standards for a profession, such as accounting, are heavily influenced by the practices of those in the profession, state laws and board of accountancy rules, and the expectations of society. Gaa and Thorne define ethics as "the field of inquiry that concerns the actions of people in situations where these actions have effects on the welfare of both oneself and others."[14] We adopt that definition and emphasize that it relies on ethical reasoning to evaluate the effects of actions on others—*the stakeholders.*

Difference between Ethics and Morals

Ethics and morals relate to "right" and "wrong" conduct. While they are sometimes used interchangeably, they are different: ethics refer to rules provided by an external source, such as codes of conduct for a group of professionals (i.e., CPAs), or for those in a particular organization. Morals refer to an individual's own principles regarding right and wrong and may be influenced by a religion or societal mores. Ethics tend to be more practical than morals, conceived as shared principles promoting fairness in social and business interactions. For example, a CEO involved in a sex scandal may involve a moral lapse, while a CEO misappropriating money from a company she is supposed to lead according to prescribed standards of behavior is an ethical problem. These terms are close and often used interchangeably, and both influence ethical decision making. In this text we oftentimes use the terms synonymously while acknowledging differences do exist.

Another important distinction can be thought of this way: When we form a moral judgment, we are employing moral standards—principles against which we compare what we see in order to form a conclusion. Such judgments might be about particular conduct, which includes a person's actions, or it might be about a person's character, which includes their attitudes and beliefs. Ethics, on the other hand, involve the study and application of those standards and judgments which people create or are established by organizations. So, we could say that ethics are the operational side of morality.

Norms, Values, and the Law

Ethics deal with well-based standards of how people *ought* to act, does *not* describe the way people *actually* act, and is prescriptive, not descriptive. Ethical people always strive to make the right decision in all circumstances. They do not rationalize their actions based on their own perceived self-interests. Ethical decision making entails following certain well-established norms of behavior. The best way to understand ethics may be to differentiate it from other concepts.

Values and Ethics

Values are basic and fundamental beliefs that guide or motivate attitudes or actions. In accounting, the values of the profession are embedded in its codes of ethics that guide the actions of accountants and auditors in meeting their professional responsibilities.

Values are concerned with how a person behaves in certain situations and is predicated on personal beliefs that may or may not be ethical, whereas ethics is concerned with how a moral person should behave to act in an ethical manner. A person who values prestige, power, and wealth is likely to act out of self-interest, whereas a person who values honesty, integrity, and trust will typically act in the best interests of others. It does not follow, however, that acting in the best interests of others always precludes acting in one's own self-interest. Indeed, the Golden Rule prescribes that we should treat others the way we want to be treated.

The Golden Rule requires that we try to understand how our actions affect others; thus, we need to put ourselves in the place of the person on the receiving end of the action. The Golden Rule is best seen as a consistency principle, in that we should not act one way toward others but have a desire to be treated differently in a similar situation. In other words, it would be wrong to think that separate standards of behavior exist to guide our personal lives but that a different standard (a lower one) exists in business.

Laws versus Ethics

Being ethical is not the same as following the law. Although ethical people always try to be law-abiding, there may be instances where their sense of ethics tells them it is best not to follow the law. These situations are rare and should be based on sound ethical reasons.

> Assume that you are driving at a speed of 45 miles per hour (mph) on a two-lane divided roadway (double yellow line) going east. All of a sudden, you see a young boy jump into the road to retrieve a ball. The boy is close enough to your vehicle so that you know you cannot continue straight down the roadway and stop in time to avoid hitting him. You quickly look to your right and notice about 10 other children off the road. You cannot avoid hitting 1 or more of them if you swerve to the right to avoid hitting the boy in the middle of the road. You glance to the left on the opposite side of the road and notice no traffic going west or any children off the road. What should you do?
>
> #### Ethical Perspective
>
> If you cross the double yellow line that divides the roadway, you have violated the motor vehicle laws. We are told never to cross a double yellow line and travel into oncoming traffic. But the ethical action would be to do just that, given that you have determined it appears to be safe. It is better to risk getting a ticket than hit the boy in the middle of your side of the road or those children off to the side of the road.

Laws and Ethical Obligations

Benjamin Disraeli (1804–1881), the noted English novelist, debater, and former prime minister, said, "When men are pure, laws are useless; when men are corrupt, laws are broken." A person of goodwill honors and respects the rules and laws and is willing to go beyond them when circumstances warrant. As indicated by the previous quote, such people do not need rules and laws to guide their actions. They always try to do the right thing. On the other hand, the existence of specific laws prohibiting certain behaviors will not stop a person who is unethical (e.g., does not care about others) from violating those laws. Just think about a Ponzi scheme such as the one engaged in by Bernie Madoff, whereby he duped others to invest with him by promising huge returns that, unbeknownst to each individual investor, would come from additional investments of scammed investors and not true returns.

Laws create a minimum set of standards. Ethical people often go beyond what the law requires because the law cannot cover every situation a person might encounter. When the facts are unclear and the legal issues uncertain, an ethical person should decide what to do on the basis of well-established standards of ethical behavior. This is where moral philosophies come in and, for accountants and auditors, the ethical standards of the profession.

Ethical people often do less than is permitted by the law and more than is required. A useful perspective is to ask these questions:

- What does the law require of me?
- What do ethical standards of behavior demand of me?
- How should I act to conform to both?

The Gray Area

When the rules are unclear, an ethical person looks beyond his / her own self-interest and evaluates the interests of the stakeholders potentially affected by the action or decision. Ethical decision making requires that a decision maker be willing, at least sometimes, to take an action that may not be in his / her best interest. This is known as the "moral point of view."

Sometimes people believe that the ends justify the means. In ethics it all depends on one's motives for acting. If one's goals are good and noble, and the means we use to achieve them are also good and noble, then the ends do justify the means. However, if one views the concept as an excuse to achieve one's goals through any means necessary, no matter how immoral, illegal, or offensive to others the means may be, then that person is attempting to justify the wrongdoing by pointing to a good outcome regardless of ethical considerations such as how one's actions affect others. Nothing could be further from the truth. The process you follow to decide on a course of action is more important than achieving the end goal. If this were not true from a moral point of view, then we could rationalize all kinds of actions in the name of achieving a desired goal, even if that goal does harm to others while satisfying our personal needs and desires.

Imagine that you work for a CPA firm and are asked to evaluate three software packages for a client. Your boss tells you that the managing partners are pushing for one of these packages, which just happens to be the firm's internal software. Your initial numerical analysis of the packages based on functionality, availability of upgrades, and customer service indicates that a competitor's package is better than the firm's software. Your boss tells you, in no uncertain terms, to redo the analysis. You know what she wants. Even though you feel uncomfortable with the situation, you decide to "tweak" the numbers to show a preference for the firm's package. The end result desired in this case is to choose the firm's package. The means to that end was to alter the analysis, an unethical act because it is dishonest and unfair to the other competitors (not to mention the client) to change the objectively determined results. In this instance, ethical decision making requires that we place the client's interests (to get the best software package for his needs) above those of the firm (to get the new business and not upset the boss.

Ethical Relativism

Ethical relativism is the philosophical view that what is right or wrong and good or bad is not absolute but variable and relative, depending on the person, circumstances, or social situation. Ethical relativism holds that morality is relative to the norms of one's culture. That is, whether an action is right or wrong depends on the moral norms of the society in which it is practiced. The same action may be morally right in one society but be morally wrong in another. For the ethical relativist, there are no universal moral standards—standards that can be universally applied to all peoples at all times. The only moral standards against which a society's practices can be judged are its own. If ethical relativism is correct, then there can be no common framework for resolving moral disputes or for reaching agreement on ethical matters among members of different societies.

Most ethicists reject the theory of ethical relativism. Some claim that while the moral practices of societies may differ, the fundamental moral principles underlying these practices do not. For example, there was a situation in Singapore in the 1990s where a young American spray-painted graffiti on several cars. The Singaporean government's penalty was to "cane" the youngster by striking him on the buttocks four times. In the United States, some said it was cruel and unusual punishment for such a minor offense. In Singapore, the issue is that to protect the interests of society, the government treats harshly those who commit relatively minor offenses. After all, it does send a message that in Singapore, this and similar types of behavior will not be tolerated. While such a practice might be condemned in the United States, most people would agree with the underlying moral principle—the duty to protect the safety and security of the public (life and liberty concerns). Societies, then, may differ in their application of fundamental moral principles but agree on the principles.

Moral Relativism in Accounting

Accountants record and report financial truths. Their conduct is regulated by state boards of accountancy, professional codes of behavior, and moral conventions directed towards fairness and accountability. However, moral dilemmas and conflicts of interest inevitably arise when determining how best to present financial information. Betty Vinson is a case in point. She rationalized that in her circumstances going along with the improper accounting was justified because if Scott Sullivan, one of the foremost chief financial officers in the country, thought the accounting was all right, who was she to question it. After all, ethical judgments can be subjective and, perhaps, this was one of those situations. Clearly, Vinson suffered from moral blindness because she failed to consider the negative effects on shareholders and other stakeholders and moral failings of Sullivan's position. There was a gap between the person she truly was and how she acted in the WorldCom fraud brought about by pressures imposed on her by Sullivan.

Situation Ethics

Situation ethics, a term first coined in 1966 by an Episcopalian priest, Joseph Fletcher, is a body of ethical thought that takes normative principles—like the virtues, natural law, and Kant's categorical imperative that relies on the universality of actions—and generalizes them so that an agent can "make sense" out of one's experience when confronting ethical dilemmas. Unlike ethical relativism that denies universal moral principles, claiming the moral codes are strictly subjective, situational ethicists recognize the existence of normative principles but question whether they should be applied as strict directives (i.e., imperatives) or, instead, as guidelines that agents should use when determining a course of ethical conduct. In other words, situationists ask: Should these norms, as generalizations about what is desired, be regarded as intrinsically valid and universally obliging of all human beings? For situationists, the circumstances surrounding an ethical dilemma can and should influence an agent's decision-making process and may alter an agent's decision when warranted. Thus, situation ethics holds that "what in some times and in some places is ethical can be in other times and in other places unethical."[15] A problem with a situation ethics perspective is that it can be used to rationalize actions such as those in the Penn State scandal.

Student Cheating

Another danger of situational ethics is it can be used to rationalize cheating. Cheating in general is at epidemic proportions in society. The *2012 Report Card on the Ethics of American Youth,* conducted by the Josephson Institute of Ethics, found that of 43,000 high school students surveyed, 51 percent admitted to having cheated on a test during 2012, 55 percent admitted to lying, and 20 percent admitted to stealing.[16]

Cheating in college is prevalent as well. The estimates of number of students engaging in some form of academic dishonesty at least once ranges from 50 to 70 percent.[17] In 1997, McCabe and Treviño surveyed 6,000 students in 31 academic institutions and found contextual factors, such as peer influence, had the most effect on student cheating behavior.[18] Contextual appropriateness, rather than what is good or right, suggests that situations alter cases, thus changing the rules and principles that guide behavior.[19]

It used to be that professors only had to worry about students copying from each other during exams and on assignments handed in, as well as bringing "notes" to an exam that are hidden from view. Plagiarizing also has been a concern. In extreme cases, students might gain unauthorized access to exams. A persistent problem has been access to past exams that some professors use over again. Here, the individual professor needs to take responsibility for changing exams and not blame students for behaviors that, while unethical, could be prevented by actions of the professor.

Now, with the advent of electronic access to a variety of online resources, term papers can be acquired or other people found to write them for a student. A disturbing trend is the availability of the solutions manual and test bank questions online. Instructors have historically relied on these resources to assess student learning. All that may be assessed now is whether an otherwise unproductive student has suddenly become productive as a result of acquiring instructor's resource materials or accessing previous exams. Here, students are to blame for irresponsible behavior and basically cheat themselves out of learning materials needed in the workplace and for the CPA Exam.

Other forms of e-cheating include using cell phones to store data and cameras to zoom in and take pictures of test questions and then posting them on Web sites where other students can access the questions for later testing. Programmable calculators have been used for awhile to store information pertinent to potential test questions. In a study of cheating in business schools, of the 40 percent of students who indicated they used various electronic methods of cheating, 99 percent indicated from occasional use up to half the time.[20]

A comprehensive study of 4,950 students at a small southwestern university identified neutralizing techniques to justify violations of accepted behavior. In the study, students rationalized their cheating behavior without challenging the norm of honesty. The most common rationale was denial of responsibility (i.e., circumstances beyond their control, such as excessive hours worked on a job, made cheating okay in that instance). Then, they blamed the faculty and testing procedures (i.e., exams that try to trick students rather than test knowledge). Finally, the students appealed to a higher loyalty by arguing that it is more important to help a friend than to avoid cheating. One student blamed the larger society for his cheating: "In America, we're taught that results aren't achieved through beneficial means, but through the easiest means." The authors concluded that the use of these techniques of neutralization conveys the message that students recognize and accept cheating as an undesirable behavior but one that can be excused under certain circumstances, reflecting a situational ethic.[21]

Student Cheating at the University of North Carolina

If you're a sports fan, by now you have heard about the paper-class scandal that we call "Tar Heel Gate" in which 3,100 student-athletes at the University of North Carolina in Chapel Hill (UNC) were essentially allowed to take classes without attending classes and given grades good enough to keep them eligible to play men's football and basketball during a 20-year period.

For five years, UNC had insisted the paper classes were the doing of one rogue professor: the department chair of the African-American studies program, Julius Nyang'oro. However, an independent report found that five counselors actively used paper classes, calling them "GPA boosters," and that at least two counselors suggested to a professor the grade an athlete needed to receive to be able to continue to play.

Many of the academic-athletic staff who were named and implicated were also named by university learning specialist Mary Willingham. Willingham said that she had worked with dozens of athletes who came to UNC and were unable to read at an acceptable level, with some of them reading on par with elementary schoolchildren. She also said there were many members of the athletic staff who knew about the paper classes, and her revelations contradicted what UNC had claimed for years—that Nyang'oro acted alone in providing the paper classes.

Willingham went public with detailed allegations about paper classes and, after an assault on her credibility by the university, filed a whistleblower lawsuit. In March 2015, UNC announced it would pay Willingham $335,000 to settle her suit.

In an unusual twist to the story, the director of UNC's Parr Center for Ethics, Jeanette M. Boxill, was accused of steering athletes into fake classes to help them maintain their eligibility with the NCAA. Moreover, she covered up her actions after the fact. Boxill violated the most basic standards of academic integrity.

Although different in kind, Tar Heel Gate and the abuse scandal at Penn State have one common element: protecting the sports programs. At UNC, the goal was to keep student athletes eligible so that the sports programs would continue to excel and promote and publicize the school, not to mention earn millions of dollars in advertising. The NCAA investigation of the program is ongoing. In June 2015, five charges were leveled against UNC including a lack of institutional control for poor oversight of an academic department popular with athletes and the counselors who advised them. In August 2015, UNC notified the NCAA's enforcement staff that it identified two new pieces of information regarding NCAA violations, including a lack of institutional control when it allowed athletes to participate in years' worth of phony paper courses.

The university's own report on the matter is highly critical of a program that knowingly steered about 1,500 athletes toward no-show courses that never met and were not taught by any faculty members, and in which the only work required was a single research paper that received a high grade no matter the content. Still, the only sanction imposed by the board of Southern Association of Colleges and Schools' Commission on Colleges was a one-year probation. The board stopped short of imposing the harshest penalty, which would have blocked the country's oldest public university from receiving federal funds, including student loan proceeds. We believe this is a slap on the wrist for such gross violations and the accrediting agency should be ashamed.

The violations of ethics by UNC raise many important questions. How could such a reputable college sports program get away with the behavior for 20 years? Who was responsible for keeping a watchful eye out for violations of NCAA rules? Where were the managers of the affected sport programs; what did they know; when did they know it; what actions, if any, did they take?

UNC suffered from ethical blindness. It failed to see the ethical violations of its actions in establishing a route for student-athletes to remain academically eligible. It acted in its own self-interest regardless of the impact of its behavior on the affected parties. The blind spots occurred because of a situational ethic whereby those who perpetrated the fraud and covered it up came to believe their actions were for the greater good of those involved in the athletic program and the UNC community, much like at Penn State, but failed to see the effects of their actions on other stakeholders including other colleges that were at a competitive disadvantage. Honesty was ignored, integrity was not in the picture, and the athletes were not provided with the education they deserved. Ironically, in the end the very stakeholders who allegedly would benefit the greatest from student-athletes taking paper classes suffered the most.

Student Cheating and Workplace Behavior

Some educators feel that a student's level of academic integrity goes hand in hand with a student's ethical values on other real-world events that present ethical challenges.[22] In other words, developing a sound set of ethical standards in one area of decision making, such as personal matters, will carry over and affect other areas such as workplace ethics.

Some educators believe that ethics scandals in the business world can be attributed to the type of education that graduates of MBA programs obtained in business schools.[23] In 2006, McCabe, Butterfield, and Treviño reported on their findings regarding the extent of cheating among MBA students compared to nonbusiness graduate students at 32 universities in the United States and Canada. The authors found that 56 percent of business students admitted to cheating, versus 47 percent of nonbusiness students.[24]

Several researchers have examined student cheating in college and the tendency of those students to cheat in the workplace. Lawson surveyed undergraduate and graduate students enrolled in business schools and found a strong relationship between "students' propensity to cheat in an academic setting and their attitude toward unethical behavior in the business world."[25] Another study looked at the issue of graduate students cheating versus workplace dishonesty. Sims surveyed MBA students and found that students who engaged in behaviors considered severely dishonest in college also engaged in behaviors considered severely dishonest at work.[26]

If students who cheat in the university setting subsequently cheat in the workplace, then ethics education is all the more important. Once a student rationalizes cheating by blaming others or circumstances, it is only a small step to blaming others in the workplace for one's inability to get things done or unethical behavior.

Social Networkers and Workplace Ethics

The Ethics Resource Center conducted a survey of social networkers in 2012 to determine the extent to which employees use social networking on the job. The survey points out that social networking is now the norm and that a growing number of employees spend some of their workday connected to a social network. More than 10 percent are "active social networkers," defined as those who spend at least 30 percent of their workday linked up to one or more networks.[27]

One concern is whether active social networkers engage in unethical practices through communications and postings on social media sites. Survey respondents say they think about risks before posting online and consider how their employers would react to what they post. But, they do admit to discussing company information online: 60 percent would comment on their personal sites about their company if it was in the news; 53 percent share information about work projects once a week or more; greater than one-third say they often comment, on their personal sites, about managers, coworkers, and even clients. The survey concludes that nothing is secret anymore and, unlike in Las Vegas, management must assume that what happens at work does not stay at work and may become publicly known.

An interesting result of the survey is active social networkers are unusually vulnerable to risks because they witness more misconduct and experience more retaliation as a result when they report it than their work colleagues. A majority (56 percent) of active social networkers who reported misdeeds experienced retaliation compared to fewer than one in five (18 percent) of other employee groups.

An encouraging result is that effective training on the use of social networks and an ongoing commitment to an ethical culture in which employees act with integrity can mitigate the risks presented by social networking at work. The survey found that in companies with both social networking policies and training, employees are more aware of what they post, think more carefully about the implications of online activity, and spend less of their worktime online. Moreover, where policies are in place, half of the social networkers say it is unacceptable to publicly post comments about their company even when they do not identify it. Without policies, only 40 percent say such posts are unacceptable. In companies with social networking policies, 88 percent consider their employer's reaction before making work-related posts, compared to the 76 percent in companies without such policies.[28]

Our conclusion about using social networking sites at work is that the burden falls both on the employees, who should know better than to discuss company business online where anyone can see it, and employers who have the responsibility to establish a culture that discourages venting one's feelings about the employer online for all to see. Organizational codes of ethics need to be expanded to create policies for the use of social networking sites, training to reinforce those policies, and consequences for those who violate the policies.

Cultural Values

Between 1967 and 1973, Dutch researcher Geert Hofstede conducted one of the most comprehensive studies of how values in the workplace are influenced by culture. Using responses to an attitude study of approximately 116,000 IBM employees in 39 countries, Hofstede identified four cultural dimensions that can be used to describe general similarities and differences in cultures around the world: (1) individualism, (2) power distance, (3) uncertainty avoidance, and (4) masculinity.[29] In 2001, a fifth dimension, long-term orientation—initially called Confucian dynamism—was identified.[30] More recently, a sixth variable was added—indulgence versus restraint—as a result of Michael Minkov's analysis of data from the World Values Survey.[31] Exhibit 1.2 summarizes the five dimensions from Hofstede's work for Japan, the United Kingdom, and the United States, representing leading industrialized nations; and the so-called BRIC countries (Brazil, Russia, India, and China), which represent four major emerging economies.[32]

EXHIBIT 1.2   Hofstede's Cultural Dimensions*

Cultural Variables	Countries/Scores						
	Brazil	Russia	India	China	Japan	U.K.	U.S.
Power Distance (PDI)	69	93	77	80	54	35	40
Individualism (IDV)	38	39	48	20	46	89	91
Masculinity (MAS)	49	36	56	66	95	66	62
Uncertainty Avoidance (UAI)	76	95	40	30	92	35	46
Long-Term Orientation (LTO)	65	N/A	61	118	80	25	29

* High scores indicate a propensity toward the cultural variable; low scores indicate the opposite.

Individualism (IDV) focuses on the degree that the society reinforces individual or collective achievement and interpersonal relationships. In individualist societies (high IDV), people are supposed to look after themselves and their direct family, while in collectivist societies (low IDV), people belong to "in-groups" that take care of them in exchange for loyalty. Imagine, for example, you are the manager of workers from different cultures and cheating/unethical behavior occurs in the workplace. A work group with collectivist values such as China and Japan (low IDV) might be more prone to covering up the behavior of one member of the group in order to "save face", whereas in the United Kingdom and United States (high IDV), there is a greater likelihood of an individual blowing the whistle.

Uncertainty Avoidance (UAI) is another cultural value that has important implications for workplace behavior, as it describes the tolerance for uncertainty and ambiguity within society. A high UAI ranking indicates that a country has a low tolerance of uncertainty and ambiguity. Such a society is likely to institute laws, rules, regulations, and controls to reduce the amount of uncertainty. A country such as Russia has a high UAI, while the United States and United Kingdom have lower scores (low UAI), indicating more tolerance for a variety of opinions. One implication is the difficulty of doing business in a country like Russia, which has strict rules and regulations about what can and cannot be done by multinational enterprises.

Other variables have important implications for workplace behavior as well, such as the Power Distance index (PDI), which focuses on the degree of equality between people in the country's society. A high PDI indicates inequalities of wealth and power have been allowed to grow within society, as has occurred in China and Russia as they develop economically. Long-term orientation (LTO) versus short-term orientation has been used to illustrate one of the differences between Asian cultures, such as China and Japan, and the United States and United Kingdom. In societies like China and Japan, high LTO scores reflect the values of long-term commitment and respect for tradition, as opposed to low-LTO countries, such as the United Kingdom and United States, where change can occur more rapidly. Time can often be a stumbling block for Western-cultured organizations entering the China market. The length of time it takes to get business deals done in China can be two or three times that in the West. One final point is to note that Brazil and India show less variability in their scores than other countries, perhaps reflecting fewer extremes in cultural dimensions.

Our discussion of cultural dimensions is meant to explain how workers from different cultures *might* interact in the workplace. The key point is that cultural sensitivity is an essential ingredient in establishing workplace values and may affect ethical behavioral patterns.

The Six Pillars of Character

LO 1-3
Describe how the pillars of character support ethical decision making.

It has been said that ethics is all about how we act when no one is looking. In other words, ethical people do not do the right thing because someone observing their actions might judge them otherwise, or because they may be punished as a result of their actions. Instead, ethical people act as they do because their "inner voice" or conscience tells them that it is the right thing to do. Assume that you are leaving a shopping mall, get into your car to drive away, and hit a parked car in the lot on the way out. Let's also assume that no one saw you hit the car. What are your options? You could simply drive away and forget about it, or you can leave a note for the owner of the parked car with your contact information. What would you do and why? Your actions will reflect the character of your inner being.

According to "virtue ethics," there are certain ideals, such as excellence or dedication to the common good, toward which we should strive and which allow the full development of our humanity. These ideals are discovered through thoughtful reflection on what we as human beings have the potential to become.

Virtues are attitudes, dispositions, or character traits that enable us to be and to act in ways that develop this potential. They enable us to pursue the ideals we have adopted. Honesty, courage, compassion, generosity, fidelity, integrity, fairness, self-control, and prudence are all examples of virtues in Aristotelian ethics. A quote attributed to Aristotle is, "We are what we repeatedly do. Therefore, excellence is not an act. It is a habit."[33]

The Josephson Institute of Ethics identifies Six Pillars of Character that provide a foundation to guide ethical decision making. These ethical values include trustworthiness, respect, responsibility, fairness, caring, and citizenship. Josephson believes that the Six Pillars act as a multilevel filter through which to process decisions. So, being trustworthy is not enough—we must also be caring. Adhering to the letter of the law is not enough; we must accept responsibility for our actions or inactions.[34]

Trustworthiness

The dimensions of trustworthiness include being honest, acting with integrity, being reliable, and exercising loyalty in dealing with others.

Honesty

Honesty is the most basic ethical value. It means that we should express the truth as we know it and without deception. In accounting, the full disclosure principle supports transparency and requires that the accounting professional disclose all the information that owners, investors, creditors, and the government need to know to make informed decisions. To withhold relevant information is dishonest. Transparent information is that which helps one understand the process followed to reach a decision. In other words it supports an ethical ends versus means belief.

Let's assume that you are a member of a discussion group in your Intermediate Accounting II class, and in an initial meeting with all members, the leader asks whether there is anyone who has not completed Intermediate I. You failed the course last term and are retaking it concurrently with Intermediate II. However, you feel embarrassed and say nothing. Now, perhaps the leader thinks that this point is important because a case study assigned to your group uses knowledge gained from Intermediate I. You internally justify the silence by thinking: Well, I did complete the course, albeit with a grade of F. This is an unethical position. You are rationalizing silence by interpreting the question in your own self-interest rather than in the interests of the entire group. The other members need to know whether you have completed Intermediate I because the leader may choose not to assign a specific project to you that requires the Intermediate I prerequisite knowledge.

Integrity

The integrity of a person is an essential element in trusting that person. MacIntyre, in his account of Aristotelian virtue, states, "There is at least one virtue recognized by tradition which cannot be specified except with reference to the wholeness of a human life—the virtue of integrity or constancy."[35] A person of integrity takes time for self-reflection, so that the events, crises, and challenges of everyday living do not determine the course of that person's moral life. Such a person is trusted by others because that person is true to her word.

Ultimately, integrity means to act on principle rather than expediency. If my superior tells me to do something wrong, I will not do it because it violates the ethical value of honesty. If my superior pressures me to compromise my values just this one time, I will not agree. I have the courage of my convictions and am true to the principles of behavior that guide my actions.

Going back to the previous example, if you encounter a conflict with another group member who pressures you to plagiarize a report available on the Internet that the two of you are working on, you will be acting with integrity if you refuse to go along. You know it's wrong to plagiarize another writer's material. Someone worked hard to get this report published. You would not want another person to take material you had published without permission and proper citation. Why do it to that person, then? If you do it simply because it might benefit you, then you act out of self-interest, or egoism, and that is wrong.

Reliability

The promises that we make to others are relied on by them, and we have a moral duty to follow through with action. Our ethical obligation for promise keeping includes avoiding bad-faith excuses and unwise commitments. Imagine that you are asked to attend a group meeting on Saturday and you agree to do so. That night, though, your best friend calls and says he has two tickets to the basketball game between the Dallas Mavericks and San Antonio Spurs. The Spurs are one of the best teams in basketball and you don't get this kind of opportunity very often, so you decide to go to the game instead of the meeting. You've broken your promise, and you did it out of self-interest. You figured, who wouldn't want to see the Spurs play? What's worse, you call the group leader and say that you can't attend the meeting because you are sick. Now you've also lied. You've started the slide down the proverbial ethical slippery slope, and it will be difficult to climb back to the top.

Loyalty

We all should value loyalty in friendship. After all, you wouldn't want the friend who invited you to the basketball game to telephone the group leader later and say that you went to the game on the day of the group meeting.

Loyalty requires that friends not violate the confidence we place in them. In accounting, loyalty requires that we keep financial and other information confidential when it deals with our employer and client. For example, if you are the in-charge accountant on an audit of a client for your CPA firm-employer and you discover that the client is "cooking the books," you shouldn't telephone the local newspaper and tell the story to a reporter. Instead, you should go to your supervisor and discuss the matter and, if necessary, go to the partner in charge of the engagement and tell her. Your ethical obligation is to report what you have observed to your supervisor and let her take the appropriate action. However, the ethics of the accounting profession allow for instances whereby informing those above your supervisor is expected, an act of internal whistleblowing, and in rare circumstances going outside the organization to report the wrongdoing. Whistleblowing obligations will be discussed in Chapter 3.

There are limits to the confidentiality obligation. For example, let's assume that you are the accounting manager at a publicly owned company and your supervisor (the controller) pressures you to keep silent about the manipulation of financial information. You then go to the CFO, who tells you that both the CEO and board of directors support the controller. Out of a misplaced duty of loyalty in this situation, you might rationalize your silence as did Betty Vinson. Ethical values sometimes conflict, and loyalty is the one value that should never take precedence over other values such as honesty and integrity. Otherwise, we can imagine all kinds of cover-ups of information in the interest of loyalty or friendship.

While attending a Josephson Institute of Ethics training program for educators, one of the authors of this book heard Michael Josephson make an analogy about loyal behavior that sticks with him to this day. Josephson said: "Dogs are loyal to their master, while cats are loyal to the house." How true it is that dogs see their ultimate allegiance to their owner while cats get attached to the place they call home—their own personal space. Now, in a business context, this means that a manager should try to encourage "cat" behavior in the organization (sorry, dog lovers). In that way, if a cover-up of a financial wrongdoing exists, the "cat loyalty" mentality incorporated into the business environment dictates that the information be disclosed because it is not in the best interests of the organization to hide or ignore it. If we act with "dog loyalty," we will cover up for our supervisor, who has a say about what happens to us in the organization. Recall our discussion of cultural values, and that someone from a country or group with a low score on individualism (a collectivist society) is more likely to hide a damaging fact out of loyalty to the controller and her superiors, while someone from a more individualistic society is more likely to come forward with information about the wrongdoing. A cover-up may be an understandable position because of internal pressures that work against voicing one's concerns and acting on one's values, but it is unethical all the same. Moreover, once we go along with the cover-up, we have started the slide down the ethical slippery slope, and there may be no turning back. In fact, our supervisor may come to us during the next period and expect us to go along with the same cover-up in a similar situation. If we refuse at that point, the first instance may be brought up and used as a threat against us because we've already violated ethical standards once and don't want to get caught. It is important to emphasize that we should not act ethically out of fear of the consequences of hiding information. Instead, we should act ethically out of a positive sense that it is the right way to behave.

Often when we cover up information in the present, it becomes public knowledge later. The consequences at that time are more serious because trust has been destroyed. We have already discussed the Penn State scandal and forfeiture of trust by Joe Paterno for failing to take steps to stop child abuse. Another example is Lance Armstrong, who for years denied taking performance-enhancing drugs while winning seven Tour de France titles. In 2012, he finally admitted to doing just that, and as a result, all those titles were stripped away by the U.S. Anti-Doping Agency. Or consider former president Richard Nixon, who went along with the cover-up in the Watergate break-in only to be forced to resign the presidency once the cover-up became public knowledge.

Respect

All people should be treated with dignity. We do not have an ethical duty to hold all people in high esteem, but we should treat everyone with respect, regardless of their circumstances in life. In today's slang, we might say that respect means giving a person "props." The Golden Rule encompasses respect for others through notions such as civility, courtesy, decency, dignity, autonomy, tolerance, and acceptance.[36]

By age 16, George Washington had copied by hand 110 *Rules of Civility & Decent Behavior in Company and Conversation.* They are based on a set of rules composed by French Jesuits in 1595. While many of the rules seem out of place in today's society, Washington's first rule is noteworthy: "Every Action done in Company, ought to be with Some Sign of Respect, to those that are Present."[37]

Washington's vernacular was consistent with the times as indicated by the last of his rules: "Labour to keep alive in your Breast that Little Spark of Celestial fire Called Conscience."[38] We have found many definitions of conscience, but the one we like best is the universal lexical English WordNet used for research and developed by the Cognitive Sciences Laboratory at Princeton University. The definition is: "Motivation deriving logically from ethical or moral principles that govern a person's thoughts and actions."[39]

As a member of the case discussion group in the previous example, it would be wrong to treat another member with discourtesy or prejudice because you have drawn conclusions about that person on the basis of national origin or some other factor rather than her abilities and conduct. You would not want to be disrespected or treated unfairly because of how you dress or walk or talk, so others should not be judged based on similar considerations. We should judge people based on their character.

Responsibility

Josephson points out that our capacity to reason and our freedom to choose make us morally responsible for our actions and decisions. We are accountable for what we do and who we are.[40]

The judgments we make in life reflect whether we have acted responsibly. Eleanor Roosevelt, the former first lady, puts it well: "One's philosophy is not best expressed in words; it is expressed in the choices one makes...and the choices we make are ultimately our responsibility."[41]

A responsible person carefully reflects on alternative courses of action using ethical principles. A responsible person acts diligently and perseveres in carrying out moral action. Imagine if you were given the task by your group to interview five CPAs in public practice about their most difficult ethical dilemma, and you decided to ask one person, who was a friend of the family, about five dilemmas that person faced in the practice of public accounting. Now, even if you made an "honest" mistake in interpreting the requirement, it is clear that you did not exercise the level of care that should be expected in this instance in carrying out the instructions to interview five different CPAs. The due care test is whether a "reasonable person" would conclude that you had acted with the level of care, or diligence, expected in the circumstance. The courts have used this test for many years to evaluate the actions of professionals.

Responsibility for accounting professionals means to meet one's ethical and professional obligations when performing services for an employer or client. Professional accountants in business often find themselves at the front line of protecting the integrity of the financial reporting process. Public accountants should approach audit services with an inquiring mind and be skeptical of what the client says and the information provided. As discussed later on, in the final analysis, the ultimate obligation of accounting professionals is to meet their public interest responsibilities. The public (i.e., investors and creditors) relies on the ethics of accountants and auditors and trusts they will act in the name of the public good.

Fairness

A person of fairness treats others equally, impartially, and openly. In business, we might say that the fair allocation of scarce resources requires that those who have earned the right to a greater share of corporate resources as judged objectively by performance measures should receive a larger share than those whose performance has not met the standard.

Let's assume that your instructor told the case study groups at the beginning of the course that the group with the highest overall numerical average would receive an A, the group with second highest a B, and so on. At the end of the term, the teacher gave the group with the second-highest average—90.5—an A and the group with the highest average—91.2—a B. Perhaps the instructor took subjective factors into account in deciding on the final grading. You might view the instructor's action as unfair to the group with the highest average. It certainly contradicts his original stated policy and is capricious and unfair, especially if the instructor does not explain his reason for doing this. As Josephson points out, "Fairness implies adherence to a balanced standard of justice without relevance to one's own feelings or inclinations."[42]

Fairness in accounting can be equated with objectivity. Objectivity means the financial and accounting information needs to presented free from bias, that is, consistent with the evidence and not based solely on one's opinion about the proper accounting treatment. Objectivity helps to ensure that financial statements are reliable and verifiable. The purpose of objectivity is to make financial statements more useful to investors and end users.

Caring

The late Edmund L. Pincoffs, a philosopher who formerly taught at the University of Texas at Austin, believed that virtues such as caring, kindness, sensitivity, altruism, and benevolence enable a person who possesses these qualities to consider the interests of others.[43] Josephson believes that caring is the "heart of ethics and ethical decision making."[44]

The essence of caring is empathy. *Empathy* is the ability to understand, be sensitive to, and care about the feelings of others. Caring and empathy support each other and enable a person to put herself in the position of another. This is essential to ethical decision making.

Let's assume that on the morning of an important group meeting, your child comes down with a temperature of 103 degrees. You call the group leader and say that you can't make it to the meeting. Instead, you suggest that the meeting be taped and you will listen to the discussions later that day and telephone the leader with any questions. The leader reacts angrily, stating that you are not living up to your responsibilities. Assuming that your behavior is not part of a pattern and you have been honest with the leader up to now, you would have a right to be upset with the leader, who seems uncaring. In the real world, emergencies do occur, and placing your child's health and welfare above all else should make sense in this situation to a person of rational thought. You also acted diligently by offering to listen to the discussions and, if necessary, follow up with the leader.

Putting yourself in the place of another is sometimes difficult to do because the circumstances are unique to the situation. For example, what would you do if a member of your team walked into a meeting all bleary-eyed? You might ignore it, or you might ask that person if everything is all right. If you do and are informed that the person was up all night with a crying baby, then you might say something like, "If there's anything I can do to lighten the load for you today, just say the word."

A person who can empathize seems to know just what to say to make the other person feel better about circumstances. On the other hand, if you have never been married and have not had children, you might not be able to understand the feelings of a mother who has just spent the night trying to comfort a screaming child.

Citizenship

Josephson points out that "citizenship includes civic virtues and duties that prescribe how we ought to behave as part of a community."[45] An important part of good citizenship is to obey the laws, be informed about the issues, volunteer in your community, and vote in elections. During his presidency, Barack Obama called for citizens to engage in some kind of public service to benefit society as a whole.

Accounting professionals are part of a community with specific ideals and ethical standards that govern behavior. These include responsibilities to one another to advance the profession and not bring discredit on oneself or others. As citizens of a community, accountants and auditors should strive to enhance the reputation of the accounting profession.

It might be said that judgments made about one's character contribute toward how another party views that person's reputation. In other words, what is the estimation in which a person is commonly held, whether favorable or not? The reputation of a CPA is critical to a client's trusting that CPA to perform services competently and maintain the confidentiality of client information (except for certain whistleblowing instances). One builds "reputational capital" through favorable actions informed by ethical behavior.

Expectations of Millennials

Universum, the global employer branding and research company, annually surveys college undergraduate and MBA students. In 2014, it surveyed about 60,000 U.S. college students from 311 institutions to find out what they were looking for as they enter the world of work, as well as their views on the attractiveness of specific employers. The results of the survey reflect a desire to join an organization that respects its people, provides a supportive environment, recognizes performance, provides development and leadership opportunities, challenges one intellectually, fosters a work/life balance, and serves the public good.[46]

Students were asked to identify up to three career goals. The top five goals (with percentages of students who selected them) were:

1. Work/life balance (79 percent)
2. Job security (50 percent)
3. Be a leader or manager of people (43 percent)
4. Be competitively or intellectually challenged (43 percent)
5. Dedicated to a cause or feel I am serving a greater good (36 percent)

It also asked students to identify the most important "attractors" an employer could offer. The responses provided by at least 40 percent of students were:

1. Leaders who will support my development (49 percent)
2. Respect for its people (46 percent)
3. Creative and dynamic work environment (43 percent)
4. Recognizing performance (meritocracy) (43 percent)
5. Friendly work environment (42 percent)

These results are interesting in that Millennials clearly recognize motivating factors other than money in selecting a career. Their values appear in many ways to be consistent with the Six Pillars of Character including respect, responsibility, fairness, and civic virtue. Moreover, they were concerned about a prospective employer's reputation and image, and 39 percent found ethical standards to be an attractive attribute in a prospective employer, second only to financial strength (40 percent). Other civic virtue issues of importance included corporate social responsibility (21 percent) and environmental sustainability (13 percent).

How did the accounting profession fare with respect to the most desirable businesses to work for? Perhaps not surprisingly, Google was the most desirable employer to work for (21 percent), followed by Walt Disney Company (14 percent) and then Apple (13 percent). Of the Big-4 international professional accounting firms, Ernst & Young (EY) was the highest rated (13 percent), followed by Deloitte (11 percent), PricewaterhouseCoopers (PwC) (10 percent), and KPMG (7 percent). We caution students not to make too much of the rank ordering of CPA firms because more prestigious surveys such as the 2015 survey conducted by Fortune Magazine of the top 500 companies to work for has KPMG at the top while another survey conducted by Vault in 2015 ranks PwC the highest. Consulting Magazine's 2014 survey lists Deloitte Consulting as the best firm to work for followed by EY. These surveys generally are based on quality of life issues and development opportunities.

Reputation

It might be said that judgments made about one's character contribute toward how another party views that person's reputation. In other words, what is the estimation in which a person is commonly held, whether favorable or not? The reputation of a CPA is critical to a client's trusting that CPA to perform services competently and maintain the confidentiality of client information (except for whistleblowing instances). One builds "reputational capital" through favorable actions informed by ethical behavior.

All too often in politics and government, a well-respected leader becomes involved in behavior that, once disclosed, tears down a reputation earned over many years of service. The example of former senator and presidential candidate John Edwards shows how quickly one's reputation can be destroyed—in this case because of the disclosure of an extramarital affair that Edwards had with a 42-year-old campaign employee, Rielle Hunter, that Edwards covered up.

In 2006, Edwards's political action committee (PAC) paid Hunter's video production firm $100,000 for work. Then the committee paid another $14,086 on April 1, 2007. The Edwards camp said the latter payment from the PAC was in exchange for 100 hours of unused videotape Hunter shot. The same day, the Edwards presidential campaign had injected $14,034.61 into the PAC for a "furniture purchase," according to federal election records.

Edwards, a U.S. senator representing North Carolina from 1998 until his vice presidential bid in 2004, acknowledged in May 2009 that federal investigators were looking into how he used campaign funds. Edwards was accused of soliciting nearly $1 million from wealthy backers to finance a cover-up of his illicit affair during his 2008 bid for the White House.

Edwards admitted to ABC News[47] in an interview with Bob Woodruff in August 2009 that he repeatedly lied about having an affair with Hunter. Edwards strenuously denied being involved in paying the woman hush money or fathering her newborn child, admitted the affair was a mistake in the interview, and said: "Two years ago, I made a very serious mistake, a mistake that I am responsible for and no one else. In 2006, I told Elizabeth [his wife] about the mistake, asked her for her forgiveness, asked God for His forgiveness. And we have kept this within our family since that time." Edwards said he told his entire family about the affair after it ended in 2006, and that his wife Elizabeth was "furious" but that their marriage would survive. On January 21, 2010, he also finally admitted to fathering Hunter's child, Quinn (and since the girl was born in 2008, that indicates pretty clearly that Edwards's statement that the affair ended in 2006 was less than truthful).

On May 31, 2012, a jury found him not guilty on one of six counts in the campaign-finance trial and deadlocked on the remaining charges; the Department of Justice decided not to retry him on those charges. On the courthouse steps, Edwards acknowledged his moral shortcomings.

Edwards violated virtually every tenet of ethical behavior and destroyed his reputation. He lied about the affair and attempted to cover it up, including allegations that he fathered Hunter's baby. He violated the trust of the public and lied after telling his family about the affair in 2006. He even had the audacity to run for the Democratic nomination for president in 2008. One has to wonder what it says about Edwards's ethics that he was willing to run for president of the United States while hiding the knowledge of his affair, without considering what might happen if he had won the Democratic nomination in 2008, and then the affair became public knowledge during the general election campaign. His behavior is the ultimate example of ethical blindness and the pursuit of one's own self-interests to the detriment of all others. Perhaps the noted Canadian-American chemist and author Orlando Aloysius Battista (1917–1995), said it best: "An error doesn't become a mistake until you refuse to correct it." In other words, when you do something wrong, admit it, take responsibility for your actions, accept the consequences, promise never to do it again, and move on. Unfortunately, most adulterers like Edwards go to great lengths to cover up their moral failings and don't admit to them until they have been caught.

Civility, Ethics, and Workplace Behavior

Can there be any doubt that incivility in society is on the rise? Not according to one of your authors. Mintz opines in his blog about incivility that daily we witness instances of inconsiderate, "in your face" behavior in communications and other forms of rudeness. There are many causes of incivility, many of which are social media–driven. The sometimes anonymous feel of posts on Twitter and other social media sites makes it relatively easy to use impersonal forms of communication to vent one's feelings without the immediate consequences of face-to-face discussions. One inappropriate Twitter rant begets another and eventually we see a further erosion of ethics in society.

Civility is not peripheral to ethics, dealing merely with manners, proper etiquette, and politeness. It runs much deeper and requires restraint, respect, and responsible action both in one's personal behavior and professional activities. Remember, ethics deals in broad terms with how we treat others.

Two pertinent questions are: Can you be civil and not entirely ethical? Can you be ethical and not terribly civil? The answer to the first is a qualified "yes." You can be well behaved and gracious to others but still be motivated by non-ethical values such as greed. The problem is you may wind up using others to advance your self-interests. The answer to the second is "no." Treating others badly and with disrespect means you have not committed to act in accordance with the pillars of character.

Taken to its extreme, uncivil behavior could manifest itself in meanness toward others, bullying, and cyberbullying. Such behaviors fly in the face of caring and empathy for others. Fair treatment is replaced by biased behaviors against others who somehow are seen as different, inferior, or just not worthy of respect. Civility should be taught in our schools at the earliest possible age. Benjamin Franklin said that "the purpose of the high school shall be to teach civility, because without civility democracy will fail."

Just as one's social networking practices in personal matters can influence workplace behavior including critical postings about fellow employees or the company, uncivil behavior in personal affairs might translate into incivility in the workplace. This may be company driven if employees feel mistreated or under extreme pressure to produce results. The result could be a lack of organizational commitment and loyalty issues that lead one to vent frustrations on social media. Of course, one's propensity to act disrespectfully toward others can translate into workplace incivility including bullying behavior.

Incivility in the workplace can lead to tangible costs for a business. In a survey of 800 managers and employees in 17 industries published in *Harvard Business Review*, Porath and Pearson report that workers who had experienced incivility indicated that they lost work time worrying about the incident (80 percent), their commitment to the organization declined (78 percent), performance declined (66 percent), lost work time avoiding the offender (63 percent), and intentionally decreased their work effort (48 percent).[48]

Civility in accounting manifests itself in the way accounting professionals market and promote their services and in their interactions with clients. The AICPA Code of Professional Conduct prohibits acts that might bring the profession into disrepute or do harm to current or prospective clients. For example, advertising of professional services and solicitation of new clients should not be made in a false, fraudulent, misleading, or deceptive manner. CPAs should not make promises in their communications that may not be kept such as to create unjustified expectations of favorable results.

Professionalism and work ethic are important qualities of accounting professionals. Professionalism is generally defined as the strict adherence to courtesy, honesty, and responsibility when dealing with individuals or other companies in business and clients in public accounting. For CPAs, this means to act in accordance with personal and professional values such as trustworthiness, integrity, transparency, and the pursuit of excellence. A strong work ethic includes completing assignments in a timely manner, diligently, and with the highest quality possible. Ethics and professionalism in accounting also means to always place the public interest ahead of one's self-interests, the interests of an employer, and the client's interests. The public expects accounting and auditing professionals to be selfless in the pursuit of the public good.

Modern Moral Philosophies

LO 1-4
Differentiate between moral philosophies and their effect on ethical reasoning in accounting.

The ancient Greeks believed that reason and thought precede the choice of action and that we deliberate about things we can influence with our decisions. In making decisions, most people want to follow laws and rules. However, rules are not always clear, and laws may not cover every situation. Therefore, it is the ethical foundation that we develop and nurture that will determine how we react to unstructured situations that challenge our sense of right and wrong. In the end, we need to rely on moral principles to guide our decision making. However, the ability to reason out ethical conflicts may not be enough to assure ethical decision making occurs in accounting. This is because while we believe that we should behave in accordance with core values, we may wind up deviating from these values that trigger ethical reasoning in accounting because of internal pressures from supervisors and others in top management. In the end, a self-interest motive may prevail over making a decision from an ethical perspective, and unethical behavior may result. This is the moral of the story of Betty Vinson's role in the WorldCom fraud. Moreover, even if we know what the right thing to do is, we still may be unable to act on our beliefs because others in the organization provide reasons and rationalizations to deviate from those beliefs and may establish barriers to ethical action. This occurred in the WorldCom fraud when Scott Sullivan, the CFO, attempted to divert Cynthia Cooper from her goal to reveal the accounting fraud.

The noted philosopher James Rest points out that moral philosophies present guidelines for "determining how conflicts in human interests are to be settled for optimizing mutual benefit of people living together in groups." However, there is no single moral philosophy everyone accepts. Notably, moral philosophies have been used to defend a particular type of economic system and individuals' behavior within these systems.[49]

Adam Smith's seminal work, *An Inquiry Into the Nature and Causes of the Wealth of Nations (1776)*, outlined the basis for free-market capitalism. Capitalism *laissez-faire* philosophies, such as minimizing the role of government intervention and taxation in the free markets, and the idea that an "invisible hand" guides supply and demand are key elements of his political philosophy. These ideas reflect the concept that each person, by looking out for his or her self-interest, inadvertently helps to create the best outcome for all. "It is not from the benevolence of the butcher, the brewer, or the baker, that we can expect our dinner, but from their regard to their own interest," Smith wrote.[50]

Even before Smith wrote *The Wealth of Nations* he produced a treatise on moral philosophy. *The Theory of Moral Sentiments* (1759) makes the case that business should be guided by the morals of good people. Smith sets forth a theory of how we come to be moral, of how morality functions on both individual and societal levels, and of what forces are likely to corrupt our sense of morality, which is derived from our capacity to sympathize directly and indirectly with other people. This occurs by feeling what others actually feel in their circumstances. We are able to achieve this moral perspective because of our consciences, which allow us to envision our own actions just as a disinterested observer might.[51]

Moral norms therefore express the feelings of an impartial spectator. A feeling, whether on the part of a person motivated to take action or on the part of a person who has been acted upon by others, is worthy of moral approval if and only if an impartial observer would sympathize with that feeling. When achieving a morally right feeling is difficult, we call that achievement "virtuous"; otherwise, we describe people as acting or failing to act within the bounds of "propriety." In the end, moral norms and ideals, and the judgments by which we guide ourselves towards those norms and ideals, arise out of the process by which we try to achieve mutual sympathy.

Smith distinguishes two kinds of normative guides to action: rules and virtues. Moral rules bar certain types of egregious behavior, such as murder, theft, and rape. They provide a basis for shared expectations of society and are essential to justice, without which societies could not survive. Virtue, on the other hand, requires more than simply following moral rules. Our emotional tendencies not only affect the sentiments of the impartial observer but we adopt those sentiments so that we identify with and become the impartial spectator to the extent possible. If we are truly virtuous, a submission to certain rules will constrain everything we do, but within that framework we can operate without rules by adopting dispositions such as kindness, empathy, patience, endurance, and courage.[52]

Moral philosophies provide specific principles and rules that we can use to decide what is right or wrong in specific instances. They can help a business decision maker formulate strategies to deal with ethical dilemmas and resolve them in a morally appropriate way. There are many such philosophies, but we limit the discussion to those that are most applicable to the study of accounting ethics, including teleology, deontology, justice, and virtue ethics. Our approach focuses on the most basic concepts needed to help you understand the ethical decision-making process in business and accounting that we outline in Chapter 2. We do not favor any one of these philosophies because there is no one correct way to resolve ethical issues in business. Instead, we present them to aid in resolving ethical dilemmas in accounting. Exhibit 1.3 summarizes the basis for making ethical judgments for each of the major moral philosophies. The discussion that follows elaborates on these principles and applies them to a common situation in accounting. One word of caution. Even though you may know what the right thing to do is, that does not mean you will act in the same way as your thoughts and feelings. Distractions occur and reasons and rationalizations are provided, making it more difficult to "give voice to your values," as will be discussed in Chapter 2.

Teleology

Recall that *telos* is the Greek word for "end" or "purpose." In *teleology,* an act is considered morally right or acceptable if it produces some desired result such as pleasure, the realization of self-interest, fame, utility, wealth, and so on. Teleologists assess the moral worth of behavior by looking at its consequences, and thus moral philosophers often refer to these theories as *consequentialism.* Two important teleological philosophies that typically guide decision making in individual business decisions are egoism and utilitarianism.

Egoism and Enlightened Egoism

Egoism defines right or acceptable behavior in terms of its consequences for the individual. *Egoists* believe that they should make decisions that maximize their own self-interest, which is defined differently by each individual. In other words, the individual should "[d]o the act that promotes the greatest good for oneself."[53] Many believe that egoistic people and companies are inherently unethical, are short-term-oriented, and will take advantage of others to achieve their goals. Our *laissez-faire* economic system enables the selfish pursuit of individual profit, so a regulated marketplace is essential to protect the interests of those affected by individual (and corporate) decision making.

There is one form of egoism that emphasizes more of a direct action to bring about the best interests of society. *Enlightened egoists* take a long-range perspective and allow for the well-being of others because they help achieve some ultimate goal for the decision maker, although their own self-interest remains paramount. For example, enlightened egoists may abide by professional codes of ethics, avoid cheating on taxes, and create safe working conditions. They do so not because their actions benefit others, but because they help achieve some ultimate goal for the egoist, such as advancement within the firm.[54]

Let's examine the following example from the perspectives of egoism and enlightened egoism. The date is Friday, January 17, 2016, and the time is 5:00 p.m. It is the last day of fieldwork on an audit, and you

EXHIBIT 1.3 Ethical Reasoning Method Bases for Making Ethical Judgments

	Teleology				Deontology		Virtue Ethics
	Egoism	Enlightened Egoism	Utilitarianism		Rights Theory	Justice	
Ethical Judgments	Defines "right" behavior by consequences for the decision maker	Considers well-being of others within the scope of deciding on a course of action based on self-interest.	Evaluates consequences of actions (harms and benefits) on stakeholders		Considers "rights" of stakeholders and related duties to them.	Emphasizes rights, fairness, and equality.	Only method where ethical reasoning methods—"virtues" (internal traits of character)—apply both to the *decision maker* and the *decision*
			Act	*Rule*	Treats people as an end and not merely as a means to an end.	Those with equal claims to justice should be treated equally; those with unequal claims should be treated unequally.	Judgments are made not by applying rules, but by possessing those traits that enable the decision maker to act for the good of others.
			Evaluate whether the intended *action* provides the greatest net benefits.	Select the action that conforms to the correct *moral rule* that produces the greatest net benefits	*Universality Perspective:* Would I want others to act in a similar manner for similar reasons in this situation?		Similar to Principles of AICPA Code and IMA Standards.
							Virtues may conflict, requiring choices to be made.
Problems with Implementation	Fails to consider interests of those affected by the decision	Interests of others are subservient to self-interest.	Can be difficult to assign values to harms and benefits.		Relies on moral absolutes—no exceptions; need to resolve conflicting rights	Can be difficult to determine the criteria to distinguish equal from unequal claims.	

are the staff auditor in charge of receivables. You are wrapping up the test of subsequent collections of accounts receivable to determine whether certain receivables that were outstanding on December 31, 2015, and that were not confirmed by the customer as being outstanding, have now been collected. If these receivables have been collected and in amounts equal to the year-end outstanding balances, then you will be confident that the December 31 balance is correct and this aspect of the receivables audit can be relied on. One account receivable for $1 million has not been collected, even though it is 90 days past due. You go to your supervisor and discuss whether to establish an allowance for uncollectibles for part of or the entire amount. Your supervisor contacts the manager in charge of the audit, who goes to the CFO to discuss the matter. The CFO says in no uncertain terms that you should not record an allowance of any amount. The CFO does not want to reduce earnings below the current level because that will cause the company to fail to meet financial analysts' estimates of earnings for the year. Your supervisor informs you that the firm will go along with the client on this matter, even though the $1 million amount is material. In fact, it is 10 percent of the overall accounts receivable balance on December 31, 2015.

The junior auditor faces a challenge to integrity in this instance. The client is attempting to circumvent GAAP. The ethical obligation of the staff auditor is not to subordinate judgment to others' judgment, including that of top management of the firm.

If you are an egoist, you might conclude that it is in your best interests to go along with the firm's position, to support the client's presumed interests. After all, you do not want to lose your job. An enlightened egoist would consider the interests of others, including the investors and creditors, but still might reason that it is in her long-run interests to go along with the firm's position to support the client because she may not advance within the firm unless she is perceived to be a "team player."

Utilitarianism

Utilitarians follow a relatively straightforward method for deciding the morally correct course of action for any particular situation. First, they identify the various courses of action that they could perform. Second, they determine the utility of the consequences of all possible alternatives and then select the one that results in the greatest net benefit. In other words, they identify all the foreseeable benefits and harms (consequences) that could result from each course of action for those affected by the action, and then choose the course of action that provides the greatest benefits after the costs have been taken into account.[55] Given its emphasis on evaluating the benefits and harms of alternatives on stakeholders, utilitarianism requires that people look beyond self-interest to consider impartially the interest of all persons affected by their actions.

The utilitarian theory was first formulated in the eighteenth century by the English writer Jeremy Bentham (1748–1832) and later refined by John Stuart Mill (1806–1873). Bentham sought an objective basis that would provide a publicly acceptable norm for determining what kinds of laws England should enact. He believed that the most promising way to reach an agreement was to choose the policy that would bring about the greatest net benefits to society once the harms had been taken into account. His motto became "the greatest good for the greatest number." Over the years, the principle of utilitarianism has been expanded and refined so that today there are many different variations of the principle. Modern utilitarians often describe benefits and harms in terms of satisfaction of personal preferences or in purely economic terms of monetary benefits over monetary costs.[56]

Utilitarians differ in their views about the kind of question we ought to ask ourselves when making an ethical decision. Some believe the proper question is: What effect will my doing this action in this situation have on the general balance of good over evil? If lying would produce the best consequences in a particular situation, we ought to lie.[57] These *act-utilitarians* examine the specific action itself, rather than the general rules governing the action, to assess whether it will result in the greatest utility. For example, a rule in accounting such as "don't subordinate judgment to the client" would serve only as a general guide for an act-utilitarian. If the overall effect of giving in to the client's demands brings net utility to all the stakeholders, then the rule is set aside.

Rule-utilitarians, on the other hand, claim that we must choose the action that conforms to the general rule that would have the best consequences. For the rule-utilitarian, actions are justified by appealing to rules such as "never compromise audit independence." According to the rule-utilitarian, an action is selected because it is required by the correct moral rules that everyone should follow. The correct moral rules are those that maximize intrinsic value and minimize intrinsic disvalue. For example, a general rule such as "don't deceive" (an element of truthfulness) might be interpreted as requiring the full disclosure of the possibility that the client will not collect on a material, $1 million receivable. A rule-utilitarian might reason that the long-term effects of deceiving the users of financial statements are a breakdown of the trust that exists between the users and preparers and auditors of financial information.

In other words, we must ask ourselves: What effect would everyone's doing this kind of action (subordination of judgment) have on the general balance of good over evil? So, for example, the rule "to always tell the truth" in general promotes the good of everyone and therefore should always be followed, even if lying would produce the best consequences in certain situations. Notwithstanding differences between act- and rule-utilitarians, most hold to the general principle that morality must depend on balancing the beneficial and harmful consequences of conduct.[58]

While utilitarianism is a very popular ethical theory, there are some difficulties in relying on it as a sole method for moral decision making because the utilitarian calculation requires that we assign values to the benefits and harms resulting from our actions. But it is often difficult, if not impossible, to measure and compare the values of certain benefits and costs. Let's go back to our receivables example. It would be difficult to quantify the possible effects of going along with the client. How can a utilitarian measure the costs to the company of possibly having to write off a potential bad debt after the fact, including possible higher interest rates to borrow money in the future because of a decline in liquidity? What is the cost to one's reputation for failing to disclose an event at a point in time that might have affected the analysis of financial results? On the other hand, how can we measure the benefits to the company of *not* recording the allowance? Does it mean the stock price will rise and, if so, by how much?

Deontology

The term *deontology* is derived from the Greek word *deon*, meaning "duty." *Deontology* refers to moral philosophies that focus on the rights of individuals and on the intentions associated with a particular behavior, rather than on its consequences. *Deontologists* believe that moral norms establish the basis for action. Deontology differs from rule-utilitarianism in that the moral norms (or rules) are based on reason, not outcomes. Fundamental to deontological theory is the idea that equal respect must be given to all persons.[59] In other words, individuals have certain inherent rights and I, as the decision maker, have a duty (obligation, commitment, or responsibility) to respect those rights.

Philosophers claim that rights and duties are correlative. That is, my rights establish your duties and my duties correspond to the rights of others. The deontological tradition focuses on duties, which can be thought of as establishing the ethical limits of my behavior. From my perspective, duties are what I owe to others. Other people have certain claims on my behavior; in other words, they have certain rights against me.[60]

As with utilitarians, deontologists may be divided into those who focus on moral rules and those who focus on the nature of the acts themselves. In *act deontology,* principles are or should be applied by individuals to each unique circumstance allowing for some space in deciding the right thing to do. *Rule deontologists* believe that general moral principles determine the relationship between the basic rights of the individual and a set of rules governing conduct. It is particularly appropriate to the accounting profession, where the Principles of the AICPA Code support the rights of investors and creditors for accurate and reliable financial information and the duty of CPAs to act in accordance with the profession's rules of conduct to meet their obligations to the users of the financial statements. Rule deontologists believe that conformity to general moral principles based on logic determines ethicalness. Examples include Kant's categorical imperative, discussed next, and the Golden Rule of the Judeo-Christian tradition: "Do unto others as you would have them do unto you." Unlike act deontologists, who hold that actions are the proper basis on which to judge morality or ethicalness and treat rules only as guidelines in the decision-making process, rule deontologists argue there are some things we should never do.[61] Similarly, unlike act-utilitarians, rule deontologists argue that some actions would be wrong regardless of utilitarian benefits. For example, rule deontologists would consider it wrong for someone who has no money to steal bread, because it violates the right of the store owner to gain from his hard work baking and selling the bread. This is the dilemma in the classic novel *Les Misérables* by Victor Hugo. The main character, Jean Valjean, serves a 19-year sentence at hard labor for stealing a loaf of bread to feed his starving family.

Rights Principles

A *right* is a justified claim on others. For example, if I have a right to freedom, then I have a justified claim to be left alone by others. Turned around, I can say that others have a duty or responsibility to leave me alone.[62] In accounting, because investors and creditors have a right to accurate and complete financial information, I have the duty to ensure that the financial statements "present fairly" the financial position, results of operations, and changes in cash flows.

Formulations of *rights theories* first appeared in the seventeenth century in writings of Thomas Hobbes and John Locke. One of the most important and influential interpretations of moral rights is based on the work of Immanuel Kant (1724–1804), an eighteenth-century philosopher. Kant maintained that each of us has a worth or dignity that must be respected. This dignity makes it wrong for others to abuse us or to use us against our will. Kant expressed this idea as a moral principle: Humanity must always be treated as an end, not merely as a means. To treat a person as a mere means is to use her to advance one's own interest. But to treat a person as an end is to respect that person's dignity by allowing each the freedom to choose for himself.[63]

An important contribution of Kantian philosophy is the so-called categorical imperative: "Act only according to that maxim by which you can at the same time will that it should become universal law."[64] The "maxim" of our acts can be thought of as the intention behind our acts. The maxim answers the question: What am I doing, and why? In other words, moral intention is a prerequisite to ethical action, as we discuss more fully in the next chapter.

Kant tells us that we should act only according to those maxims that could be universally accepted and acted on. For example, Kant believed that truth telling could be made a universal law, but lying could not. If we all lied whenever it suited us, rational communication would be impossible. Thus, lying is unethical. Imagine if every company falsified its financial statements. It would be impossible to evaluate the financial results of one company accurately over time and in comparison to other companies. The financial markets might ultimately collapse because reported results were meaningless, or even misleading. This condition of universality, not unlike the Golden Rule, prohibits us from giving our own personal point of view special status over the point of view of others. It is a strong requirement of impartiality and equality for ethics.[65]

One problem with deontological theory is that it relies on moral absolutes—absolute principles and absolute conclusions. Kant believed that a moral rule must function without exception. The notions of rights and duties are completely separate from the consequences of one's actions. This could lead to making decisions that might adhere to one's moral rights and another's attendant duties to those rights, but which also produce disastrous consequences for other people. For example, imagine if you were the person hiding Anne Frank and her family in the attic of your home and the Nazis came banging at the door and demanded, "Do you know where the Franks are?" Now, a strict application of rights theory requires that you tell the truth to the Nazi soldiers. However, isn't this situation one in which an exception to the rule should come into play for humanitarian reasons?

Whenever we are confronted with a moral dilemma, we need to consider whether the action would respect the basic rights of each of the individuals involved. How would the action affect the well-being of those individuals? Would it involve manipulation or deception—either of which would undermine the right to truth that is a crucial personal right? Actions are wrong to the extent that they violate the rights of individuals.[66]

Sometimes the rights of individuals will come into conflict, and one has to decide which right has priority. There is no clear way to resolve conflicts between rights and the corresponding moral duties to respect those rights. One of the most widely discussed cases of this kind is taken from William Styron's novel *Sophie's Choice*. Sophie and her two children are at a Nazi concentration camp. A guard confronts Sophie and tells her that one of her children will be allowed to live and one will be killed. Sophie must decide which child will be killed. She can prevent the death of either of her children, but only by condemning the other to be killed. The guard makes the situation even more painful for Sophie by telling her that if she chooses neither, then both will be killed. With this added factor, Sophie has a morally compelling reason to choose one of her children. But for each child, Sophie has an equally strong reason to save him or her. Thus, the same moral precept gives rise to conflicting obligations.[67]

Now, we do not face such morally excruciating decisions in accounting (thank goodness). The ultimate obligation of accountants and auditors is to honor the public trust. The public interest obligation that is embedded in the profession's codes of ethics requires that if a conflict exists between the obligations of a decision maker to others, the decision maker should always decide based on protecting the public's right (i.e., investors and creditors), such as in the receivables example, to receive accurate and reliable financial information about uncollectibles.

Justice

Justice is usually associated with issues of rights, fairness, and equality. A just act respects your rights and treats you fairly. Justice means giving each person what she or he deserves. *Justice* and *fairness* are closely related terms that are often used interchangeably, although differences do exist. While *justice* usually has been used with reference to a standard of rightness, *fairness* often has been used with regard to an ability to judge without reference to one's feelings or interests.

Justice as Fairness

John Rawls (1921–2002) developed a conception of justice as fairness using elements of both Kantian and utilitarian philosophy. He described a method for the moral evaluation of social and political institutions this way.

> Imagine that you have set for yourself the task of developing a totally new social contract for today's society. How could you do so fairly? Although you could never actually eliminate all of your personal biases and prejudices, you would need to take steps at least to minimize them. Rawls suggests that you imagine yourself in an original position behind a veil of ignorance. Behind this veil, you know nothing of yourself and your natural abilities, or your position in society. You know nothing of your sex, race, nationality, or individual tastes. Behind such a veil of ignorance all individuals are simply specified as rational, free, and morally equal beings. You do know that in the "real world," however, there will be a wide variety in the natural distribution of natural assets and

abilities, and that there will be differences of sex, race, and culture that will distinguish groups of people from each other.

Rawls says that behind the veil of ignorance the only safe principles will be fair principles, for you do not know whether you would suffer or benefit from the structure of any biased institutions. The safest principles will provide for the highest minimum standards of justice in the projected society.

Rawls argues that in a similar manner, the rational individual would only choose to establish a society that would at least conform to the following two rules:

1. *Each person is to have an equal right to the most extensive basic liberty compatible with similar liberty for others.*

2. *Social and economic inequalities are to be arranged so that they are both:*

    (a) reasonably expected to be to everyone's advantage and

    (b) attached to positions and offices open to all.

The first principle—often called the *Liberty Principle*—is very Kantian in that it provides for basic and universal respect for persons as a minimum standard for all just institutions. But while all persons may be morally equal, we also know that in the "real world" there are significant differences between individuals that under conditions of liberty will lead to social and economic inequalities.

The second principle—called the *Difference Principle*—permits such inequalities and even suggests that it will be to the advantage of all (similar to the utility principle), but only if they meet the two specific conditions. Thus the principles are not strictly egalitarian, but they are not laissez-faire either. Rawls is locating his vision of justice in between these two extremes.

When people differ over what they believe should be given, or when decisions have to be made about how benefits and burdens should be distributed among a group of people, questions of justice or fairness inevitably arise. These are questions of *distributive justice*.[68]

The most fundamental principle of justice, defined by Aristotle more than 2,000 years ago, is that "equals should be treated equally and unequals unequally." In other words, individuals should be treated the same unless they differ in ways that are relevant to the situation in which they are involved. The problem with this interpretation is in determining which criteria are morally relevant to distinguish between those who are equal and those who are not. It can be a difficult theory to apply in business if, for example, a CEO of a company decides to allocate a larger share of the resources than is warranted (justified), based on the results of operations, to one product line over another to promote that operation because it is judged to have more long-term expansion and income potential. If I am the manager in charge of the operation getting fewer resources but producing equal or better results, then I may believe that my operation has been (I have been) treated unfairly. On the other hand, it could be said that the other manager deserves to receive a larger share of the resources because of the long-term potential of that other product line. That is, the product lines are not equal; the former deserves more resources because of its greater upside potential.

Justice as fairness is the basis of the objectivity principle in the AICPA Code that establishes a standard of providing unbiased financial information. In our discussion of ethical behavior in this and the following chapters, questions of fairness will be tied to making objective judgments. Auditors should render objective judgments about the fair presentation of financial results. In this regard, auditors should act as impartial arbiters of the truth, just as judges who make decisions in court cases should. The ethical principle of objectivity requires that such judgments be made impartially, unaffected by pressures that may exist to do otherwise. An objective auditor with knowledge about the failure to allow for the uncollectible receivables would not stand idly by and allow the financial statements to be materially misleading.

For purposes of future discussions about ethical decision making, we elaborate on the concept of *procedural justice*. Procedural justice considers the processes and activities that produce a particular outcome. For example, an ethical organization environment should positively influence employees' attitudes and behaviors toward work-group cohesion. When there is strong employee support for decisions, decision makers, organizations, and outcomes, procedural justice is less important to the individual. In contrast, when employees' support for decisions, decision makers, organizations, or outcomes is not very strong, then procedural justice becomes more important.[69] Consider, for example, a potential whistleblower who feels confident about bringing her concerns to top management because specific procedures are in place to support that person. Unlike the Betty Vinson situation, an environment built on procedural justice supports the whistleblower, who perceives the fairness of procedures used to make decisions.

Virtue Ethics

Virtue considerations apply both to the decision maker and to the act under consideration by that party. This is one of the differences between virtue theory and the other moral philosophies that focus on the act. To make an ethical decision, I must internalize the traits of character that make me an ethical (virtuous) person, such as the Six Pillars of Character. This philosophy is called *virtue ethics,* and it posits that what is moral in a given situation is not only what conventional morality or moral rules require but also what a well-intentioned person with a "good" moral character would deem appropriate.

Virtue theorists place less emphasis on learning rules and instead stress the importance of developing *good habits of character,* such as benevolence. Plato emphasized four virtues in particular, which were later called *cardinal virtues:* wisdom, courage, temperance, and justice. Other important virtues are fortitude, generosity, self-respect, good temper, and sincerity. In addition to advocating good habits of character, virtue theorists hold that we should avoid acquiring bad character traits, or vices, such as cowardice, insensibility, injustice, and vanity. Virtue theory emphasizes moral education because virtuous character traits are developed in one's youth. Adults, therefore, are responsible for instilling virtues in the young.

The philosopher Alasdair MacIntyre states that the exercise of virtue requires "a capacity to judge and to do the right thing in the right place at the right time in the right way." Judgment is exercised not through a routinizable application of the rules, but as a function of possessing those dispositions (tendencies) that enable choices to be made about what is good for people and by holding in check desires for something other than what will help achieve this goal.[70]

At the heart of the virtue approach to ethics is the idea of "community." A person's character traits are not developed in isolation, but within and by the communities to which he belongs, such as the Principles in the AICPA Code that pertain to standards of acceptable behavior in the accounting profession (its community).

MacIntyre relates virtues to the internal rewards of a practice (i.e., the accounting profession). He differentiates between the external rewards of a practice (such as money, fame, and power) and the internal rewards, which relate to the intrinsic value of a particular practice. MacIntyre points out that every practice requires a certain kind of relationship between those who participate in it. The virtues are the standards of excellence (i.e., AICPA Code principles) that characterize relationships within the practice. To enter into a practice is to accept the authority of those standards, obedience to the rules, and commitment to achieve the internal rewards. Some of the virtues that MacIntyre identifies are truthfulness, trust, justice, courage, and honesty.[71]

Mintz points out that the accounting profession is a practice with inherent virtues that enable accountants to meet their ethical obligations to clients, employers, the government, and the public at large. For instance, for auditors to render an objective opinion of a client's financial statements, they must be committed to perform such services without bias and to avoid conflicts of interest. Impartiality is an essential virtue for judges in our judicial system. CPAs render judgments on the fairness of financial statements. Therefore, they should act impartially in carrying out their professional responsibilities.[72]

The virtues enable accounting professionals to resolve conflicting duties and loyalties in a morally appropriate way. They provide accountants with the inner strength of character to withstand pressures that might otherwise overwhelm and negatively influence their professional judgment in a relationship of trust.[73] For example, if your boss, the CFO, pressures you to overlook a material misstatement in financial statements, the virtues of honesty and trustworthiness will lead you to place your obligation to investors and creditors ahead of any perceived loyalty obligation to your immediate supervisor or other members of top management. The virtue of integrity enables you to withstand the pressure to look the other way. Now, in the real world, this is easier said than done. You may be tempted to be silent because you fear losing your job. However, the ethical standards of the accounting profession obligate accountants and auditors to bring these issues to the attention of those in the highest positions in an organization, including the audit committee of the board of directors, as Cynthia Cooper did in the WorldCom fraud.

We realize that for students, it may be difficult to internalize the concept that, when forced into a corner by one's supervisor to go along with financial wrongdoing, you should stand up for what you know to be right, even if it means losing your job. However, ask yourself the following questions: Do I even want to work for an organization that does not value my professional opinion? If I go along with it this time, might the same demand be made at a later date? Will I begin to slide down that ethical slippery slope where there is no turning back? How much is my reputation for honesty and integrity worth? Would I be proud if others found out what I did (or didn't do)? To quote the noted Swiss psychologist and psychiatrist, Carl Jung: "You are what you do, not what you say you'll do."

The Public Interest in Accounting

LO 1-5
Explain the concept of the public interest in accounting.

Following the disclosure of numerous accounting scandals in the early 2000s at companies such as Enron and WorldCom, the accounting profession, professional bodies, and regulatory agencies turned their attention to examining how to rebuild the public trust and confidence in financial reporting. Stuebs and Wilkinson point out that restoring the accounting profession's public interest focus is a crucial first step in recapturing the public trust and securing the profession's future.[74] Copeland believes that in order to regain the trust and respect the profession enjoyed prior to the scandals, the profession must rebuild its reputation on its historical foundation of ethics and integrity.[75]

In the United States, the state boards of accountancy are charged with protecting the public interest in licensing candidates to become CPAs. The behavior of licensed CPAs and their ability to meet ethical and professional obligations is regulated by the state boards. Regulatory oversight is based on the statutorily defined scope of practice of public accountancy. There are 54 state boards including four U.S. territories. The National Association of State Boards of Accountancy (NASBA) provides a forum for discussion of the different state board requirements to develop an ideal set of regulations in the Uniform Accountancy Act.

The accounting profession is a community with values and standards of behavior. These are embodied in the various codes of conduct in the professional bodies, including the American Institute of Certified Public Accountants (AICPA). The AICPA is a voluntary association of CPAs with more than 400,000 members in 145 countries, including CPAs in business and industry, public accounting, government, and education; student affiliates; and international associates. CPA state societies also exist in the United States.

The Institute of Management Accountants (IMA), with a membership of more than 70,000, is the worldwide association for accountants and financial professionals working in business. We discuss ethics standards of the IMA later in this chapter. The Institute of Internal Auditors (IIA) is an international professional association representing the internal audit profession with more than 180,000 members. The IIA also has a code of ethics for its professionals.

On an international level, the largest professional accounting association is the Institute of Chartered Accountants [equivalent to CPAs] in England and Wales (ICAEW) that has over 142,000 members worldwide. A truly global professional association is the International Federation of Accountants (IFAC). IFAC is a global professional body dedicated to serve the public interest with over 175 members and associate members in 130 countries representing approximately 2.5 million accountants.

Typically, licensed CPAs work for public accounting firms, and in business, government, and education. It is important to note that state board rules and statutory regulations always supersede rules of professional associations, such as the AICPA, so that when the rules conflict a licensed CPA should follow the state board rules. A good example is when a licensed CPA has possession of client records while performing professional services. Under Rule 501.76 of the Texas State Board of Public Accountancy, a licensee must not withhold client records, including workpapers that constitute client records, once a demand has been made for them regardless of whether fees due to the licensee are outstanding for services already provided. However, under Rule 501 (Section 1.400.200) of the AICPA Code of Professional Conduct (AICPA Code), members of the AICPA can withhold member work product if there are fees due for the specific work product. In this instance, the more restrictive requirement of the Texas State Board must be followed.

Regulation of the Accounting Profession

Professions are defined by the knowledge, skills, attitudes, behaviors, and ethics of those in the (accounting) profession. Regulation of a profession is a specific response to the need for certain standards to be met by the members of the profession. The accounting profession provides an important public service through audits and other assurance services and those who choose to join the community pledge to act in the public interest.

According to IFAC Policy Position Statement 1, a number of reasons exist why regulation might be necessary to ensure that appropriate quality is provided in the market for professional accounting services. These include compliance with ethics, technical, and professional standards and the need to represent the interests of users of those services (i.e., investors and creditors).[76]

Regulations exist to address the knowledge imbalance between the client and the provider of services, who has professional expertise. Regulation also helps when there are significant benefits or costs from the provision of accountancy services that accrue to third parties, other than those acquiring and producing the services.

Effective regulation is predicated on serving the interests of those who are the beneficiaries of professional accounting services. To meet the public interest, regulation must be objectively determined, transparent, and implemented fairly and consistently. The benefits of regulation to the economy and society should outweigh the costs of that regulation.

While regulation is important, it is a necessary but insufficient condition to ensure ethical and professional behavior. Regulations should be designed to promote and achieve this behavior. It is the ethical behavior of the professional accountant that is the ultimate guarantee of good service and quality.

AICPA Code of Conduct

LO 1-6
Discuss the Principles section of the AICPA Code of Professional Conduct.

Given the broader scope of membership in the AICPA and the fact that state boards of accountancy generally recognize its ethical standards in state board rules of conduct, we emphasize the AICPA Code in most of this book. The Principles section of the AICPA Code, which mirrors virtues-based principles, are discussed next. We discuss the rules of conduct that are the enforceable provisions of the AICPA Code in Chapter 4. Later in this chapter, we explain the IMA Statement of Ethical Professional Practice to apply a framework of professional values along with ethical reasoning to a dilemma faced by management accountants.

The Principles of the AICPA Code are aspirational statements that form the foundation for the Code's enforceable rules. The Principles guide members in the performance of their professional responsibilities and call for an unyielding commitment to honor the public trust, even at the sacrifice of personal benefits. While CPAs cannot be legally held to the Principles, they do represent the expectations for CPAs on the part of the public in the performance of professional services. In this regard, the Principles are based on values of the profession and traits of character (virtues) that enable CPAs to meet their obligations to the public.

The Principles include (1) Responsibilities, (2) The Public Interest, (3) Integrity, (4) Objectivity and Independence, (5) Due Care, and (6) Scope and Nature of Services.[77]

The umbrella statement in the Code is that the overriding responsibility of CPAs is to exercise sensitive professional and moral judgments in all activities. By linking professional conduct to moral judgment, the AICPA Code recognizes the importance of moral reasoning in meeting professional obligations.

The second principle defines the public interest to include "clients, credit grantors, governments, employers, investors, the business and financial community, and others who rely on the objectivity and integrity of CPAs to maintain the orderly functioning of commerce." This principle calls for resolving conflicts between these stakeholder groups by recognizing the primacy of a CPA's responsibility to the public as the way to best serve clients' and employers' interests. In discharging their professional responsibilities, CPAs may encounter conflicting pressures from each of these groups. According to the public interest principle, when conflicts arise, the actions taken to resolve them should be based on integrity, guided by the precept that when CPAs fulfill their responsibilities to the public, clients' and employers' interests are best served.

As a principle of CPA conduct, integrity recognizes that the public trust is served by (1) being honest and candid within the constraints of client confidentiality, (2) not subordinating the public trust to personal gain and advantage, (3) observing both the form and spirit of technical and ethical standards, and (4) observing the principles of objectivity and independence and of due care.

Objectivity requires that all CPAs maintain a mental attitude of impartiality and intellectual honesty and be free of conflicts of interest in meeting professional responsibilities. Objectivity pertains to all CPAs in their performance of all professional services. Independence applies only to CPAs who provide attestation services (i.e., auditing and other assurance services), not tax and advisory services. The reason lies in the scope and purpose of an audit. When conducting an audit of a client's financial statements, the CPA gathers evidence to support an opinion on whether the financial statements present fairly, in all material respects, the client's financial position and the results of operations and cash flows in accordance with GAAP. The audit opinion is relied on by investors and creditors (external users), thereby triggering the need to be independent of the client entity to enhance assurances. In tax and advisory engagements, the service is provided primarily for the client (internal user) so that the CPA might become involved in some relationships with the client that might otherwise impair audit independence but do not come into play when providing nonattest services; nonattest services do require objectivity in decision making and the exercise of due care to protect the public interest.

Independence is required both in fact and in appearance. Because it is difficult to determine independence in fact inasmuch as it involves identifying a mindset, CPAs should avoid relationships with a client entity that may be seen as impairing objective judgment by a "reasonable" observer. The foundational standard of independence is discussed in the context of the audit function in Chapter 4.

The due care standard (diligence) calls for continued improvement in the level of competency and quality of services by (1) performing professional services to the best of one's abilities, (2) carrying out professional responsibilities with concern for the best interests of those for whom the services are performed, (3) carrying out those responsibilities in accordance with the public interest, (4) following relevant technical and ethical standards, and (5) properly planning and supervising engagements. A key element of due care is professional skepticism, which means to have a questioning mind and critical assessment of audit evidence.

The importance of the due care standard is as follows. Imagine if a CPA were asked to perform an audit of a school district and the CPA never engaged in governmental auditing before and never completed a course of study in governmental auditing. While the CPA or CPA firm may still obtain the necessary skills to perform the audit—for example, by hiring someone with the required skills—the CPA/firm would have a hard time supervising such work without the proper background and knowledge.

The due care standard also relates to the scope and nature of services performed by a CPA. The latter requires that CPAs practice in firms that have in place internal quality control procedures to ensure that services are competently delivered and adequately supervised and that such services are consistent with one's role as a professional. Also, CPAs should determine, in their individual judgments, whether the scope and nature of other services provided to an audit client would create a conflict of interest in performing an audit for that client.

A high-quality audit features the exercise of professional judgment by the auditor and professional skepticism throughout the planning and performance of the audit. Professional skepticism is an essential attitude that enhances the auditor's ability to identify and respond to conditions that may indicate possible misstatement of the financial statements. Professional judgment is a critical component of ethical behavior in accounting. The qualities of behavior that enable professional judgment come not only from the profession's codes of conduct, but also the virtues and ability to reason through ethical conflicts using ethical reasoning methods.

Virtue, Character, and CPA Obligations

Traits of character such as honesty, integrity, and trustworthiness enable a person to act with virtue and apply the moral point of view. Kurt Baier, a well-known moral philosopher, discusses the moral point of view as being one that emphasizes practical reason and rational choice.[78] To act ethically means to incorporate ethical values into decision making and to reflect on the rightness or wrongness of alternative courses of action. The core values of integrity, objectivity, and independence; attitudes for exercising professional skepticism; and a framework for ethical reasoning all underlie virtue-based decision making in accounting.

Aristotle believed that deliberation (reason and thought) precedes the choice of action and we deliberate about things that are in our power (voluntary) and can be realized by action. The deliberation that leads to the action always concerns choices, not the ends. We take the end for granted—a life of excellence or virtue—and then consider in what manner and by what means it can be realized. In accounting, we might say that the end is to gain the public trust and serve the public interest, and the means to achieve that end is by acting in accordance with the profession's ethical standards.

Aristotle's conception of virtue incorporates positive traits of character that enable reasoned judgments to be made, and in accounting, they support integrity—the inner strength of character to withstand pressures that might otherwise overwhelm and negatively influence their professional judgment. A summary of the virtues is listed in Exhibit 1.4.[79]

EXHIBIT 1.4   Virtues and Ethical Obligations of CPAs

Aristotle's Virtues	Ethical Standards for CPAs
Trustworthiness, benevolence, altruism	Integrity
Honesty, integrity	Truthfulness, non-deception
Impartiality, open-mindedness	Objectivity, independence
Reliability, dependability, faithfulness	Loyalty (confidentiality)
Trustworthiness	Due care (competence and prudence)

Application of Ethical Reasoning in Accounting

LO 1-7
Apply the IMA Statement of Ethical and Professional Practice to a case study.

In this section, we discuss the application of ethical reasoning in its entirety to a common dilemma faced by internal accountants and auditors. The case deals with the classic example of when pressure is imposed on accountants by top management to ignore material misstatements in financial statements.

Many internal accountants, such as controllers and CFOs, are CPAs and members of the IMA. The IMA's Statement of Ethical Professional Practice[80] is presented in Exhibit 1.5. Other than independence, which is a specific ethical requirement of an external audit, the standards of the IMA are similar to the Principles of Professional Conduct in the AICPA Code. Most important, read through the "Resolution of Ethical Conflict" section, which defines the steps to be taken by members when they are pressured to go along with financial statement improprieties. Specific steps to be taken include discussing matters of concern with the highest levels of the organization, including the audit committee.

DigitPrint Case Study

DigitPrint was formed in March 2015 with the goal of developing an outsource business for high-speed digital printing. The company is small and does not yet have a board of directors. The comparative advantage of the company is that its founder and president, Henry Higgins, owned his own print shop for several years before starting DigitPrint. Higgins recently hired Liza Doolittle to run the start-up business. Wally Wonderful, who holds the Certified Management Accountant (CMA) certification from the IMA, was hired to help set up a computerized system to track incoming purchase orders, sales invoices, cash receipts, and cash payments for the printing business.

EXHIBIT 1.5   Institute of Management Accountants Statement of Ethical Professional Practice

Members of IMA shall behave ethically. A commitment to ethical professional practice includes overarching principles that express our values, and standards that guide our conduct.

Principles

IMA's overarching ethical principles include: Honesty, Fairness, Objectivity, and Responsibility. Members shall act in accordance with these principles and shall encourage others within their organizations to adhere to them.

Standards

A member's failure to comply with the following standards may result in disciplinary action.

I. Competence

Each member has a responsibility to:

1. Maintain an appropriate level of professional expertise by continually developing knowledge and skills.
2. Perform professional duties in accordance with relevant laws, regulations, and technical standards.
3. Provide decision support information and recommendations that are accurate, clear, concise, and timely.
4. Recognize and communicate professional limitations or other constraints that would preclude responsible judgment or successful performance of an activity.

II. Confidentiality

Each member has a responsibility to:

1. Keep information confidential except when disclosure is authorized or legally required.
2. Inform all relevant parties regarding appropriate use of confidential information. Monitor subordinates' activities to ensure compliance.
3. Refrain from using confidential information for unethical or illegal advantage.

III. Integrity

Each member has a responsibility to:

1. Mitigate actual conflicts of interest, regularly communicate with business associates to avoid apparent conflicts of interest. Advise all parties of any potential conflicts.
2. Refrain from engaging in any conduct that would prejudice carrying out duties ethically.
3. Abstain from engaging in or supporting any activity that might discredit the profession.

IV. Credibility

Each member has a responsibility to:

1. Communicate information fairly and objectively.
2. Disclose all relevant information that could reasonably be expected to influence an intended user's understanding of the reports, analyses, or recommendations.
3. Disclose delays or deficiencies in information, timeliness, processing, or internal controls in conformance with organization policy and/or applicable law.

Resolution of Ethical Conduct

In applying the Standards of Ethical Professional Practice, you may encounter problems identifying unethical behavior or resolving an ethical conflict. When faced with ethical issues, you should follow your organization's established policies on the resolution of such conflict. If

(Continued)

these policies do not resolve the ethical conflict, you should consider the following courses of action:

1. Discuss the issue with your immediate supervisor except when it appears that the supervisor is involved. In that case, present the issue to the next level. If you cannot achieve a satisfactory resolution, submit the issue to the next management level. If your immediate superior is the chief executive officer or equivalent, the acceptable reviewing authority may be a group such as the audit committee, executive committee, board of directors, board of trustees, or owners. Contact with levels above the immediate superior should be initiated only with your superior's knowledge, assuming he or she is not involved. Communication of such problems to authorities or individuals not employed or engaged by the organization is not considered appropriate, unless you believe there is a clear violation of the law.

2. Clarify relevant ethical issues by initiating a confidential discussion with an IMA Ethics Counselor or other impartial advisor to obtain a better understanding of possible courses of action.

3. Consult your own attorney as to legal obligations and rights concerning the ethical conflict.

DigitPrint received $2 million as venture capital to start the business. The venture capitalists were given an equity share in return. From the beginning, they were concerned about the inability of the management to bring in customer orders and earn profits. In fact, only $200,000 net income had been recorded during the first year. Unfortunately, Wonderful had just discovered that $1 million of accrued expenses had not been recorded at year-end. Had that amount been recorded, the $200,000 net income of DigitPrint would have changed to an $800,000 loss.

Wonderful approached his supervisor, Doolittle, with what he had uncovered. She told him in no uncertain terms that the $1 million of expenses and liabilities could not be recorded, and warned him of the consequences of pursuing the matter any further. The reason was that the venture capitalists might pull out from financing DigitPrint because of the reduction of net income, working capital, and higher level of liabilities. Wonderful is uncertain whether to inform Higgins. On one hand, he feels a loyalty obligation to go along with Doolittle. On the other hand, he believes he has an ethical obligation to the venture capitalists and other financiers that might help fund company operations.

We provide a brief analysis of ethical reasoning methods based on the following. First, consider the ethical standards of the IMA and evaluate potential actions for Wonderful. Then, use ethical reasoning with reference to the obligations of an accountant to analyze what you think Wonderful should do.

IMA Standards

Wonderful is obligated by the competence standard to follow relevant laws, regulations, and technical standards, including GAAP, in reporting financial information. Of particular importance is his obligation to disclose all relevant information, including the accrued expenses, that could reasonably be expected to influence an intended user's understanding (i.e., venture capitalists) of the financial reports. Doolittle has refused to support his position and told him in no uncertain terms not to pursue the matter. At this point, Wonderful should follow the Resolution of Ethical Conduct procedures outlined in the IMA Standards and take the matter up the chain of command. Typically, in a public corporation, this would mean to go as far as the audit committee of the board of directors. However, DigitPrint is a small company without a board, so Henry Higgins, the founder and president, is the final authority. If Higgins backs Doolittle's position of nondisclosure, then Wonderful should seek outside advice from a trusted adviser, including an attorney, to help evaluate legal obligations and rights concerning the ethical conflict. The danger for Wonderful would be if he goes along with the improper accounting for the accrued expenses, and the venture capitalists find out about the material misstatement in the financial statements at a later date, then Wonderful would be blamed both by the company and the venture capitalists.

Utilitarianism

Wonderful should attempt to identify the harms and benefits of the act of recording the transactions versus not recording them. The consequences of failing to inform the venture capitalists about the accrued expenses are severe, not only for Wonderful but also for DigitPrint. These include a possible lawsuit, investigation by regulators for failing to record the information, and, most important, a loss of reputational capital in the marketplace. The primary benefit to Wonderful is acceptance by his superiors, and he can be secure in the knowledge that he'll keep his job. Utilitarian values are difficult to assign to each potential act. Still, Wonderful should act in accordance with the moral rule that honesty requires not only truth telling, but disclosing all the information that another party has a need (or right) to know.

Rights Theory

The venture capitalists have an ethical right to know about the higher level of payables, the lower income, and the effect of the unrecorded transactions on working capital; the company has a duty to the venture capitalists to record the information. Wonderful should take the necessary steps to support such an outcome. The end goal of securing needed financing should not cloud Wonderful's judgment about the means chosen to accomplish the goal (i.e., nondisclosure). Wonderful should ask whether he believes that others in a similar situation should cover up the existence of $1 million in accrued expenses. Assuming that this is not the case, he shouldn't act in this way.

Justice

In this case, the justice principle is linked to the fairness of the presentation of the financial statements. The omission of the $1 million of unrecorded expenses means that the statements would not "present fairly" financial position and results of operations. It violates the rights of the venture capitalists to receive accurate and reliable financial information. As previously explained, a procedural justice perspective applied to the case means to assess the support for employee decisions on the part of the company. As a new employee, Wonderful needs to understand the corporate culture at DigitPrint.

Virtue Considerations

Wonderful is expected to reason through the ethical dilemma and make a decision that is consistent with virtue considerations. The virtue of integrity requires Wonderful to have the courage to withstand the pressure imposed by Doolittle and not subordinate his judgment to hers. Integrity is the virtue that enables Wonderful to act in this way. While he has a loyalty obligation to his employer, it should not override his obligation to the venture capitalists, who expect to receive truthful financial information. A lie by omission is dishonest and inconsistent with the standards of behavior in the accounting profession.

What Should Wonderful Do?

Wonderful should inform Doolittle that he will take his concerns to Higgins. That may force Doolittle's hand and cause her to back off from pressuring Wonderful. As president of the company, Higgins has a right to know about the situation. After all, he hired Doolittle because of her expertise and, presumably, based on certain ethical expectations. Higgins may decide to disclose the matter immediately and cut his losses because this is the right thing to do. On the other hand, if Higgins persists in covering up the matter, then, after seeking outside/legal advice, Wonderful must decide whether to go outside the company. His conscience may move him in this direction. However, the confidentiality standard requires that he not do so unless legally required.

A Message for Students

As you can tell from the DigitPrint case, ethical matters in accounting are not easy to resolve. On one hand, the accountant feels an ethical obligation to his employer or the client. On the other hand, the profession has strong codes of ethics that require accountants and auditors to place the public interest ahead of all other interests. Accounting professionals should analyze conflicting situations and evaluate the ethics by considering professional standards and the moral principles discussed in this chapter. A decision should be made after careful consideration of these factors and by applying logical reasoning to resolve the dilemma.

Keep in mind that you may be in a position during your career where you feel pressured to remain silent about financial wrongdoing. You might rationalize that you didn't commit the unethical act, so your hands are clean. That's not good enough, though, as your ethical obligation to the public and the profession is to do whatever it takes to prevent a fraud from occurring and, if it does, take the necessary steps to correct the matter. We hope that you will internalize the ethical standards of the accounting profession, and look at the bigger picture when pressured by a superior to go along with financial wrongdoing. The road is littered with CFOs/CPAs who masterminded (or at least directed) financial frauds at companies such as Enron, WorldCom, and Tyco. The result of their trials was a jail sentence for Andy Fastow of 10 years, Scott Sullivan of 5 years, and Mark Swartz of 8 1/3 to 25 years. Most important is they lost their livelihood, as well as the respect of the community. A reputation for trust takes a long time to build, but it can be destroyed in no time at all.

Scope and Organization of the Text

The overriding philosophy of this text is that the obligations of accountants and auditors are best understood in the context of ethical and professional responsibilities and organizational ethics. Ethical leadership is a critical component of creating the kind of ethical organization environment that supports ethical decision making.

Ethical decision making in accounting is predicated on moral reasoning. In this chapter, we have attempted to introduce the complex philosophical reasoning methods that help to fulfill the ethical obligations of accounting professionals. In Chapter 2, we address behavioral ethics issues and cognitive development to lay the groundwork for discussions of professional judgment and professional skepticism that form the basis of a sound audit. We introduce a decision-making model that provides a framework for ethical decision making and can be used to help analyze cases presented at the end of each chapter. A critical component of ethical behavior is to go beyond knowledge of what the right thing to do is and translate such knowledge into action. Cognitive development theories address this issue. We also explain the "Giving Voice to Values" methodology that has become an integral part of values-based decision making. In Chapter 3, we transition to the culture of an organization and how processes and procedures can help to create and sustain an ethical organization environment, including effective corporate governance systems. We also address whistleblowing considerations for accounting professionals and the confidentiality requirement.

The remainder of this book focuses more directly on accounting ethics. Chapter 4 addresses the AICPA Code and provisions that establish standards of ethical behavior for accounting professionals. In Chapter 5, we address fraud in financial statements, including the Fraud Triangle, and the obligations of auditors to assess the risk of material misstatements in the financial statements. We also address the PCAOB inspection process.

Auditors can be the target of lawsuits because of business failures and deficient audit work. In Chapter 6, we look at legal liability issues and regulatory requirements. The techniques used to manipulate earnings and obscure financial statement items are discussed in the context of earnings management in Chapter 7. These "financial shenanigans" threaten the reliability of the financial reports and can lead to legal liabilities for accountants and auditors. Finally, in Chapter 8, we look at ethical leadership, the heart and soul of an ethical organization. Leadership in the accounting profession is examined from the perspective of auditor and firm behavior. This chapter ties together much of the discussion in this book and discusses challenges to ethical decision making in the accounting profession going forward.

Concluding Thoughts

Our culture seems to have morphed toward exhibitionist tendencies where people do silly (stupid) things just to get their 15 minutes of fame through a YouTube video and with the promise of their own reality television show. Think about the "balloon boy" incident in October 2009, when the whole world watched a giant balloon fly through the air as a tearful family expressed fears that their six-year-old boy could be inside, all the while knowing the whole thing was staged. The messages sent by some reality programs is anti-ethics, such as MTV's "16 and Pregnant." Then there is the Canadian-based online dating service and social networking service, Ashley Madison. Its tacky Web site aims to facilitate cheating (Slogan: "Life is short. Have an affair.")

When was the last time you picked up a newspaper and read a story about someone doing the right thing because it was the right thing to do? It is rare these days. We seem to read and hear more about pursuing one's own selfish interests, even to the detriment of others. It might be called the "What's in it for me?" approach to life. Nothing could be more contrary to leading a life of virtue, and, as the ancient Greeks knew, benevolence is an important virtue.

In a classic essay on friendship, Ralph Waldo Emerson said: "The only reward of virtue is virtue; the only way to have a friend is to be one."[81] In other words, virtue is its own reward, just as we gain friendship in life by being a friend to someone else. In accounting, integrity is its own reward because it builds trust in client relationships and helps honor the public trust that is the foundation of the accounting profession.

We want to conclude on a positive note. Heroes in accounting do exist: brave people who have spoken out about irregularities in their organizations, such as Cynthia Cooper from WorldCom, whom we have already discussed. Another such hero is David Walker, who served as comptroller general of the United States and head of the Government Accountability Office from 1998 to 2008. Walker appeared before an appropriations committee of the U.S. Senate in 2008 and spoke out about billions of dollars in waste spent by the U.S. government, including on the Iraqi war effort. Then there was auditor Joseph St. Denis, who spoke out about improper accounting practices at his former company, AIG, which received a $150 billion bailout from the U.S. government during the financial crisis of 2008. All three received the Accounting Exemplar Award from the Public Interest Section of the American Accounting Association and serve as role models in the profession.

Discussion Questions

1. A common ethical dilemma used to distinguish between philosophical reasoning methods is the following. Imagine that you are standing on a footbridge spanning some trolley tracks. You see that a runaway trolley is threatening to kill five people. Standing next to you, in between the oncoming trolley and the five people, is a railway worker wearing a large backpack. You quickly realize that the only way to save the people is to push the man off the bridge and onto the tracks below. The man will die, but the bulk of his body and the pack will stop the trolley from reaching the others. (You quickly understand that you can't jump yourself because you aren't large enough to stop the trolley, and there's no time to put on the man's backpack.) Legal concerns aside, would it be ethical for you to save the five people by pushing this stranger to his death? Use the deontological and teleological methods to reason out what you would do and why.

2. Another ethical dilemma deals with a runaway trolley heading for five railway workers who will be killed if it proceeds on its present course. The only way to save these people is to hit a switch that will turn the trolley onto a side track, where it will run over and kill one worker instead of five. Ignoring legal concerns, would it be ethically acceptable for you to turn the trolley by hitting the switch in order to save five people at the expense of one person? Use the deontological and teleological methods to reason out what you would do and why.

3. The following two statements about virtue were made by noted philosophers/writers:

   a. MacIntyre, in his account of Aristotelian virtue, states that integrity is the one trait of character that encompasses all the others. How does integrity relate to, as MacIntrye said, "the wholeness of a human life"?

   b. David Starr Jordan (1851–1931), an educator and writer, said, "Wisdom is knowing what to do next; virtue is doing it." Explain the meaning of this phrase as you see it.

4. a. Do you think it is the same to act in your own self-interest as it is to act in a selfish way? Why or why not?

   b. Do you think "enlightened self-interest" is a contradiction in terms, or is it a valid basis for all actions? Evaluate whether our laissez-faire, free-market economic system does (or should) operate under this philosophy.

5. In this chapter, we have discussed the Joe Paterno matter at Penn State. Another situation where a respected individual's reputation was tarnished by personal decisions is the resignation of David Petraeus, former U.S. military general and head of the Central Intelligence Agency (CIA). On November 9, 2012, Petraeus resigned from the CIA after it was announced he had an extramarital affair with a biographer, Paula Broadwell, who wrote a glowing book about his life. Petraeus acknowledged that he exercised poor judgment by engaging in the affair. When Federal Bureau of Investigation (FBI) agents investigated the matter because of concerns there may have been security leaks, they discovered a substantial number of classified documents on her computer. Broadwell told investigators that she ended up with the secret military documents after taking them from a government building. No security leaks had been found. In accepting Petraeus's resignation, President Obama praised Petraeus's leadership during the Iraq and Afghanistan wars and said: "By any measure, through his lifetime of service, David Petraeus has made our country safer and stronger." Should our evaluation of Petraeus's lifetime of hard work and Petraeus's success in his career be tainted by one act having nothing to do with job performance?

6. One explanation about rights is that there is a difference between what we have the right to do and

what the right thing to do is. Explain what you think is meant by this statement. Do you believe that if someone is rude to you, you have a right to be rude right back?

7. Steroid use in baseball is an important societal issue. Many members of society are concerned that their young sons and daughters may be negatively influenced by what apparently has been done at the major league level to gain an advantage and the possibility of severe health problems for young children from continued use of the body mass enhancer now and in the future. Mark McGwire, who broke Roger Maris's 60-home-run record, initially denied using steroids. He has never come close to the 75 percent positive vote to be in the Hall of Fame. Unfortunately for McGwire, his approval rating has been declining each year since he received 23.7 percent of the vote in 2010 and only 10 percent of the sportscasters voted in 2015 to elect him into the Hall. Some believe that Barry Bonds and Roger Clemens, who were the best at what they did, should be listed in the record books with an asterisk after their names and an explanation that their records were established at a time when baseball productivity might have been positively affected by the use of steroids. Some even believe they should be denied entrance to the baseball Hall of Fame altogether. The results for Bonds (36.8 percent) and Clemens (37.5 percent) in their third year of eligibility (2015) were not close to meeting the 75 percent requirement, and that led some to question whether these superstars would ever be voted into the Hall.[82] Evaluate whether Bonds and Clemens should be elected to the Hall of Fame from a situational ethics point of view.

8. Your best friend is from another country. One day after a particularly stimulating lecture on the meaning of ethics by your instructor, you and your friend disagree about whether culture plays a role in ethical behavior. You state that good ethics are good ethics, and it doesn't matter where you live and work. Your friend tells you that in her country it is common to pay bribes to gain favor with important people. Comment on both positions from a relativistic ethics point of view. What do you believe and why?

9. Hofstede's Cultural Dimensions in Exhibit 1.2 indicate that China has a score of only 20 in Individualism, while the U.S. score is 91. How might the differences in scores manifest itself when the public interest is threatened by harmful actions taken by a member of management who has direct control over an employee's standing within the organization? Should cultural considerations in this instance influence ethical behavior?

10. a. What is the relationship between the ethical obligation of honesty and truth telling?

   b. Is it ever proper to not tell someone something that he or she has an expectation of knowing? If so, describe under what circumstances this might be the case. How does this square with rights theory?

11. Is there a difference between cheating on a math test, lying about your age to purchase a cheaper ticket at a movie theater, and using someone else's ID to get a drink at a bar?

12. Do you think it is ethical for an employer to use social media information as a factor when considering whether to hire an employee? What about monitoring social networking activities of employees while on the job? Use ethical reasoning in answering these questions.

13. In a 2014 segment of *Shark Tank*, Trevor Hiltbrand, the founder of nootropic supplement maker Cerebral Success, sought funding from the "Sharks" to introduce a line of nootropic shots to be sold on college campuses in Five Hour Energy-style containers, but encountered some pushback from some of the Sharks who questioned the ethics of marketing to stressed-out, sleep-deprived college students anxious to get good grades. Should it matter if Hiltbrand was trying to capitalize on the need to gain a competitive edge in college by selling something that may not have received FDA approval?

14. According to Adam Smith's *The Wealth of Nations*, when it comes to government oversight in the free market and regulations, the less intervention, the better. Does the government play an important

role in encouraging businesses to behave in an ethical manner? Explain the basis for your answer. What role do environmental laws have in a capitalistic system?

15. According to the 2011 National Business Ethics Survey conducted by the Ethics Resource Center, *Generational Differences in Workplace Ethics,*[83] a relatively high percentage of Millennials consider certain behaviors in the workplace ethical when compared with their earlier counterparts. These include:

   - Use social networking to find out about the company's competitors (37%),
   - "Friend" a client or customer on a social network (36%),
   - Upload personal photos on a company network (26%),
   - Keep copies of confidential documents (22%),
   - Work less to compensate for cuts in benefits or pay (18%),
   - Buy personal items using a company credit card (15%),
   - Blog or tweet negatively about a company (14%), and
   - Take a copy of work software home for personal use (13%).

   The report further concludes that younger workers are significantly more willing to ignore the presence of misconduct if they think that behavior will help save jobs.

   a. Choose one or more behaviors and explain why Millennials might view the behavior as ethical.
   b. Choose one or more behaviors and explain why you think it is unethical.

   Use ethical reasoning to support your points of view.

16. How should an accounting professional go about determining whether a proposed action is in the public interest?

17. Distinguish between ethical rights and obligations from the perspective of accountants and auditors.

18. Using the concept of justice, evaluate how an auditor would assess the equality of interests in the financial reporting process.

19. Why is it important for a CPA to promote professional services in an ethical manner? Do you believe it would be ethical for a CPA to advertise professional services using testimonials and endorsements? Why or why not?

20. Do you think it would be ethical for a CPA to have someone else do for her that which she is prohibited from doing by the AICPA Code of Professional Conduct? Why or why not? Do you think a CPA can justify allowing the unethical behavior of a supervisor by claiming, "It's not my job to police the behavior of others?"

21. Assume in the DigitPrint case that the venture capitalists do not provide additional financing to the company, even though the accrued expense adjustments have not been made. The company hires an audit firm to conduct an audit of its financial statements to take to a local bank for a loan. The auditors become aware of the unrecorded $1 million in accrued expenses. Liza Doolittle pressures them to delay recording the expenses until after the loan is secured. The auditors do not know whether Henry Higgins is aware of all the facts. Identify the stakeholders in this case. What alternatives are available to the auditors? Use the AICPA Code of Professional Conduct and Josephson's Six Pillars of Character to evaluate the ethics of the alternative courses of action.

22. In the discussion of loyalty in this chapter, a statement is made that "your ethical obligation is to report what you have observed to your supervisor and let her take the appropriate action." We point out that you may want to take your concerns to others. The IMA Statement of Ethical Professional

Practice includes a confidentiality standard that requires members to "keep information confidential except when disclosure is authorized or legally required.

23. Do you think there are any circumstances when you should go outside the company to report financial wrongdoing? If so, to what person/organization would you go? Why? If not, why would you not take the information outside the company?

24. Assume that a corporate officer or other executive asks you, as the accountant for the company, to omit or leave out certain financial figures from the balance sheet that may paint the business in a bad light to the public and investors. Because the request does not involve a direct manipulation of numbers or records, would you agree to go along with the request? What ethical considerations exist for you in deciding on a course of action?

25. Sir Walter Scott (1771–1832), the Scottish novelist and poet, wrote: "Oh what a tangled web we weave, when first we practice to deceive." Comment on what you think Scott meant by this phrase.

26. Assume you are preparing for an interview with the director of personnel and you are considering some of the questions that you might be asked. Craft a response that you would feel comfortable giving for each one.

- Describe an experience in the workplace when your attitudes and beliefs were ethically challenged. Use a personal example if you have not experienced a workplace dilemma.

- What are the most important values that would drive your behavior as a new staff accountant in a CPA firm?

- Describe your ethical expectations of the culture in an accounting firm.

- What would you do if your position on an accounting issue differs from that of firm management?

Endnotes

1. Freeh, Sporkin, and Sullivan, LLP, *Report of the Special Investigative Counsel Regarding the Actions of The Pennsylvania State University Related to the Child Sexual Abuse Committed by Gerald A. Sandusky,* July 12, 2012, Available at: www.thefreehreportonpsu.com/REPORT_FINAL_071212.pdf.

2. Graham Winch, "Witness: I Saw Sandusky Raping Boy in Shower," June 12, 2012, Available at: www.hlntv.com/article/2012/06/12/witness-i-saw-sandusky-raping-child.

3. Eyder Peralta, "Paterno, Others Slammed In Report For Failing To Protect Sandusky's Victims," July 12, 2012, Available at: www.npr.org/blogs/thetwo-way/2012/07/12/156654260/was-there-a-coverup-report-on-penn-state-scandal-may-tell-us.

4. Jeffrey Toobin, "Former Penn State President Graham Spanier Speaks," the *New Yorker* online, August 22, 2012, Available at: www.newyorker.com/online/blogs/newsdesk/2012/08/graham-spanier-interview-on-sandusky-scandal.html#ixzz2PQ326lkq.

5. Max H. Bazerman and Ann E. Trebrunsel, *Blind Spots: Why We Fail to Do What's Right and What to Do about It* (Princeton, NJ: Princeton University Press, 2011).

6. Steven M. Mintz, "Virtue Ethics and Accounting Education," *Issues in Accounting Education* 10, no. 2 (Fall 1995), p. 257.

7. Susan Pulliam and Deborah Solomon, "Ms. Cooper Says No to Her Boss," *The Wall Street Journal,* October 30, 2002, p. A1.

8. Lynne W. Jeter, *Disconnected: Deceit and Betrayal at WorldCom* (Hoboken, NJ: Wiley, 2003).

9. Securities Litigation Watch, *Betty Vinson Gets 5 Months in Prison,* Available at: http://slw.issproxy.com /securities_litigation_blo/2005/08/betty_vinson_ge.html.

10. Cynthia Cooper, *Extraordinary Circumstances* (Hoboken, NJ: Wiley, 2008).

11. Teaching Values, *The Golden Rule in World Religions,* Available at: www.teachingvalues.com/ goldenrule.html.

12. William J. Prior, *Virtue and Knowledge: An Introduction to Ancient Greek Ethics* (London: Routledge, 1991).

13. William H. Shaw and Vincent Barry, *Moral Issues in Business* (Belmont, CA: Wadsworth Cengage Learning, 2010), p. 5.

14. James C. Gaa and Linda Thorne, "An Introduction to the Special Issue on Professionalism and Ethics in Accounting Education," *Issues in Accounting Education* 1, no. 1 (February 2004), p. 1.

15. Joseph Fletcher, *Situation Ethics: The New Morality* (Louisville: KY: Westminster John Knox Press), 1966.

16. Josephson Institute of Ethics, *2012 Report Card on the Ethics of American Youth's Values and Actions,* Available at: http://charactercounts.org/programs/reportcard/2012/index.html.

17. Eric G. Lambert, Nancy Lynee Hogan, and Shannon M. Barton, "Collegiate Academic Dishonesty Revisited: What Have They Done, How Often Have They Done It, Who Does It, and Why Do They Do It?" *Electronic Journal of Sociology,* 2003, Available at: www.sociology.org/content/vol7.4 /lambert_etal.html.

18. Donald L. McCabe and Linda Klebe Treviño, "Individual and Contextual Influences on Academic Dishonesty: A Multicampus Investigation," *Research in Higher Education* 38, no. 3, 1997.

19. Paul Edwards, ed., *The Encyclopedia of Philosophy,* Vol. 3 (New York: Macmillan Company and Free Press, 1967).

20. Brenda Sheets and Paula Waddill, "E-Cheating Among College Business Students," *Information Technology, Learning, and Performance Journal,* Fall 2009, Volume 25, Issue 2, p. 4.

21. Emily E. LaBeff, Robert E. Clark, Valerie J. Haines, and George M. Diekhoff, "Situational Ethics and College Student Cheating," *Sociological Inquiry* 60, no. 2 (May 1990), pp. 190–197.

22. See, for example: Donald L. McCabe, Kenneth D. Butterfield, and Linda Klebe Treviño, "Academic Dishonesty in Graduate Business Programs: Prevalance, Causes, and Proposed Action," *Academy of Management Learning & Education* 5 (2006): 294–305.

23. See, for example, Kathy Lund Dean and Jeri Mullins Beggs, "University Professors and Teaching Ethics: Conceptualizations and Expectations," *Journal of Management Education* 30, no. 1 (2006), pp. 15–44.

24. McCabe, Butterfield, and Treviño.

25. Raef A. Lawson, "Is Classroom Cheating Related to Business Students' Propensity to Cheat in the 'Real World'?" *Journal of Business Ethics* 49, no. 2, (2004), pp. 189–199.

26. Randi L. Sims, "The Relationship between Academic Dishonesty and Unethical Business Practices," *Journal of Education for Business* 68, no. 12, (1993), pp. 37–50.

27. Ethics Resource Center, 2013 National Business Ethics Survey of Social Networkers, Available at: http://www.ethics.org/nbes/key-findings/social-networking/.

28. Ethics Resource Center, 2013 National Business Ethics Survey of Social Networkers, Available at: http://www.ethics.org/nbes/key-findings/social-networking/, pp. 8–10.

29. Geert Hofstede, *Culture's Consequences: International Differences in Work-Related Values* (London: Sage, 1980).

30. Geert Hofstede, *Culture's Consequences: Comparing Values, Behaviours, Institutions, and Organizations* (Thousand Oaks, CA: Sage, 2001), p. 359.

31. Michael Minkov, *What Makes Us Different and Similar: A New Interpretation of the World Values Survey and Other Cross-Cultural Data* (Sofia, Bulgaria: Klasika y Stil Publishing House, 2007).

32. The results are published on a Web site devoted to Hofstede's work: http://geert-hofstede.com /countries.html.

33. Aristotle, *Nicomachean Ethics,* trans. W. D. Ross (Oxford, UK: Oxford University Press, 1925).

34. Michael Josephson, *Making Ethical Decisions,* rev. ed. (Los Angeles: Josephson Institute of Ethics, 2002).

35. Alasdair MacIntyre, *After Virtue,* 2nd ed. (Notre Dame, IN: University of Notre Dame Press, 1984).

36. Josephson.

37. George Washington, *George Washington's Rules of Civility and Decent Behavior in Company and Conversation* (Bedford, ME: Applewood Books, 1994), p. 9.

38. Washington.

39. Cognitive Sciences Laboratory at Princeton University, *WordNet,* Available at: http://wordnet.princeton.edu.

40. Josephson.

41. Amy Anderson, "Profiles in Greatness - Eleanor Roosevelt," Success, December 1, 2008, http://www.success.com/article/profiles-in-greatness-eleanor-roosevelt.

42. Josephson.

43. Edmund L. Pincoffs, *Quandaries and Virtues against Reductivism in Ethics* (Lawrence: University Press of Kansas, 1986).

44. Josephson.

45. Josephson.

46. Michigan Technological University/Business, Universum Student Survey 2014, University Report/ US Edition, Available at: http://www.mtu.edu/career/employers/partner/2014/presentations/usss 2014 university report - ug - business - michigan technological university.pdf.

47. Rhonda Schwartz, Brian Ross, and Chris Francescani, "Edwards Admits Sexual Affair; Lied as Presidential Candidate" (Interview with "Nightline"), August 8, 2008.

48. Christine Porath and Christine Pearson, "The Price of Incivility," *Harvard Business Review,* January–February 2013, Available at: https://hbr.org/2013/01/the-price-of-incivility.

49. James R. Rest, *Moral Development: Advances in Research and Theory* (NY: Praeger, 1986).

50. Adam Smith, *An Inquiry into the Nature and Causes of the Wealth of Nations* (1776), eds. R. H. Campbell, A. S. Skinner, and W. B. Todd (Oxford: Oxford University Press, 1976).

51. Adam Smith, *The Theory of Moral Sentiments* (1759), eds. D. D. Raphael and A. L. Macfie (Oxford: Oxford University Press, 1976).

52. Samuel Fleischacker, "Adam Smith's Moral and Political Philosophy," *The Stanford Encyclopedia of Philosophy* (Spring 2013 Edition), ed. Edward N. Zalta, Available at: http://plato.stanford.edu/archives /spr2013/entries/smith-moral-political/.

53. O. C. Ferrell, John Fraedrich, and Linda Ferrell, *Business Ethics: Ethical Decision Making and Cases,* 9th ed. (Mason, OH: South-Western, Cengage Learning, 2011), p. 157.

54. Ferrell et al., p. 157.

55. Ferrell et al., p. 158.

56. Manuel Velasquez, Claire Andre, Thomas Shanks, and Michael J. Meyer, "Calculating Consequences: The Utilitarian Approach to Ethics," *Issues in Ethics* 2, no. 1 (Winter 1989), Available at: www.scu.edu/ethics.

57. Velasquez et al., 1989.

58. Velasquez et al., 1989.

59. Velasquez et al., 1989

60. Velasquez et al., 1989.

61. Ferrell et al., pp. 160–161.

62. Claire Andre and Manuel Velasquez, "Rights Stuff," Markkula Center for Applied Ethics' *Issues in Ethics* 3, no. 1 (Winter 1990), Available at: www.scu.edu/ethics/publications/iie/v3n1/.

63. Velasquez et al., 1990.

64. Immanuel Kant, *Foundations of Metaphysics of Morals*, trans. Lewis White Beck (New York: Liberal Arts Press, 1959), p. 39.

65. Velasquez et al., 1990.

66. Velasquez, et al. 1990.

67. William Styron, *Sophie's Choice* (London: Chelsea House, 2001).

68. Manuel Velasquez, Claire Andre, Thomas Shanks, and Michael J. Meyer, "Justice and Fairness," *Issues in Ethics* 3, no. 2 (Spring 1990).

69. Ferrell et al., p. 165.

70. MacIntyre, pp. 187–190.

71. MacIntyre, pp. 190–192.

72. Mintz, 1995.

73. Mintz, 1995.

74. Martin Stuebs and Brett Wilkinson, "Restoring the Profession's Public Interest Role," *The CPA Journal* 79, no. 11, (2009) pp. 62–66.

75. James E. Copeland, Jr., "Ethics as an Imperative," *Accounting Horizons* 19, no. 1 (2005), pp. 35–43.

76. International Federation of Accountants (IFAC), *IFAC Policy Position Statement 1,* September 2011, Available at: http://www.ifac.org/system/files/publications/files/PPP1-Regulation-of-the-Accountancy-Profession.pdf.

77. American Institute of Certified Public Accountants, *Code of Professional Conduct* at June 1, 2012 (New York: AICPA, 2012); Available at: www.aicpa.org/Research/Standards/CodeofConduct/Pages/default.aspx.

78. Kurt Baier, *The Rational and Moral Order: The Social Roots of Reason and Morality* (Oxford, U.K.: Oxford University Press, 1994).

79. Steven M. Mintz, "Virtue Ethics and Accounting Education," *Issues in Accounting Education* 10, no. 2 (1995), p. 260.

80. IMA—The Association of Accountants and Financial Professionals in Business, *IMA Statement of Ethical Professional Practice*, Available at: www.imanet.org/pdfs/statement%20of%20Ethics_web.pdf.

81. Ralph Waldo Emerson, *Essays: First and Second Series* (New York: Vintage Paperback, 1990).

82. See: www.espn.go.com/mlb/story/_/id/8828339/no-players-elected-baseball-hall-fame-writers.

83. Ethics Resource Center, Generational Differences in Workplace Ethics: A Supplemental Report of the 2011 National Business Ethics Survey, Available at: http://www.ethics.org/files/u5/2011 GenDiffFinal_0.pdf.

Chapter 1 Cases

Case 1-1 Harvard Cheating Scandal

Yes. Cheating occurs at the prestigious Harvard University. In 2012, Harvard forced dozens of students to leave in its largest cheating scandal in memory, but the institution would not address assertions that the blame rested partly with a professor and his teaching assistants. The issue is whether cheating is truly cheating when students collaborate with each other to find the right answer—in a take-home final exam.

Harvard released the results of its investigation into the controversy, in which 125 undergraduates were alleged to have cheated on an exam in May 2012.[1] The university said that more than half of the students were forced to withdraw, a penalty that typically lasts from two to four semesters. Many returned by 2015. Of the remaining cases, about half were put on disciplinary probation—a strong warning that becomes part of a student's official record. The rest of the students avoided punishment.

In previous years, students thought of Government 1310 as an easy class with optional attendance and frequent collaboration. But students who took it in spring 2012 said that it had suddenly become quite difficult, with tests that were hard to comprehend, so they sought help from the graduate teaching assistants who ran the class discussion groups, graded assignments, and advised them on interpreting exam questions.

Administrators said that on final-exam questions, some students supplied identical answers (right down to typographical errors in some cases), indicating that they had written them together or plagiarized them. But some students claimed that the similarities in their answers were due to sharing notes or sitting in on sessions with the same teaching assistants. The instructions on the take-home exam explicitly prohibited collaboration, but many students said they did not think that included talking with teaching assistants.

The first page of the exam contained these instructions: "The exam is completely open book, open note, open Internet, etc. However, in all other regards, this should fall under similar guidelines that apply to in-class exams. More specifically, students may not discuss the exam with others—this includes resident tutors, writing centers, etc."

Students complained about confusing questions on the final exam. Due to "some good questions" from students, the instructor clarified three exam questions by e-mail before the due date of the exams.

Students claim to have believed that collaboration was allowed in the course. The course's instructor and the teaching assistants sometimes encouraged collaboration, in fact. The teaching assistants—graduate students who graded the exams and ran weekly discussion sessions—varied widely in how they prepared students for the exams, so it was common for students in different sections to share lecture notes and reading materials. During the final exam, some teaching assistants even worked with students to define unfamiliar terms and help them figure out exactly what certain test questions were asking.

Some have questioned whether it is the test's design, rather than the students' conduct, that should be criticized. Others place the blame on the teaching assistants who opened the door to collaboration outside of class by their own behavior in helping students to understand the questions better.

An interesting part of the scandal is that, in March 2013, administrators searched e-mail accounts of some junior faculty members, looking for the source of leaks to the news media about the cheating investigation, prompting much of the faculty to protest what it called a breach of trust.

Harvard adopted an honor code on May 6, 2014. The goal is to establish a culture of academic integrity at the university.

---

[1] The facts of this case are taken from Richard Perez-Peña," Students Disciplined in Harvard Scandal," February 1, 2013, Available at www.nytimes.com/2013/02/02/education/harvard-forced-dozens-to-leave-in-cheating-scandal.html?_r=0.

Answer the following questions about the Harvard cheating scandal.

1. Using Josephson's Six Pillars of Character, which of the character traits (virtues) apply to the Harvard cheating scandal and how do they apply with respect to the actions of each of the stakeholders in this case?
2. Who is at fault for the cheating scandal? Is it the students, the teaching assistants, the professor, or the institution? Use ethical reasoning to support your answer.
3. Do you think Harvard had a right to search the e-mail accounts of junior faculty, looking for the source of leaks to the news media? Explain.
4. What is meant by the culture of an organization? Can an honor code establish a culture of academic integrity in an institution such as Harvard University?

Case 1-2 Giles and Regas

Ed Giles and Susan Regas have never been happier than during the past four months since they have been seeing each other. Giles is a 35-year-old CPA and a partner in the medium-sized accounting firm of Saduga & Mihca. Regas is a 25-year-old senior accountant in the same firm. Although it is acceptable for peers to date, the firm does not permit two members of different ranks within the firm to do so. A partner should not date a senior in the firm any more than a senior should date a junior staff accountant. If such dating eventually leads to marriage, then one of the two must resign because of the conflicts of interest. Both Giles and Regas know the firm's policy on dating, and they have tried to be discreet about their relationship because they don't want to raise any suspicions.

While most of the staff seem to know about Giles and Regas, it is not common knowledge among the partners that the two of them are dating. Perhaps that is why Regas was assigned to work on the audit of CAA Industries for a second year, even though Giles is the supervising partner on the engagement.

As the audit progresses, it becomes clear to the junior staff members that Giles and Regas are spending personal time together during the workday. On one occasion, they were observed leaving for lunch together. Regas did not return to the client's office until three hours later. On another occasion, Regas seemed distracted from her work, and later that day, she received a dozen roses from Giles. A friend of Regas's who knew about the relationship, Ruth Revilo, became concerned when she happened to see the flowers and a card that accompanied them. The card was signed, "Love, Poochie." Regas had once told Revilo that it was the nickname that Regas gave to Giles.

Revilo pulls Regas aside at the end of the day and says, "We have to talk."

"What is it?" Regas asks.

"I know the flowers are from Giles," Revilo says. "Are you crazy?"

"It's none of your business," Regas responds.

Revilo goes on to explain that others on the audit engagement team are aware of the relationship between the two. Revilo cautions Regas about jeopardizing her future with the firm by getting involved in a serious dating relationship with someone of a higher rank. Regas does not respond to this comment. Instead, she admits to being distracted lately because of an argument that she had with Giles. It all started when Regas had suggested to Giles that it might be best if they did not go out during the workweek because she was having a hard time getting to work on time. Giles was upset at the suggestion and called her ungrateful. He said, "I've put everything on the line for you. There's no turning back for me." She points out to Revilo that the flowers are Giles's way of saying he is sorry for some of the comments he had made about her.

Regas promises to talk to Giles and thanks Revilo for her concern. That same day, Regas telephones Giles and tells him she wants to put aside her personal relationship with him until the CAA audit is complete in two weeks. She suggests that, at the end of the two-week period, they get together and thoroughly examine the possible implications of their continued relationship. Giles reluctantly agrees, but he conditions his acceptance on having a "farewell" dinner at their favorite restaurant. Regas agrees to the dinner.

Giles and Regas have dinner that Saturday night. As luck would have it, the controller of CAA Industries, Mark Sax, is at the restaurant with his wife. Sax is startled when he sees Giles and Regas together. He wonders about the possible seriousness of their relationship, while reflecting on the recent progress billings of the accounting firm. Sax believes that the number of hours billed is out of line with work of a similar nature and the fee estimate. He had planned to discuss the matter with Herb Morris, the managing partner of the firm. He decides to call Morris on Monday morning.

"Herb, you son of a gun, it's Mark Sax."

"Mark. How goes the audit?"

"That's why I'm calling," Sax responds. "Can we meet to discuss a few items?"

"Sure," Morris replies. "Just name the time and place."

"How about first thing tomorrow morning?" asks Sax.

"I'll be in your office at 8:00 a.m.," says Morris.

"Better make it at 7:00 a.m., Herb, before your auditors arrive."

Sax and Morris meet to discuss Sax's concerns about seeing Giles and Regas at the restaurant and the possibility that their relationship is negatively affecting audit efficiency. Morris asks whether any other incidents have occurred to make him suspicious about the billings. Sax says that he is only aware of this one instance, although he sensed some apprehension on the part of Regas last week when they discussed why it was taking so long to get the audit recommendations for adjusting entries. Morris listens attentively until Sax finishes and then asks him to be patient while he sets up a meeting to discuss the situation with Giles. Morris promises to get back to Sax by the end of the week.

Questions

1. Analyze the behavior of each party from the perspective of the Six Pillars of Character. Assess the personal responsibility of Ed Giles and Susan Regas for the relationship that developed between them. Who do you think is mostly to blame?

2. If Giles were a person of integrity but just happened to have a "weak moment" in starting a relationship with Regas, what do you think he will say when he meets with Herb Morris? Why?

3. Assume that Ed Giles is the biggest "rainmaker" in the firm. What would you do if you were in Herb Morris's position when you meet with Giles? In your response, consider how you would resolve the situation in regard to both the completion of the CAA Industries audit and the longer-term issue of the continued employment of Giles and Regas in the accounting firm.

Case 1-3 NYC Subway Death: Bystander Effect or Moral Blindness

On December 3, 2012, a terrible incident occurred in the New York City subway when Ki-Suck Han was pushed off a subway platform by Naeem Davis. Han was hit and killed by the train, while observers did nothing other than snap photos on their cell phones as Han was struggling to climb back onto the platform before the oncoming train struck him. Davis was arraigned on a second-degree murder charge and held without bail in the death of Han.

One of the most controversial aspects of this story is that of R. Umar Abbasi, a freelance photographer for the *New York Post,* who was waiting for a train when he said he saw a man approach Han at the Times Square station, get into an altercation with him, and push him into the train's path. He too chose to take pictures of the incident, and the next day, the *Post* published the photographer's handiwork: a photo of Han with his head turned toward the approaching train, his arms reaching up but unable to climb off the tracks in time.

Abbasi told NBC's "Today" show that he was trying to alert the motorman to what was going on by flashing his camera. He said he was shocked that people nearer to the victim didn't try to help in the 22 seconds before the train struck. "It took me a second to figure out what was happening . . . I saw the lights in the distance. My mind was to alert the train," Abbasi said. "The people who were standing close to him . . . they could have moved and grabbed him and pulled him up. No one made an effort."

In a written account Abbasi gave the *Post,* he said that the crowd took videos and snapped photos on their cell phones after Han's mangled body was pulled onto the platform. He said that he shoved the onlookers back while a doctor and another man tried to resuscitate the victim, but Han died in front of them.

Some have attributed the lack of any attempt by those on the subway platform to get involved and go to Han's aid as the bystander effect. The term *bystander effect* refers to the phenomenon in which the greater the number of people present, the less likely people will be to help a person in distress. When an emergency situation occurs, observers are more likely to take action if there are few or no other witnesses. One explanation for the bystander effect is that each individual thinks that others will come to the aid of the threatened person. But when you are alone, either you will help, or no one will.

Questions

1. Do you think the bystander effect was at work in the subway death incident? What role might situational ethics have played in Abbasi's response? How might the bystander effect translate to a situation where members of a work group observe financial improprieties committed by one of their group that threatens the organization? In general, do you think that someone would come forward?

2. Another explanation for the inaction in the subway incident is a kind of *moral blindness,* where a person fails to perceive the existence of moral issues in a particular situation. Do you believe moral blindness existed in the incident? Be sure to address the specific moral issues that give rise to your answer.

3. What would you have done if you were in Abbasi's place and why?

Case 1-4 Lone Star School District

Jose and Emily work as auditors for the state of Texas. They have been assigned to the audit of the Lone Star School District. There have been some problems with audit documentation for the travel and entertainment reimbursement claims of the manager of the school district. The manager knows about the concerns of Jose and Emily, and he approaches them about the matter. The following conversation takes place:

Manager: Listen, I've requested the documentation you asked for, but the hotel says it's no longer in its system.

Jose: Don't you have the credit card receipt or credit card statement?

Manager: I paid cash.

Jose: What about a copy of the hotel bill?

Manager: I threw it out.

Emily: That's a problem. We have to document all your travel and entertainment expenses for the city manager's office.

Manager: Well, I can't produce documents that the hotel can't find. What do you want me to do?

Questions

1. Assume that Jose and Emily are CPAs and members of the AICPA. What ethical standards in the Code of Professional Conduct should guide them in dealing with the manager's inability to support travel and entertainment expenses?

2. Using Josephson's Six Pillars of Character as a guide, evaluate the statements and behavior of the manager.

3. a. Assume that Jose and Emily report to Sharon, the manager of the school district audit. Should they inform Sharon of their concerns? Why or why not?

   b. Assume that they don't inform Sharon, but she finds out from another source. What would you do if you were in Sharon's position?

Case 1-5 Reneging on a Promise

Part A

Billy Tushoes recently received an offer to join the accounting firm of Tick and Check LLP. Billy would prefer to work for Foot and Balance LLP but has not received an offer from the firm the day before he must decide whether to accept the position at Tick and Check. Billy has a friend at Foot and Balance and is thinking about calling her to see if she can find out whether an offer is forthcoming.

Question

1. Should Billy call his friend? Provide reasons why you think he should or should not. Is there any other action you suggest Billy take prior to deciding on the offer of Tick and Check? Why do you recommend that action?

Part B

Assume that Billy calls his friend at Foot and Balance and she explains the delay is due to the recent merger of Vouch and Trace LLP with Foot and Balance. She tells Billy that the offer should be forthcoming. However, Billy gets nervous about the situation and decides to accept the offer of Tick and Check. A week later, he receives a phone call from the partner at Foot and Balance who had promised to contact him about the firm's offer. Billy is offered a position at Foot and Balance at the same salary as Tick and Check. He has one week to decide whether to accept that offer. Billy is not sure what to do. On one hand, he knows it's wrong to accept an offer and then renege on it. On the other hand, Billy hasn't signed a contract with Tick and Check, and the offer with Foot and Balance is his clear preference because he has many friends at that firm.

Questions

1. Identify the stakeholders in this case. Evaluate the alternative courses of action for Billy using ethical reasoning. What should Billy do? Why?
2. Do you think it is ever right to back out of a promise that you gave to someone else? If so, under what circumstances? If not, why not?

Case 1-6 Capitalization versus Expensing

Gloria Hernandez is the controller of a public company. She just completed a meeting with her superior, John Harrison, who is the CFO of the company. Harrison tried to convince Hernandez to go along with his proposal to combine 12 expenditures for repair and maintenance of a plant asset into one amount ($1 million). Each of the expenditures is less than $100,000, the cutoff point for capitalizing expenditures as an asset and depreciating it over the useful life. Hernandez asked for time to think about the matter. As the controller and chief accounting officer of the company, Hernandez knows it's her responsibility to decide how to record the expenditures. She knows that the $1 million amount is material to earnings and the rules in accounting require expensing of each individual item, not capitalization. However, she is under a great deal of pressure to go along with capitalization to boost earnings and meet financial analysts' earnings expectations, and provide for a bonus to top management including herself. Her job may be at stake, and she doesn't want to disappoint her boss.

Questions

Assume both Hernandez and Harrison hold the CPA and CMA designations.

1. What are the loyalty obligations of both parties in this case?
2. Assume that you were in Gloria Hernandez's position. What would motivate you to speak up and act or to stay silent? Would it make a difference if Harrison promised this was a one-time request?
3. What would you do and why?

Case 1-7 Eating Time

Kevin Lowe is depressed. He has been with the CPA firm Stooges LLP for only three months. Yet the partners in charge of the firm—Bo Chambers and his brother, Moe—have asked for a "sit-down." Here's how it goes:

"Kevin, we asked to see you because your time reports indicate that it takes you 50 percent longer to complete audit work than your predecessor," Moe said.

"Well, I am new and still learning on the job," replied Lowe.

"That's true," Bo responded, "but you have to appreciate that we have fixed budgets for these audits. Every hour over the budgeted time costs us money. While we can handle it in the short run, we will have to bill the clients whose audit you work on a larger fee in the future. We don't want to lose clients as a result."

"Are you asking me to cut down on the work I do?" Lowe asked.

"We would never compromise the quality of our audit work," Moe said. "We're trying to figure out why it takes you so much longer than other staff members."

At this point, Lowe started to perspire. He wiped his forehead, took a glass of water, and asked, "Would it be better if I took some of the work home at night and on weekends, completed it, but didn't charge the firm or the client for my time?"

Bo and Moe were surprised by Kevin's openness. On one hand, they valued that trait in their employees. On the other hand, they couldn't answer with a yes. Moe looked at Bo, and then turned to Kevin and said, "It's up to you to decide how to increase your productivity on audits. As you know, this is an important element of performance evaluation."

Kevin cringed. Was the handwriting on the wall in terms of his future with the firm?

"I understand what you're saying," Kevin said. "I will do better in the future—I promise."

"Good," responded Bo and Moe. "Let's meet 30 days from now and we'll discuss your progress on the matters we've discussed today and your future with the firm."

In an effort to deal with the problem, Kevin contacts Joyce, a friend and fellow employee, and asks if she has faced similar problems. Joyce answers "yes" and goes on to explain she handles it by "ghost-ticking." Kevin asks her to explain. "Ghost-ticking is when we document audit procedures that have not been completed." Kevin, dumbfounded, wonders, what kind of a firm am I working for?

Questions

1. Kevin is not a CPA yet. What are his ethical obligations in this case?
2. Given the facts in the case, evaluate using deontological and teleological reasoning whether Kevin should take work home and not charge it to the job. What about engaging in ghost-ticking?
3. What would you do if you were Kevin and why? How would you explain your position to Bo and Moe when you meet in 30 days?

Case 1-8 Shifty Industries

Shifty Industries is a small business that sells home beauty products in the San Luis Obispo, California, area. The company has experienced a cash crunch and is unable to pay its bills on a timely basis. A great deal of pressure exists to minimize cash outflows such as income tax payments to the Internal Revenue Service (IRS) by interpreting income tax regulations as liberally as possible.

You are the tax accountant and a CPA working at the company and you report to the tax manager. He reports to the controller. You are concerned about the fact that your supervisor has asked you to go along with an improper treatment of section 179 depreciation on the 2015 tax return so you can deduct the $100,000 full cost of eligible equipment against taxable income. The problem as you see it is the 2014 limitation of $500,000, which would have been fine for 2015 had Congress extended it, was rolled back to a maximum of $25,000. Therefore, your supervisor is planning to allow Shifty to deduct $75,000 more than allowed by law. Using a 35 percent tax rate it means the company is "increasing" its cash flow by $26,250.

Answer the following questions to prepare for a meeting you will have tomorrow morning with the tax manager.

Questions

1. What values are most important to you in deciding on a course of action? Why?

2. Who are the stakeholders in this case and how might they be affected by your course of action?

3. What would you do and why, assuming your approach will be based on the application of the ethical reasoning methods discussed in the chapter?

Case 1-9 Cleveland Custom Cabinets

Cleveland Custom Cabinets is a specialty cabinet manufacturer for high-end homes in the Cleveland Heights and Shaker Heights areas. The company manufactures cabinets built to the specifications of homeowners and employs 125 custom cabinetmakers and installers. There are 30 administrative and sales staff members working for the company.

James Leroy owns Cleveland Custom Cabinets. His accounting manager is Marcus Sims, who reports to the director of finance. Sims manages 15 accountants. The staff is responsible for keeping track of manufacturing costs by job and preparing internal and external financial reports. The internal reports are used by management for decision making. The external reports are used to support bank loan applications.

The company applies overhead to jobs based on direct labor hours. For 2016, it estimated total overhead to be $4.8 million and 80,000 direct labor hours. The cost of direct materials used during the first quarter of the year is $600,000, and direct labor cost is $400,000 (based on 20,000 hours worked). The company's accounting system is old and does not provide actual overhead information until about four weeks after the close of a quarter. As a result, the applied overhead amount is used for quarterly reports.

On April 10, 2016, Leroy came into Sims's office to pick up the quarterly report. He looked at it aghast. Leroy had planned to take the statements to the bank the next day and meet with the vice president to discuss a $1 million working capital loan. He knew the bank would be reluctant to grant the loan based on the income numbers in Exhibit 1. Without the money, Cleveland could have problems financing everyday operations.

EXHIBIT 1   Cleveland Custom Cabinets

Net Income for the Quarter Ended March 31, 2016	
Sales	$6,400,000
Cost of goods sold	4,800,000
Gross margin	$1,600,000
Selling and administrative expenses	1,510,000
Net income	$ 90,000

Leroy asked Sims to explain how net income could have gone from 14.2 percent of sales for the year ended December 31, 2015, to 1.4 percent for March 31, 2016. Sims pointed out that the estimated overhead cost had doubled for 2016 compared to the actual cost for 2015. He explained to Leroy that rent had doubled and the cost of utilities skyrocketed. In addition, the custom-making machinery was wearing out more rapidly, so the company's repair and maintenance costs also doubled from 2015.

Leroy wouldn't accept Sims's explanation. Instead, he told Sims that the quarterly income had to be at least the same percentage of sales as at December 31, 2015. Sims looked confused and reminded Leroy that the external auditors would wrap up their audit on April 30. Leroy told Sims not to worry about the auditors. He would take care of them. Furthermore, "as the sole owner of the company, there is no reason not to 'tweak' the numbers on a one-time basis. I own the board of directors, so no worries there." He went on to say, "Do it this one time and I won't ask you to do it again." He then reminded Sims of his obligation to remain loyal to the company and its interests. Sims started to soften and asked Leroy just how he expected the tweaking to happen. Leroy flinched, held up his hands, and said, "I'll leave the creative accounting to you."

Questions

1. Do you agree with Leroy's statement that it doesn't matter what the numbers look like because he is the sole owner? Even if it is true that Sims "owns" the board of directors, what should be their role in this matter? What about the external auditors? Should Sims simply accept Leroy's statement that he would handle them?

2. a. Assume that Sims is a CPA and holds the CMA. Put yourself in Sims's position. What are your ethical considerations in deciding whether to tweak the numbers?

   b. Assume you do a utilitarian analysis to help decide what to do. Evaluate the harms and benefits of alternative courses of action. What would you do? Would your analysis change if you use a rights theory approach?

3. Think about how you would actually implement your chosen action. What barriers could you face? How would you overcome them? Is it worth jeopardizing your job in this case? Why or why not?

Case 1-10 Better Boston Beans

Better Boston Beans is a coffee shop located in the Faneuil Hall Marketplace near the waterfront and Government Center in Boston. It specializes in exotic blends of coffee, including Sumatra Dark Roast Black, India Mysore "Gold Nuggets," and Guatemala Antigua. It also serves a number of blended coffees, including Reggae Blend, Jamaican Blue Mountain Blend, and Marrakesh Blend. For those with more pedestrian tastes, the shop serves French Vanilla, Hazelnut, and Hawaiian Macadamia Nut varieties. The coffee of the day varies, but the most popular is Colombia Supremo. The coffee shop also serves a variety of cold-blended coffees.

Cyndie Rosen has worked for Better Boston Beans for six months. She took the job right out of college because she wasn't sure whether she wanted to go to graduate school before beginning a career in financial services. Cyndie hoped that by taking a year off before starting her career or going on to graduate school, she would experience "the real world" and find out firsthand what it is like to work a 40-hour week. (She did not have a full-time job during her college years because her parents paid for the tuition and books.)

Because Cyndie is the "new kid on the block," she is often asked to work the late shift, from 4 p.m. to midnight. She works with one other person, Jeffrey Levy, who is the assistant shift supervisor. Jeffrey has been with Boston Beans for three years but recently was demoted from shift supervisor. Jeffrey reports to Sarah Hoffman, the new shift supervisor. Sarah reports to David Cohen, the owner of the store.

For the past two weeks, Jeffrey has been leaving before 11 p.m., after most of the stores in the Marketplace close, and he has asked Cyndie to close up by herself. Cyndie feels that this is wrong and it is starting to concern her, but she hasn't spoken to Jeffrey or anyone else. Basically, she is afraid to lose her job. Her parents have told her that financially she is on her own. They were disappointed that Cyndie did not go to graduate school or interview for a professional position after graduating from college.

Something happened that is stressing Cyndie out and she doesn't know what to do about it. At 11 p.m. one night, 10 Japanese tourists came into the store for coffee. Cyndie was alone and had to rush around and make five different cold-blended drinks and five different hot-blended coffees. While she was working, one of the Japanese tourists, who spoke English very well, approached her and said that he was shocked that such a famous American coffee shop would only have one worker in the store at any time during the workday. Cyndie didn't want to ignore the man's comments, so she answered that her coworker had to go home early because he was sick. That seemed to satisfy the tourist.

It took Cyndie almost 20 minutes to make all the drinks and also field two phone calls that came in during that time. After she closed for the night, she reflected on the experience. Cyndie realized that it could get worse before it gets better because Jeffrey was now making it a habit to leave work early.

At this point, Cyndie realizes that she either has to approach Jeffrey about her concerns or speak to Sarah. She feels much more comfortable talking to Sarah because, in Cyndie's own words, "Levy gives me the creeps."

Questions

1. Do you think it was right for Cyndie to tell the Japanese tourist that "her coworker had to go home early because he was sick?"

2. Cyndie decided to speak with Jeffrey. From an ethical perspective, do you think Cyndie made the right decision as opposed to speaking directly with either Sarah Hoffman or David Cohen? Would you have done the same thing? Why or why not?

3. During their discussion, Jeffrey tells Cyndie that he has an alcohol problem. Lately, it's gotten to him really bad. That's why he's left early—to get a drink and calm his nerves. Jeffrey also explains that this is the real reason he was demoted. He had been warned that if one more incident occurred, David would fire him. He pleaded with Cyndie to work with him through these hard times. How would you react to Jeffrey's request if you were Cyndie? Would your answer change if Jeffrey was a close personal friend instead of someone who gave you the creeps? Why or why not?

4. Assume that Cyndie keeps quiet. The following week, another incident occurs. Cyndie gets into a shouting match with a customer who became tired of waiting for his coffee after 10 minutes. Cyndie felt terrible about it, apologized to the customer after serving his coffee, and left work that night wondering if it was time to apply to graduate school. The customer was so irate that he contacted David and expressed his displeasure about both the service and Cyndie's attitude. David asks to meet with Jeffrey, Sarah, and Cyndie the next day. What are Cyndie's ethical responsibilities at this point?

Chapter

2

Cognitive Processes and Ethical Decision Making in Accounting

---

Learning Objectives

After studying Chapter 2, you should be able to:

LO 2-1 Describe Kohlberg's stages of moral development.

LO 2-2 Explain the components of Rest's model and how it influences ethical decision making.

LO 2-3 Describe the link between moral intensity and ethical decision making.

LO 2-4 Explain how moral reasoning and virtue influence ethical decision making.

LO 2-5 Apply the steps in the Integrated Ethical Decision-Making Model to a case study.

LO 2-6 Analyze the thought process involved in making decisions and taking ethical action.

LO 2-7 Describe the "Giving Voice to Values" technique and apply it to a case study.

Ethics Reflection

Arthur Andersen and Enron

One event more than any other that demonstrates the failure of professional judgment and ethical reasoning in the period of accounting frauds of the late 1990s and early 2000s is the relationship between Enron and its auditors, Arthur Andersen. Bazerman and Tenbrunsel characterize it as *motivated blindness,* a term that describes the common failure of people to notice others' unethical behavior when seeing that behavior would harm the observer.[1] In 2000, Enron paid Andersen a total of $52 million: $25 million in audit fees and $27 million for consulting services. This amount was enough to make Enron Andersen's second largest account and the largest client in the Houston office. Andersen's judgment was compromised by this relationship and led to moral blindness with respect to Enron's accounting for so-called special-purpose entities (SPEs)—entities set up by the firm and kept off the balance sheet. When Enron declared bankruptcy, there was $13.1 billion in debt on the company's books, $18.1 billion on its nonconsolidated subsidiaries' books, and an estimated $20 billion more off the balance sheets.[2] Barbara Toffler pinpoints Andersen's failures in *Final Accounting,* her book about the rise and fall of Andersen,[3] noting that *The Powers Report* denounced Andersen for failing to fulfill its professional and ethical obligations in connection with its auditing of Enron's financial statements, as well as to bring to the attention of Enron's board of directors concerns about Enron's internal controls over these related-party transactions.

The possibility of an accounting fraud at Enron was first raised in an article by two *Fortune* magazine reporters, Bethany McLean and Peter Elkind, who in 2004 wrote a book that became the basis for a movie of the same name, titled *The Smartest Guys in the Room,*[4] in which they criticized Andersen for failing to use the professional skepticism that requires that an auditor approach the audit with a questioning mind and a critical assessment of audit evidence.

Andersen's ethics were called into question shortly after Enron disclosed that a large portion of the 1997 earnings restatement consisted of adjustments that the auditors had proposed at the end of the 1997 audit but had allowed to go uncorrected. Congressional investigators wanted to know why Andersen tolerated $51 million of known misstatements during a year when Enron reported only $105 million of earnings. Andersen chief executive officer (CEO) Joseph Berardino explained that Enron's 1997 earnings were artificially low due to several hundred million dollars of nonrecurring expenses and write-offs. The proposed adjustments were not material, Berardino testified, because they represented less than 8 percent of "normalized" earnings.[5]

The Enron-Andersen relationship illustrates how a CPA firm can lose sight of its professional obligations. While examining Enron's financial statements, the auditors at Andersen knew that diligent application of strict auditing standards required one decision, but that the consequences for the firm were harmful to its own business interests. It placed the client's interests ahead of its own and the public interest.

Some Andersen auditors paid a steep price for their ethical failings: Their licenses to practice as CPAs in Texas were revoked. David Duncan was charged with failing to exercise due care and professional skepticism in failing to conduct an audit in accordance with generally accepted auditing standards (GAAS) and acting recklessly in issuing unqualified opinions on the 1998–2000 audits, thus violating Section 10(b) of the Securities and Exchange Act.[6]

In this chapter, we explore the process of ethical decision making and how it influences professional judgment. Ethical decision making relies on the ability to make moral judgments using the reasoning methods discussed in Chapter 1. However, the ability to reason ethically does not ensure that ethical action will be taken. The decision maker must follow up ethical intent with ethical action. That may be more difficult than it sounds because the accountant may encounter resistance from those who have a vested interest in the outcome and provide reasons and rationalizations for deviating from sound ethical decisions in a particular instance. In such cases, the decision maker needs to find a way to give "voice" to values -- express one's beliefs and act on them. Think about the following questions as you read this chapter: (1) What are the cognitive processes that guide ethical decision making? (2) What would you do if your attitudes and beliefs conflict with your intended behavior? (3) If you encounter resistance to ethical action, ask yourself: Who can I speak to, what can I say, and what actions can I take to act in accordance with my values?

As we practice resolving dilemmas we find ethics to be less a goal than a pathway, less a destination than a trip, less an inoculation than a process.

Ethicist Rushworth Kidder (1944–2012)

Kidder believed that self-reflection was the key to resolving ethical dilemmas, and a conscious sense of vision and deep core of ethical values provide the courage to stand up to the tough choices.

Kohlberg and the Cognitive Development Approach

LO 2-1
Describe Kohlberg's stages of moral development.

Cognitive development refers to the thought process followed in one's moral development. An individual's ability to make reasoned judgments about moral matters develops in stages. The psychologist Lawrence Kohlberg concluded, on the basis of 20 years of research, that people develop from childhood to adulthood through a sequential and hierarchical series of cognitive stages that characterize the way they think about ethical dilemmas. Moral reasoning processes become more complex and sophisticated with development. Higher stages rely upon cognitive operations that are not available to individuals at lower stages, and higher stages are thought to be "morally better" because they are consistent with philosophical theories of justice and rights.[7] Kohlberg's views on ethical development are helpful in understanding how individuals may internalize moral standards and, as they become more sophisticated in their use, apply them more critically to resolve ethical conflicts.

Kohlberg developed his theory by using data from studies on how decisions are made by individuals. The example of Heinz and the Drug, given here, illustrates a moral dilemma used by Kohlberg to develop his stage-sequence model.

Heinz and the Drug

In Europe, a woman was near death from a rare type of cancer. There was one drug that the doctors thought might save her. It was a form of radium that a druggist in the same town had recently discovered. The drug was expensive to make, but the druggist was charging 10 times what the drug cost him to make: It cost $200 for the radium, and he charged $2,000 for a small dose of the drug. The sick woman's husband, Heinz, went to everyone he knew to borrow the money, but he could get together only about $1,000—half the cost. He told the druggist that his wife was dying and asked him to sell it cheaper or let him pay later. But the druggist said, "No, I discovered the drug and I'm going to make money from it." Heinz got desperate and broke into the man's store to steal the drug for his wife.

Should the husband have done that? Was it right or wrong? Most people say that Heinz's theft was morally justified, but Kohlberg was less concerned about whether they approved or disapproved than with the reasons they gave for their answers. Kohlberg monitored the reasons for judgments given by a group of 75 boys ranging in age from 10 to 16 years and isolated the six stages of moral thought. The boys progressed in reasoning sequentially, with most never reaching the highest stages. He concluded that the universal principle of justice is the highest claim of morality. Kohlberg's justice orientation has been criticized by Carol Gilligan, a noted psychologist and educator.[8] Gilligan claims that because the stages were derived exclusively from interviews with boys, the stages reflect a decidedly male orientation and they ignore the care-and-response orientation that characterizes female moral judgment. For males, advanced moral thought revolves around rules, rights, and abstract principles. The ideal is formal justice, in which all parties evaluate one another's claims in an impartial manner. But this conception of morality, Gilligan argues, fails to capture the distinctly female voice on moral matters. Gilligan believes that women need more information before answering the question: Should Heinz steal the drug? Females look for ways of resolving the dilemma where no one—Heinz, his wife, or the druggist—will experience pain. Gilligan sees the hesitation to judge as a laudable quest for nonviolence, an aversion to cruel situations where someone will get hurt. However, much about her theories has been challenged in the literature. For example, Kohlberg considered it a sign of ethical relativism, a waffling that results from trying to please everyone (Stage 3). Moreover, Gilligan's beliefs seem to imply that men lack a caring response when compared to females. Rest argues that Gilligan has exaggerated the extent of the sex differences found on Kohlberg's scale.[9]

The dilemma of Heinz illustrates the challenge of evaluating the ethics of a decision. Table 2.1 displays three types of responses.[10]

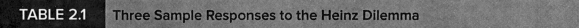

TABLE 2.1	Three Sample Responses to the Heinz Dilemma
A:	It really depends on how much Heinz likes his wife and how much risk there is in taking the drug. If he can get the drug in no other way and if he really likes his wife, he'll have to steal it.
B:	I think that a husband would care so much for his wife that he couldn't just sit around and let her die. He wouldn't be stealing for his own profit; he'd be doing it to help someone he loves.
C:	Regardless of his personal feelings, Heinz has to realize that the druggist is protected by the law. Since no one is above the law, Heinz shouldn't steal it. If we allowed Heinz to steal, then all society would be in danger of anarchy.

Kohlberg considered how the responses were different and what problem-solving strategies underlie the three responses. Response A (Preconventional) presents a rather uncomplicated approach to moral problems. Choices are made based on the wants of the individual decision maker (egoism). Response B (Conventional) also considers the wife's needs. Here, Heinz is concerned that his actions should be motivated by good intentions (i.e., the ends justify the means). In Response C (Postconventional), a societywide perspective is used in decision making. Law is the key in making moral decisions[11] (for example, rule utilitarianism; justice orientation).

The examples in Table 2.2 demonstrate the application of Kohlberg's model of cognitive development to possible decision making in business.

TABLE 2.2	Kohlberg's Stages of Moral Development

Level 1—Preconventional

At the preconventional level, the individual is very self-centered. Rules are seen as something external imposed on the self.

Stage 1: Obedience to Rules; Avoidance of Punishment

At this stage, what is right is judged by one's obedience to rules and authority.

Example: A company forbids making payoffs to government or other officials to gain business. Susan, the company's contract negotiator, might justify refusing the request of a foreign government official to make a payment to gain a contract as being contrary to company rules, or Susan might make the payment if she believes there is little chance of being caught and punished.

Stage 2: Satisfying One's Own Needs

In Stage 2, rules and authority are important only if acting in accordance with them satisfies one's own needs (egoism).

Example: Here, Susan might make the payment even though it is against company rules if she perceives that such payments are a necessary part of doing business. She views the payment as essential to gain the contract. Susan may believe that competitors are willing to make payments, and that making such payments are part of the culture of the host country. She concludes that if she does not make the payment, it might jeopardize her ability to move up the ladder within the organization and possibly forgo personal rewards of salary increases, bonuses, or both. Because everything is *relative,* each person is free to pursue her individual interests.

Level 2—Conventional

At the conventional level, the individual becomes aware of the interests of others and one's duty to society. Personal responsibility becomes an important consideration in decision making.

Stage 3: Fairness to Others

In Stage 3, an individual is not only motivated by rules but seeks to do what is in the perceived best interests of others, especially those in a family, peer group, or work organization. There is a commitment to loyalty in the relationship.

Example: Susan wants to be liked by others. She might be reluctant to make the payment but agrees to do so, not because it benefits her interests, but in response to the pressure imposed by her supervisor, who claims that the company will lose a major contract and employees will be fired if she refuses to go along.

Stage 4: Law and Order

Stage 4 behavior emphasizes the morality of law and duty to the social order. One's duty to society, respect for authority, and maintaining the social order become the focus of decision making.

Example: Susan might refuse to make the illegal payment, even though it leads to a loss of jobs in her company (or maybe even the closing of the company itself), because she views it as her duty to do so in the best interests of society. She does not want to violate the law.

(Continued)

Level 3—Postconventional
Principled morality underlies decision making at this level. The individual recognizes that there must be a societywide basis for cooperation. There is an orientation to principles that shape whatever laws and role systems a society may have.

Stage 5: Social Contract

In Stage 5, an individual is motivated by upholding the basic rights, values, and legal contracts of society. That person recognizes in some cases that legal and moral points of view may conflict. To reduce such conflict, individuals at this stage base their decisions on a rational calculation of benefits and harms to society.

Example: Susan might weigh the alternative courses of action by evaluating how each of the groups is affected by her decision to make the payment. For instance, the company might benefit by gaining the contract. Susan might even be rewarded for her action. The employees are more secure in their jobs. The customer in the other country gets what it wants. On the other hand, the company will be in violation of the Foreign Corrupt Practices Act (FCPA), which prohibits (bribery) payments to foreign government officials. Susan then weighs the consequences of making an illegal payment, including any resulting penalties, against the ability to gain additional business. Susan might conclude that the harms of prosecution, fines, other sanctions, and the loss of one's reputational capital are greater than the benefits.

Stage 6: Universal Ethical Principles

Kohlberg was still working on Stage 6 at the time of his death in 1987. He believed that this stage rarely occurred. Still, a person at this stage believes that right and wrong are determined by universal ethical principles that everyone should follow. Stage 6 individuals believe that there are inalienable rights, which are universal in nature and consequence. These rights, laws, and social agreements are valid not because of a particular society's laws or customs, but because they rest on the premise of universality. Justice and equality are examples of principles that are deemed universal. If a law conflicts with an ethical principle, then an individual should act in accordance with the principle.

An example of such a principle is Immanuel Kant's categorical imperative, the first formulation of which can be stated as: "Act only according to that maxim [reason for acting] by which you can at the same time will that it would become a universal law."[12] Kant's categorical imperative creates an absolute, unconditional requirement that exerts its authority in all circumstances, and is both required and justified as an end in itself.

Example: Susan would go beyond the norms, laws, and authority of groups or individuals. She would disregard pressure from her supervisor or the perceived best interests of the company when deciding what to do. Her action would be guided only by universal ethical principles that would apply to others in a similar situation.

Let's return to the receivables example in Chapter 1 that applies ethical reasoning to the methods discussed in Exhibit 1.3 (Ethical Reasoning Method Bases for Making Ethical Judgments). In the receivables example, an auditor who reasons at Stage 3 might go along with the demands of a client out of loyalty or because she thinks the company will benefit by such inaction. At Stage 4, the auditor places the needs of society and abiding by the law (GAAP, in this instance) above all else, so the auditor will insist on recording an allowance for uncollectibles.

An auditor who reasons at Stage 5 would not want to violate the public interest principle embedded in the profession's ethical standards, which values the public trust above all else. Investors and creditors have a right to know about the uncertainty surrounding collectibility of the receivables. At Stage 6, the auditor would ask whether she would want other auditors to insist on providing an allowance for the uncollectibles if they were involved in a similar situation. This creates an objective standard for determining the right decision. The auditor reasons that the orderly functioning of markets and a level playing field require that financial information should be accurate and reliable, so another auditor should also decide that the allowance needs to be recorded. The application of virtues such as objectivity and integrity enables her to carry out the ethical action and act in a responsible manner.

Kohlberg's model suggests that people continue to change their decision priorities over time and with additional education and experience. They may experience a change in values and ethical behavior.[13] In the context of business, an individual's moral development can be influenced by corporate culture, especially ethics training.[14] Ethics training and education have been shown to improve managers' moral development. More will be said about corporate culture in Chapter 3.

Universal Sequence

Kohlberg maintains that his stage sequence is universal; it is the same in all cultures. This seems to run contrary to Geert Hofstede's five cultural dimensions discussed in Chapter 1. For example, we might expect those in a highly collectivist-oriented society to exhibit Stage 3 features more than in an individualistic one that reflects Stage 2 behavior.

William Crain addresses whether different cultures socialize their children differently, thereby teaching them different moral beliefs.[15] He points out that Kohlberg's response has been that different cultures do teach different beliefs, but that his stages refer not to specific beliefs, but to underlying modes of reasoning. We might assume, then, that in a collectivist society, blowing the whistle on a member of a work group would be considered improper because of the "family" orientation (Stage 3), while in a more individualistic one, it is considered acceptable because it is in the best interests of society (Stage 4). Thus, individuals in different cultures at the same stage-sequence might hold different beliefs about the appropriateness of whistleblowing but still reason the same because, from a fairness perspective, it is the right way to behave.

The Ethical Domain in Accounting and Auditing

Professions, such as accounting, are characterized by their unique expertise gained through education and training, a commitment to lifelong learning, service to society, a code of ethics, and an agreement to abide by the profession's code, and participation in the self-governance and monitoring of the profession.[16] A commitment to serve the public interest is the bedrock of the accounting profession. Snoeyenbos, Almeder, and Humber have described this as a "social contract," in which the professional discharges her obligation by operating with high standards of expertise and integrity. When the profession does not maintain these standards, the social contract is broken, and society may decide to limit the role or the autonomy of the profession. This occurred in the aftermath of the accounting scandals when Congress passed the Sarbanes-Oxley Act (SOX) and established the Public Company Accounting Oversight Board (PCAOB) to oversee the auditing, ethics, and independence practices of CPA firms that audit companies with stock listed on the New York Stock Exchange (NYSE) and NASDAQ. For nonpublicly-owned companies, the standards of the AICPA still apply.[17]

The ethical domain for accountants and auditors usually involves four key constituent groups, including (1) the client organization that hires and pays for accounting services; (2) the accounting firm that employs the practitioner, typically represented by the collective interests of the firm's management; (3) the accounting profession, including various regulatory bodies such as the Securities and Exchange Commission (SEC) and the PCAOB; and (4) the general public, who rely on the attestations and representations of the practitioner and the firm.[18] Responsibilities to each of these groups may conflict. For example, fees are paid by the client organization rather than by the general public, including investors and creditors who are the direct beneficiary of the independent auditing services, so the public interest may conflict with client interests. These conflicts might influence the cognitive development of auditors, thereby influencing their ethical reasoning.

The accounting profession's codes of conduct (i.e., the AICPA Code and IMA Ethical Standards) encourage the individual practitioner's ethical behavior in a way that is consistent with the stated rules and guidelines of the profession. These positive factors work in conjunction with an individual's attitudes and beliefs and ethical reasoning capacity to influence professional judgment and ethical decision making.

Kohlberg's theory of ethical development provides a framework that can be used to consider the effects of conflict areas on ethical reasoning in accounting. For example, if an individual accountant is influenced by the firm's desire to "make the client happy," then the result may be reasoning at Stage 3. The results of published studies during the 1990s by accounting researchers indicate that CPAs reason primarily at Stages 3 and 4. One possible implication of these results is that a larger percentage of CPAs may be overly influenced by their relationship with peers, superiors, and clients (Stage 3) or by rules (Stage 4). A CPA who is unable to apply the technical accounting standards and rules of conduct critically when these requirements are unclear is likely to be influenced by others in the decision-making process.[19] If an auditor reasons at the postconventional level, then that person may refuse to give in to the pressure applied by the supervisor to overlook the client's failure to follow GAAP. This is the ethical position to take, although it may go against the culture of the firm to "go along to get along."

Empirical studies have explored the underlying ethical reasoning processes of accountants and auditors in practice. Findings show that ethical reasoning may be an important determinant of professional judgment, such as the disclosure of sensitive information[20] and auditor independence.[21] Results also show that unethical and dysfunctional audit behavior, such as the underreporting of time on an audit budget, may be systematically related to the auditor's level of ethical reasoning.[22] In reviewing these and other works, Ponemon and Gabhart conclude that the results imply that ethical reasoning may be an important cognitive characteristic that may affect individual judgment and behavior under a wide array of conditions and events in extant professional practice.[23]

The role of an accountant is to tell a story—to make an account—of a series of business activities. This story can be told from a variety of perspectives (i.e., employer or client) and can therefore result in many accounts. It is the role of the accountant to determine the perspective that will fairly present the information in accordance with laws and accounting standards, but they contain options and ambiguities. A higher level of understanding is required to deal with these different perspectives, the options and ambiguities that exist within the standards, and the uncertainties of business life. This higher level of understanding is encapsulated in the postconventional level of reasoning.[24]

Moral Reasoning and Moral Behavior

Within the cognitive-developmental paradigm the most distinguishing characteristic of morality is the human capacity to reason. Moral judgment has long been regarded as the single most influential factor—and the only truly moral determinant—of a person's moral behavior.[25] By definition, morality requires that a person's actions be rational, motivated by purpose or intent, and carried out with autonomous free will. Kohlberg maintained that it is as a result of development in moral reasoning that one becomes truly a moral person, in both mind and deed.[26]

Kohlberg's work is not without its critics. Some philosophers complain it draws too heavily from Rawls's Theory of Justice and makes deontological ethics superior to other ethical perspectives. They note that the theory applies more to societal issues than to individual ethical decisions. A number of psychologists have challenged the notion that people go through "rigid" stages of moral reasoning, arguing instead that they can engage in many ways of thinking about a problem, regardless of their age.[27]

Although he later admitted to having underestimated the complexity of the relation between moral stage and action and revised his thinking to include two intervening cognitive functions to explain it—a prescriptive judgment of the moral right and a personal judgment of responsibility to act accordingly —Kohlberg still contended that it is the logic of a person's reasoning that most strongly influences her moral behavior. Thus, reason constitutes the essential core and strength of character of a person's moral maturity in Kohlberg's theory.[28]

Kohlberg's commitment to reason has been challenged by some who claim he disregarded other factors also associated with moral functioning, such as emotion[29] and traits of character.[30] Others have criticized Kohlberg's emphasis on reason without considering its interaction with other components of morality, and its link to moral behavior in particular.[31] Still others claim the over-reliance on dilemmas, such as Heinz and the Drug, to evaluate moral reasoning shortchanges the role of virtue ethics and its focus on the character of individuals and their overall approach to life.[32]

Noted moral psychologist James Rest attempted to address some of the problems that are recognized in Kohlberg's work, and in doing so has moved from the six-stage model to one with three levels of understanding: personal interest, maintaining norms, and postconventional. Rest focuses on the maintaining norms (similar to the conventional level) and postconventional schemas. By maintaining norms, Rest means recognizing the need for societywide norms; a duty orientation; the need for cooperation; uniform and categorical application of norms, laws, and rules; and that individuals will obey the norms and laws and expect others to do the same even though it may not benefit all affected parties equally.[33]

Rest's conception has particular appeal for accountants who at this level of moral development recognize the importance of various laws and standards, comply with them, understand that sometimes compliance would benefit them and sometimes not, but recognize that obeying these norms is important for society. Rest recognized that, while operating at this level would be ideal for an accountant, it does not ensure that the accountant can make good decisions when there are options and ambiguities within accounting and auditing standards, nor does it ensure that he will have the ability to make good decisions when business circumstances arise that are outside the current laws, norms, or standards.[34]

A higher level of understanding is needed to deal with these different perspectives. The postconventional schema integrates such issues by recognizing that accountants do not have to follow the norms but should seek the moral criteria behind the norms for guidance in action. In accounting this means the fair presentation of financial information in a way that benefits society—that is, the public interest.

Rest's Four-Component Model of Ethical Decision Making

LO 2-2
Explain the components of Rest's model and how it influences ethical decision making.

Cognitive-developmental researchers have attempted to understand the process of ethical decision making. In particular, Rest asserts that ethical actions are not the outcome of a single, unitary decision process, but result from a combination of various cognitive structures and psychological processes. Rest's model of ethical action is based on the presumption that an individual's behavior is related to her level of moral development. Rest built on Kohlberg's work by developing a four-component model of the ethical decision-making process. The four-component model describes the cognitive processes that individuals use in ethical decision making; that is, it depicts how an individual first identifies an ethical dilemma and then continues through to his intention and finally finds courage to behave ethically. Each component of the model must be present before the moral action will be undertaken.[35]

Rest built his four-component model by working backward. He started with the end product—moral action—and then determined the steps that produce such behavior. He concluded that ethical action is the result of four psychological processes: (1) moral sensitivity (recognition), moral judgment, (3) moral focus (motivation), and (4) moral character.

Moral Sensitivity

The first step in moral behavior requires that the individual interpret the situation as moral. Absent the ability to recognize that one's actions affect the welfare of others, it would be virtually impossible to make the most ethical decision when faced with a moral dilemma.

A good example of failing to spot the ethical issues is Dennis Kozlowski, the former CEO of Tyco International. On June 17, 2005, Kozlowski was convicted of crimes related to his receipt of $81 million in purportedly unauthorized bonuses, the purchase of art for his Manhattan apartment of $14.725 million, and the payment by Tyco of a $20 million investment banking fee to Frank Walsh, a former Tyco director. He also had Tyco pay the $30 million for his apartment, which included $6,000 shower curtains and $15,000 "dog umbrella stands," not to mention charging the company one-half of the $2 million, 40th birthday party for his wife held on the Italian island of Sardinia under the guise of having a board of directors meeting.

On September 19, 2005, Kozlowski was sentenced to serve from eight years and four months to twenty-five years in prison for his role in the scandal. On January 17, 2014, he was granted conditional release.

Kozlowski, commenting on his trial in a March 2007 interview with Morley Safer for "60 Minutes," said, "I am absolutely not guilty of the charges. There was no criminal intent here. Nothing was hidden. There were no shredded documents. All the information the prosecutors got was directly off the books and records of the company." He also claimed to have done nothing different from his predecessors. He invoked "ethical legalism" in his defense -- if it is legal, it is ethical.

Kozlowski was blinded by his ambition and never remotely thought about the ethics of his actions. He was not sensitive to these issues because of a desire to keep up with "The Masters of the Universe," by which he meant other CEOs who, at the time, were raking in hundreds of millions of dollars in executive compensation.

Our ability to identify an ethical situation enables us to focus on how alternative courses of action might affect ourselves and others. Kozlowski acted without reflecting on the ethics of the situation. He failed even the most basic test of ethical behavior, which is ethics is all about how we act when no one is looking.

Moral Judgment

An individual's ethical cognition of what "ideally" ought to be done to resolve an ethical dilemma is called *prescriptive reasoning*.[36] The outcome of one's prescriptive reasoning is his ethical judgment of the ideal solution to an ethical dilemma. Generally, an individual's prescriptive reasoning reflects his cognitive understanding of an ethical situation as measured by his level of moral development.[37] Once a person is aware of possible lines of action and how people would be affected by the alternatives, a process aided by the philosophical reasoning methods, a judgment must be made about which course of action is more morally justifiable (which alternative is just or right).

Moral judgment relates to developing moral reasoning abilities over time. Kohlberg argued that individuals progress through a series of moral stages just as they do physical stages. Each stage is more advanced than the one before. People engage in more complex reasoning as they progress up the stages and become less self-centered and develop broader definitions of morality. Rest added that developing moral judgment is a social and cognitive construct that progressed from a self-focused view of moral issues, through a group-based moral perspective, to a reliance on postconventional moral principles, and a primary factor in the understanding of moral actions and emotions.

Making moral judgments is crucial for moral behavior. Carpendale suggests that moral reasoning is viewed as a process of coordinating all perspectives involved in a moral dilemma. He contends that Kohlberg's stages entail a view of moral reasoning as the application of a moral principle or rule to a dilemma in order to generate a solution. Once an individual has internalized a moral principle or rule she would then be expected to apply it to all moral conflicts encountered. If reasoning consists of understanding and coordinating conflicting perspectives in a moral dilemma, consistency in reasoning across different situations should not be expected.[38]

Moral Motivation

After concluding what course of action is best, decision makers must be focused on taking the moral action and follow through with ethical decision making. Moral values may conflict with other values. Moral motivation reflects an individual's willingness to place ethical values (e.g., honesty, integrity, trustworthiness, caring, and empathy) ahead of nonethical values (e.g., wealth, power, and fame) that relate to self-interest. An individual's ethical motivation influences her intention to comply or not comply with her ethical judgment in the resolution of an ethical dilemma.

Sometimes individuals want to do the right thing but are overwhelmed by countervailing pressures that may overpower their ethical intentions because of perceived personal costs. The loss of a job or a client can be motivating factors that compromise integrity and block ethical action.

What would you do if the primary revenue-producing client in your tax practice threatens to fire you and take his bookkeeping work elsewhere unless you ignore a 1099 form showing a significant amount of income that is reportable to the IRS? We can imagine some tax accountants rationalizing not reporting income especially if the client makes a convincing, albeit unethical case to go along just this one time.

Emotions also play a part in moral motivation. Organizations should create ethically rewarding environments to increase moral motivation. To reduce the costs of behaving morally, policies and procedures should be instituted that make it easier to report unethical behavior, prevent retaliation, and create an ethical culture in the organization. Leaders have to inspire employees and build confidence that their ethical intentions are supported by organizational systems.

Moral Character

Individuals do not always behave in accordance with their ethical intention. An individual's intention to act ethically and her ethical actions may not be aligned because of a lack of ethical character. Individuals with strong ethical character will be more likely to carry out their ethical intentions with ethical action than individuals with a weak ethical character because they are better able to withstand any pressures (i.e., have courage and maintain integrity to do otherwise). Once a moral person has considered the ethics of the alternatives, she must construct an appropriate plan of action, avoid distractions, and maintain the courage to continue.

Executing a plan of action takes character. Moral agents have to overcome indifference and opposition, resist distractions, cope with fatigue, and develop tactics and strategies for reaching their goals. Johnson points out that this helps to explain why there is only a moderate correlation between moral judgment and moral behavior. Many times deciding does not lead to doing.[39]

The character traits and virtues discussed in this chapter contribute to ethical follow-through. Courage helps leaders implement their plans despite the risks and costs of doing so while prudence helps them choose the best course of action. Integrity encourages leaders to be true to themselves and their choices. Compassion and justice focus the attention of leaders on the needs of others rather than on personal priorities. Selflessness is the underlying virtue that, in accounting, enables an accounting professional to place the public interest ahead of those of one's employer or client.

The four components of Rest's model are processes that must take place for moral behavior to occur. Rest does not offer the framework as a linear decision-making model, suggesting instead that the components interact through a complicated sequence of "feed-back" and "feed-forward" loops. An individual who demonstrates adequacy in one component may not necessarily be adequate in another, and moral failure can occur when there is a deficiency in any one component.[40] For example, an individual who has good moral reasoning capacity, a skill that can be developed (Component 2), may fail to perceive an ethical problem because she does not clearly understand how others might feel or react—a lack of empathy (Component 1).

Moral Intensity

LO 2-3
Describe the link between moral intensity and ethical decision making.

The lack of research on the characteristics of a moral issue prompted Thomas Jones to develop the moral intensity model. He argued that the characteristics of the moral issue—what he collectively termed moral intensity—influence ethical decision making. Jones's model links moral intensity to Rest's Four-Component Model. The six dimensions are briefly explained below.[41]

Magnitude of Consequences refers to the degree to which an individual may be harmed or benefited by the decision maker's action. A greater degree of harm or benefit results in an increase in moral intensity.

Temporal Immediacy refers to the length of time between the action and its consequences. An action with immediate negative consequences will cause a greater increase in moral intensity than an action for which the consequences are delayed.

Social Consensus refers to the degree of agreement among a social group that an action is good or bad. This social group could be society as a whole (e.g., a fraudulent financial statement is not morally accepted by society because accounting rules and SEC laws prohibit it). A strong Social Consensus that an act is morally wrong increases moral intensity.

Proximity refers to the nearness of the decision maker to the individuals potentially affected by the consequences. An increase in proximity results in an increase of moral intensity. An auditor who becomes too close to a client and is dealing with fraudulent financial statements is likely to feel more pressure from the client because of their close relationship.

Probability of Effect refers to the likelihood that the predicted consequences and the expected level of harm/benefit will occur. Moral intensity increases with an action that has a high probability of occurrence and high likelihood of causing predicted harm. Pressures increase on auditors when harm to the public interest intensifies with the likelihood of fraudulent financial statements.

Concentration of Effect refers to the relationship between the number of people affected and the magnitude of harm. Moral intensity increases if the Concentration of Effect is great. Fraudulent financial statements issued by a publicly owned company that is also using the statements for a significant loan creates additional pressures on auditors to make the most ethical decision possible.[42]

Our contention is there is an important link between moral intensity and ethical decision making. As individuals face morally intense situations, their awareness of the moral dilemma, their judgments about choices and consequences, and their intention to act are significantly affected by specific characteristics of the moral situation. One study found that Social Consensus is significantly associated with moral awareness, judgment, and intention. As subjects in the study recognized a moral issue, formed a judgment, and decided on their intention to act, they were strongly affected by what they believed others within their social group considered morally right or wrong.[43]

The link between Social Consensus and ethical decision making makes sense in accounting because it is a community with shared values and beliefs and expectations for ethical actions. On the other hand, if the CPA firm has a culture of placing the client's interests ahead of the public interest, then intensity increases and moral action may not occur.[44]

Aligning Ethical Behavior and Ethical Intent: Virtue-Based Decision Making

LO 2-4
Explain how moral reasoning and virtue influence ethical decision making.

One question that arises from Rest's model is how to align ethical behavior with ethical intent. The answer is through the exercise of virtue, according to a study conducted by Libby and Thorne.[45] The authors point out that audit failures at companies such as Enron and WorldCom demonstrate that the rules in accounting cannot replace auditors' professional judgment. Transactions (i.e., special-purpose entities at Enron) can be structured around rules, and rules cannot be made to fit every situation. The rules may be unclear or nonexistent, in which case professional judgment is necessary for decisions to be made in accordance with the values of the profession as embodied in its codes of conduct. Professional judgment requires not only technical competence, but also depends on auditors' ethics and virtues.

Libby and Thorne surveyed members of the Canadian accounting community with the help of the Canadian Institute of Chartered Accountants (CICA), the equivalent of the AICPA in the United States, to develop a set of virtues important in the practice of auditing.[46] The authors divided the virtues into two categories: intellectual virtues, which indirectly influence an individual's intentions to exercise professional judgment; and instrumental virtues, which directly influence an individual's actions. The most important intellectual virtues were found to be integrity, truthfulness, independence, objectivity, dependability, being principled, and healthy skepticism. The most important instrumental virtues were diligence (i.e., due care) and being alert, careful, resourceful, consultative, persistence, and courageous. The authors concluded from their study that virtue plays an integral role in both the intention to exercise professional judgment and the exercise of professional judgment, and the necessity of possessing both intellectual and instrumental virtues for auditors.

Returning now to Rest's model, in her seminal paper on the role of virtue on auditors' ethical decision making, Thorne contends that the model fails to provide a theoretical description of the role of personal characteristics, except for level of moral development, in auditors' ethical decision processes. Thorne develops a model of individuals' ethical decision processes that integrates Rest's components with the basic tenets of virtue ethics theory. Her model relies on virtue-based characteristics, which tend to increase the decision maker's propensity to exercise sound ethical judgment. Thorne believes that virtue theory is similar to the approach advocated by the cognitive-developmental perspective in three ways. First, both perspectives suggest that ethical action is the result of a rational decision-making process. Second, both perspectives are concerned with an individual's ethical decision-making process. Third, both perspectives acknowledge the critical role of cognition in individuals' ethical decision making. Exhibit 2.1 presents Thorne's integrated model of the ethical decision-making process.[47]

EXHIBIT 2.1   **Thorne's Integrated Model of Ethical Decision Making[*]**

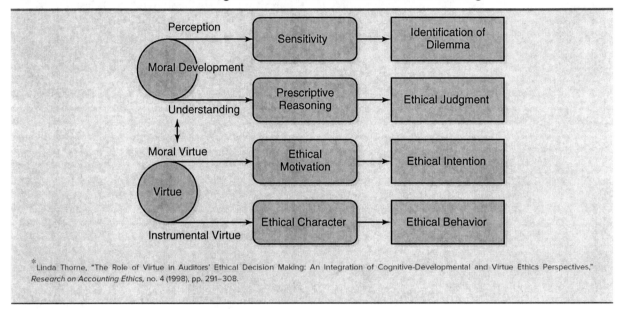

[*]Linda Thorne, "The Role of Virtue in Auditors' Ethical Decision Making: An Integration of Cognitive-Developmental and Virtue Ethics Perspectives," *Research on Accounting Ethics*, no. 4 (1998), pp. 291–308.

Exhibit 2.1 indicates that moral development and virtue are both required for ethical behavior. In her examination of the model, Armstrong suggests that moral development comprises sensitivity to the moral content of a situation or dilemma and prescriptive reasoning, or the ability to understand the issues, think them through, and arrive at an ethical judgment. Similarly, virtue comprises ethical motivation, which describes an individual's willingness to place the interests of others ahead of her own interest; and ethical character, which leads to ethical behavior.[48]

Even though virtue is a critical component of ethical behavior, other factors may get in the way of taking ethical action including situational pressures, business norms, and the moral intensity of the issue itself that influences ethical decision making. Also, one's strength of character deepens with experience, and reflection on ethical dilemmas can bolster one's resolve.

Ethical Decision-Making Models

LO 2-5
Apply the steps in the Integrated Ethical Decision-Making Model to a case study.

Dealing with moral issues can be perplexing. How, exactly, should we think through an ethical issue? What questions should we ask? What factors should we consider? The philosophical methods of moral reasoning suggest that once we have ascertained the facts, we should ask ourselves five questions when trying to resolve a moral issue:

- What benefits and what harms will each course of action produce, and which alternative will lead to the best overall consequences?

- What moral rights do the affected parties have, and which course of action best respects those rights?
- Which course of action treats everyone the same, except where there is a morally justifiable reason not to, and does not show favoritism or discrimination?
- Which course of action advances the common good?
- Which course of action develops moral virtues?

In commenting on the method, Velasquez points out that it does not provide an automatic solution to moral problems. It is not meant to. The method is merely meant to help identify most of the important ethical considerations. In the end, we must deliberate on moral issues for ourselves, keeping a careful eye on both the facts and on the ethical considerations involved.[49]

Virtue is not specifically recognized in the philosophical model, although it is implied by the considerations. It would be difficult to answer these questions in a morally appropriate way without being an honest, trustworthy person in evaluating these considerations and willing to act out of integrity in deciding on the preferred course of action.

Decision-making guidelines can help us make better ethical choices. Johnson points out that taking a systematic approach encourages teams and individuals to carefully define the problem, gather information, apply ethical standards and values, identify and evaluate alternative courses of action, and follow through on their choices. They are also better equipped to defend their decisions.

Kidder's Ethical Checkpoints

Ethicist Rushworth Kidder acknowledges that ethical issues can be "disorderly and sometimes downright confusing." They can arise suddenly, create complex issues, and have unexpected consequences. However, Kidder argues that there is an underlying structure to the ethical decision-making process.[50] Kidder suggests that nine steps or checkpoints can help bring order to otherwise confusing ethical issues. What follows is a brief summary of the major points.

1. *Recognize that there is a moral issue.* Similar to Rest's notion of ethical sensitivity, we must acknowledge that an issue deserves our attention and moral questions exist.

2. *Determine the actor.* Kidder distinguishes between involvement and responsibility. Because we are members of larger communities, we are involved in any ethical issue that arises in the group. Yet we are only responsible for dealing with problems that we can do something about. For example, I may be concerned that clients threaten to fire their auditors if they plan to give a negative opinion on the financial statements. However, there is little I can do about it unless it happens in my firm.

3. *Gather the relevant facts.* Adequate, accurate, and current information is important for making effective decisions of all kinds, including ethical ones. Consider the motives of affected parties, patterns of behavior, likely consequences if the problem persists, and likely outcome of one course of action or another.

4. *Test for right-versus-wrong issues.* Kidder suggests using four determinations including a *legal test*. If lawbreaking is involved (i.e., fraudulent financial statements), then the problem becomes a legal matter, not a moral one. The *smell test* relies on intuition. If you have an uneasy feeling about the decision or course of action, chances are it involves right-versus-wrong issues. The *front-page test* asks how you would feel if your decision made it to the front page of the local newspaper. If you feel uncomfortable about it, then you should consider choosing another alternative. The *mom test*

asks how you would feel if your mother or some other important role model became aware of your choice. If you have a queasy feeling, then it is best to reconsider your choice.

5. *Test for right-versus-right paradigms.* If an issue does not involve wrong behavior, then it likely pits two important positive values against each other. Kidder identified four such models: truth-telling versus loyalty to others and institutions; personal needs versus needs of the community; short-term benefits versus long-term negative consequences; and justice versus mercy. When an ethical dilemma pits two core values against each other, a determination should be made whether they are in conflict with one another in this situation.

6. *Apply the ethical standards and perspectives.* Consider which ethical principle is most relevant and useful to this specific issue. Is it utilitarianism? Kant's categorical imperative? Justice as fairness? Or, is it a combination of perspectives?

7. *Look for a third way.* Compromise is one way to reveal a new alternative that will resolve the problem or to develop a creative solution. A third way can also be the product of moral imagination. One's conception of the moral and ethical issues can change when considering different perspectives from a moral point of view. We may discover a better, economically viable, and morally justifiable solution.

8. *Make the decision.* At some point we have to make the decision. However, we may be mentally exhausted from wrestling with the problem, get caught up in analysis paralysis, or lack the necessary courage to come to a decision.

9. *Revisit and reflect on the decision.* Return to the decision later, after the issue has been resolved, to debrief. Reflect on the lessons to be learned. How can you apply them to future decisions? What ethical issues did it raise?

Johnson evaluates Kidder's approach to ethical decision making by pointing out it seems to cover all the bases, beginning with defining the issue all the way through to learning from the situation in the aftermath of the decision. He recognizes that some decisions involve deciding between two "goods" and leaves the door open for creative solutions. Making a choice is an act of courage, as Kidder points out, and we can apply lessons learned in one dilemma to future problems.[51]

On the flip side, Johnson points out that it is not easy to determine who has responsibility for solving a problem, the facts may not be available, or a time constraint prevents gathering all the relevant information, and decisions do not always lead to action. The model seems to equate deciding with doing and, as we saw in our earlier discussion of moral action, we can decide on a course of action but not follow through. Johnson concludes that Kidder is right to say that making ethical choices takes courage. However, it takes even more courage to put the choice into effect.

We believe that a decision-making process in accounting helps to organize one's thoughts about the ethical issues that accounting professionals face and can serve as a basis for analysis in many of the cases in this book. The integrated model explained below draws on Rest's Model and Kidder's Checkpoints to provide a basis for ethical decision making when accounting issues create ethical dilemmas. Consideration is given to moral intensity and how intellectual instrumental virtues enable ethical action to occur.

The integrated model links to Rest's framework as follows:

Integrated Ethical Decision-Making Process

1. Identify the ethical and professional issues (ethical sensitivity).

- *What are the ethical and professional issues in this case (i.e., GAAP and GAAS)?*
- *Who are the stakeholders (i.e., investors, creditors, employees, management, the organization)?*
- *Which ethical/professional standards apply (i.e., AICPA Code Principles, IMA Ethical Standards, and IFAC standards)?*

2. Identify and evaluate alternative courses of action (ethical judgment).

- *What legal issues exist?*
- *What can and cannot be done in resolving the conflict under professional standards?*
- *Which ethical reasoning methods apply to help reason through alternatives (i.e., rights theory, utilitarianism, justice, and virtue)?*

3. Reflect on the moral intensity of the situation and virtues that enable ethical action to occur (ethical intent).

- *Evaluate the magnitude of the consequences if specific actions are taken; likelihood of those consequences; ability to effect ethical responses by one's actions; consensus view within the profession about the appropriateness of the intended actions.*
- *Consider whether anyone's rights are at stake and how they manifest in the decision-making process*
- *Consider how virtue (i.e., intellectual virtues) motivates ethical actions.*

4. Take action (ethical behavior).

- *Decide on a course of action consistent with one's professional obligations.*
- *How can virtue (i.e., instrumental virtue) support turning ethical intent into ethical action?*
- *What steps can I take to strengthen my position and argument?*
- *How can I counter reasons and rationalizations that mitigate against taking ethical action? Who can I go to for support?*

Reflection would follow after the decision has been made. What was the outcome? How should it affect my approach to ethical decision making? How can I do better in the future?

Application of the Integrated Ethical Decision-Making Model: Ace Manufacturing

In order to illustrate the use of the model, a short case appears in Exhibit 2.2. The facts of the case and ethical issues are analyzed below using the Integrated Model. It is not our intention to cover all points; instead, it is to illustrate the application of the model and consideration of Rest's framework, moral intensity, and the virtues previously discussed and identified in Thorne's study.

Ace Manufacturing: Integrated Ethical Decision-Making Process

1.   Identify the ethical and professional issues (ethical sensitivity).

GAAP

- Appears there may be fraud in the financial statements. Expense accounts were charged for personal withdrawals.

- Financial statements do not fairly present financial position and results of operations due to improper expensing of personal expenditures.
- Taxable income may be similarly misstated.

Stakeholders

- Owners including Jack Jones
- Paul Jones (son)
- Larry Davis (new accountant/CPA)
- IRS
- Banks that may be approached about the loan

Ethical/professional standards

- Objectivity: Davis should not permit bias or influence, because of his relationship with Paul, to interfere with making the right choice.
- Integrity: Don't subordinate judgment to Paul even though he is your boss.
- Due care: Professional skepticism has been exercised; carry through diligently and insist on supporting evidence for the recorded expenditures.

2.   Identify and evaluate alternative courses of action (ethical judgment).

Legal issues

- GAAP appears to be violated; financial statements are fraudulent. Legal liabilities may exist.
- Tax payments will be understated assuming the improper accounting carries over to taxable income.

Alternatives/ethical analysis

- Do nothing: Moral blindness is not a defense to unethical action; violates the rights of the owners of the business; Davis will have violated his ethical responsibilities under the AICPA Code.
- Confront Paul and insist on an explanation: (a) allow him to repay the amount if he agrees to do so, or (b) bring the matter to the attention of the owners regardless of what Paul says.
- Report the matter to Jack Jones—let Paul's dad deal with it: He may pay back the amounts for his son, which sweeps the ethical problem under the rug; he may read the riot act to his son.
- Report the matter to all of the owners: Davis may be fired; the other owners may be grateful and negate any negative action against Davis by Paul or his dad.

Prevailing ethical theories: Rule utilitarianism dictates that certain rules should never be violated regardless of any utilitarian benefits. Owners have a right to know about Paul's ethical lapse.

3.   Reflect on the moral intensity of the situation and virtues that enable ethical action to occur (ethical intent).

- Do I want to be responsible for getting Paul in trouble with his dad, possibly fired? Paul may be prosecuted for his actions. The consequences for Ace are severe so I need to be sure of my decision.

- I want to do the right thing but will my actions do irreparable harm to others? Should I be concerned about "caring about others" given the profession's standards?

- Can I ever trust Paul again? What he did is wrong and I shouldn't become a party to a cover-up.

- I am accountable for my actions; I need to maintain my integrity and not subordinate judgment to Paul.

4.   Take action (ethical behavior).

- Insist that steps be taken to correct the accounting; have the courage to stand up for my beliefs.

- I should give Paul an opportunity to explain why he did what he did, out of fairness, but be prepared to approach the other owners if his explanation and intended actions are not satisfactory.

Once I decide what to do and why, I need to assess how best to express myself and be true to my values. This entails considering how others may react to my decision. This is where a "Giving Voice to Values" framework comes in handy, as discussed below.

Traditional philosophical reasoning methods have limitations. We have already pointed out the need for a link between moral judgment, moral intent, and moral behavior. Beyond that, even if a decision maker has followed a sound ethical analysis, knows what to do, and has made the ethical choice, it still does not mean that her voice will be heard within the organization and it may require a different approach to make a real difference. In the Ace Manufacturing case, Larry Davis needs to prepare for what might happen when he meets with Paul. As explained later on, scripting responses is a sound way of ensuring that one's voice is heard in the resolution of the matter. This is where tools that are provided through behavioral ethics come into play.

EXHIBIT 2.2   Ace Manufacturing

Ace Manufacturing is a privately held company in Anytown, USA. There are three stockholders of the company—Joe Smith, Sue Williams, and Jack Jones. Jones manages the business including the responsibility for the financial statements. Smith and Williams are in charge of sales and marketing. Each owner has a one-third stake in the business.

Jones recently hired his son, Paul, to manage the office. Paul has limited managerial experience, but his father hopes Paul will take over in a few years when he retires, and this is a good opportunity for Paul to learn the business.

Paul is given complete control over payroll, and he approves disbursements, signs checks, and reconciles the general ledger cash account to the bank statement balance. Previously, the bookkeeper was the only employee with such authority. However, the bookkeeper recently left the company, and Jack Jones needed someone he could trust to be in charge of these sensitive operations. He did ask his son to hire someone as soon as possible to help with these and other accounting functions. Paul hired Larry Davis shortly thereafter based on a friend's recommendation. While Davis is relatively inexperienced, he did graduate with honors in Accounting from Anytown University and recently passed all parts of the CPA Exam.

On March 21, one year after hiring Davis, Paul discovered that he needed surgery. Even though the procedure was fairly common and the risks were minimal, Paul planned to take three weeks off after the surgery because of other medical conditions that might complicate the recovery. He told Davis to approve vouchers for payment and present them to his father during the four-week period for payment. Paul had previously discussed this plan with his father, and they both agreed that Davis was ready to assume the additional responsibilities. They did not, however, discuss the matter with either Smith or Williams.

(Continued)

The bank statement for March arrived on April 4. Paul did not tell Davis to reconcile the bank statement. In fact, he specifically told Davis to just put it aside until he returned. But Davis looked at the March statement while trying to trace a payment to a vendor who had billed the company for an invoice that Davis thought had already been paid. In the course of examining the bank statement, Davis noticed five separate payments to Paul, each for $2,000, during March. He became suspicious because Paul's salary was $3,950 per month. What's more, a check for that amount appeared on the statement.

Curiosity got the better of Davis and he decided to trace the checks paid to Paul to the cash disbursements journal. He looked for supporting documentation but couldn't find any. He noticed that the five checks were coded to different accounts including supplies, travel and entertainment, office expense, and two miscellaneous expenses. He then reviewed the banks statements for January and February and found five separate check payments each month to Paul each for $2,000.

Davis didn't know what to do at this point. He was quite certain there was no business justification for the $30,000 payments to Paul for the first three months of the year and he was concerned that if the same pattern continued unabated for the next three months, the total of $60,000 payments to Paul might threaten the ability of the company to secure a $100,000 loan for working capital.

What would you do if you were in the position of Larry Davis? Use the Integrated Ethical Decision-Making Model to craft your responses.

Behavioral Ethics

LO 2-6
Analyze the thought process involved in making decisions and taking ethical action.

The field of behavioral ethics emphasizes the need to consider how individuals actually make decisions, rather than how they would make decisions in an ideal world. Research in behavioral ethics reveals that our minds have two distinct modes of decision making— "System 1" and "System 2" thinking.[52] Daniel Kahneman, the Nobel Prize–winning behavioral economist, points out that System 1 thinking is our intuitive system of processing information: fast, automatic, effortless, and emotional decision processes; on the other hand, System 2 thinking is slower, conscious, effortful, explicit, and a more reasoned decision process. For example, System 1 thinking is detecting that one object is more distant than another, while an example of System 2 thinking is parking in a narrow space.[53]

Kahneman's fundamental proposition is that we identify with System 2, *"the conscious, reasoning self that has beliefs, makes choices and decides what to think about and what to do."* But the one that is really in charge is System 1 as it *"effortlessly originates impressions and feelings that are the main sources of the explicit beliefs and deliberate choices of System 2."*[54]

What follows is an example of using System 1 thinking instead of the more deliberate approach of System 2, and drawing the wrong conclusion as a result. To illustrate, answer the following question: A baseball bat and ball together cost $110. If the bat costs $100 more than the ball, how much does the ball cost? Most people say $10. They decide quickly, without doing the math or thinking through the question. However, it is the wrong answer. The ball actually cost $5, and the bat cost $105.

The broader point of this exercise is to explain how System 1 thinking can lead to snap decisions that make it more difficult to resolve an ethical dilemma in a morally appropriate way. It may occur because you lack important information regarding a decision, fail to notice available information, or face time and cost constraints. You don't have the time or inclination and fail to see the dangers of deciding too quickly.

Many decisions in business and accounting have ethical challenges. This is because of the impacts of those decisions and the fact that outcomes are likely to affect stakeholders in different ways and will express different ethical values. A decision-making model built on System 2 thinking can provide a more systematic analysis that enables comprehensible judgment, clearer reasons, and a more justifiable and defensible action than otherwise would have been the case.

One limitation of the philosophical reasoning approaches incorporated into decision-making models is that how we think we should behave is different from how we decide to behave. This creates a problem of *cognitive dissonance*, a term first coined by Leon Festinger in 1956. The inconsistency between our thoughts, beliefs, or attitudes and our behavior creates the need to resolve contradictory or conflicting beliefs, values, and perceptions.[54] Tompkins and Lawley point out that:

> This dissonance only occurs when we are "attached" to our attitudes or beliefs, i.e., they have emotional significance or consequences for our self-concept or sense of coherence about how the world works. The psychological opposition of irreconcilable ideas (cognitions) held simultaneously by one individual, create[s] a motivated force that [c]ould lead, under proper conditions, to the adjustment of one's beliefs to fit one's behavior instead of changing one's behavior to fit one's beliefs (the sequence conventionally assumed).[55]

Cognitive dissonance suggests that we have an inner drive to hold all our attitudes and beliefs in harmony and avoid disharmony. When there is inconsistency between attitudes or behaviors (dissonance), something must change to eliminate the dissonance. Festinger posits that dissonance can be reduced in one of three ways: (1) change one or more of the attitudes, behavior, or beliefs so as to make the relationship between the two elements a consonant one; (2) acquire new information that outweighs the dissonant beliefs; or (3) reduce the importance of the cognitions (beliefs, attitudes).[56]

The Betty Vinson situation at WorldCom, discussed in Chapter 1, is a case in point about the dangers of reducing dissonance by changing one's attitudes and behaviors. Vinson knew it was wrong to "cook the books." She felt it in her inner being, but she did not act on those beliefs. Instead, she followed the orders from superiors and later justified her behavior by rationalizing it as a one-time act and demanded by people who knew accounting better than herself. In a sense she reduced the importance of her own intuitions about the appropriateness of what she was asked to do.

Bazerman and Gino ask: What makes even good people cross ethical boundaries?[57] Wittmer asks: Do individuals in organizations always act and behave consistently with what they know or believe to be the right thing to do?[58] The behavioral approach to ethics leads to understanding and explaining moral and immoral behavior in systematic ways. In reality, whether behaviors are viewed legally or ethically, we hold individuals accountable for their behaviors and choices, at least in part because they *should have* known better. Even if we agree on what someone should ethically do in a given situation, our judgment is often clouded by other factors that cause us to act against our intuition of what good sense dictates.

Why did CEO Richard Scrushy certify HealthSouth Corporation's financial statements when he knew or was reckless in not knowing they were materially false and misleading? What influenced him to behave unethically? Once we start asking these questions, we shift our attention from inquiring about what the right thing to do is, or what a good person should do. Rather, we are attempting to understand why such an individual acted the way he did, trying to identify the factors that influenced or caused the behaviors. We have moved from a prescriptive framework, such as with the philosophical reasoning methods, to a more descriptive mode of analysis. Such a perspective is important in leading organizations toward more ethical behavior.[59]

Behavioral ethics looks at how human beings actually behave in moral contexts and describes the actual behavior of people, how situational and social forces influence it, and ways in which decisions can be nudged in a more ethical direction through simple interventions. This approach to ethics requires understanding and explaining moral and immoral behavior in systematic ways. It requires understanding the antecedents and consequences of both ethical and unethical actions. Finally, it requires identifying levers at both the individual and the institutional level to change ethically questionable behaviors when individuals are acting in unethical ways that they would not endorse with greater reflection.[60]

Giving Voice to Values

LO 2-7
Describe the "Giving Voice to Values" technique and apply it to a case study.

"Giving Voice to Values (GVV)" is a behavioral ethics approach that shifts the focus away from traditional philosophical reasoning to an emphasis on developing the capacity to effectively express one's values in a way that positively influences others by finding the levers to effectively voice and enact one's values.[61] The methodology asks the protagonist to think about the arguments others might make that create barriers to expressing one's values in the workplace and how best to counteract these "reasons and rationalizations."[62]

GVV links to ethical intent and ethical action in Rest's Model. An ethical decision maker should start by committing to expressing her values in the workplace. The intent is there, but it may fall short of the mark of taking ethical action unless a pathway can be found to express one's values in the workplace. It is the pathway that GVV addresses.

GVV is used post–decision making; that is, you have already decided what to do and have chosen to voice your values. In the Ace Manufacturing case, elaborated on below, Davis knows he must act and we assume he has decided to give Paul a chance to explain about the "personal" expenditures. Other decisions might be made by students, but we use the alternative of giving Paul a chance to explain his actions as the basis for the following discussion.

Davis wants to do what he thinks is right, but he needs to be prepared for the eventuality that Paul will pressure him to stay silent. Davis needs to find a way to communicate his values powerfully and persuasively in the face of strong countervailing organizational or individuals norms, reasons, and rationalizations. In other words, how can Davis find a way to effectively articulate his point of view so that others can be convinced of its rightness?

According to Mary Gentile who developed the GVV methodology, "It shifts the focus away from awareness and analysis to action by addressing a series of questions for protagonists after identifying the right thing to do," including: How can you get it done effectively and efficiently? What do you need to say, to whom, and in what sequence? What will the objections or pushback be and, then, what will you say next? What data and examples do you need to support your point of view?[63]

Kohlberg argued that higher moral development requires role-taking ability. Role-taking ability involves understanding the cognitive and affective (i.e., relating to moods, emotions, and attitudes) aspects of another person's point of view. Davis needs to consider how Paul might react; what he might say; and how Davis might counter those statements when he meets with Paul.

The underlying theme of GVV is that we can effectively voice values in the workplace if we have the proper tools to do so. GVV relies on developing arguments and action plans, and rehearsing how to voice/enact not just any values, but moral values specifically. For our purposes, the pillars of character and virtues discussed in this and the previous chapter are our target behaviors.

Reasons and Rationalizations

An important part of the GVV methodology is to develop ways to confront barriers we may encounter when value conflicts exist in the workplace. These barriers often appear in the form of "reasons and rationalizations" that can confound our best attempts to fulfill our sense of organizational and personal purpose. These are the objections one might hear from colleagues when attempting to point out an ethical problem in the way things are being done, as Cynthia Cooper experienced in the WorldCom case. Or, sometimes you do not hear them because they are the unspoken assumptions of the organization.[64]

GVV provides a framework to deal with the opposing points of view based on the following series of questions.[65]

- What are the main arguments you are trying to counter? That is, what are the *reasons and rationalizations* you need to address?

- What is at *stake* for the key parties, including those who disagree with you?

- What *levers* can you use to influence those who disagree with you?

- What is your most *powerful and persuasive response* to the reasons and rationalizations you need to address? To whom should the argument be made? When and in what context?

Gentile identifies the most frequent categories of argument or rationalization that we face when we speak out against unethical practice. Some of the most common arguments include:

Expected or Standard Practice: "Everyone does this, so it's really standard practice. It's even expected."

Materiality: "The impact of this action is not material. It doesn't really hurt anyone."

Locus of Responsibility: "This is not my responsibility; I'm just following orders here."

Locus of Loyalty: "I know this isn't quite fair to the customer, but I don't want to hurt my reports/team /boss/company."

An additional argument we include is:

Isolated Incident: "This is a one-time request; you won't be asked to do it again."

Basic Exercise in GVV

GVV Brief Exercise: Doing Good by Being Good

Matt and Becca volunteered to head up the Accounting Club efforts to organize volunteers for a clean-up effort and raise donations to help the students, faculty, and staff at the college affected by Hurricane Debits. Over 1,200 had been displaced from their homes, apartments, and dorm rooms due to the severe weather. Over the next month the 25 students of the club helped clean up debris left by the storm and donated over 2,000 hours of time. Matt set up a GoFundMe Web page and posted pictures of the devastation on Instagram. Donations from the community totaled $20,367. The relief agencies in town suggested the club purchase $100 Visa and MasterCard gift cards to be distributed to the affected community members. Matt purchased 200 such cards and Becca delivered them.

Later that afternoon at the Accounting Club meeting, Matt announced that $20,000 was raised for the GoFundMe program and 200 locals received a $100 gift card each. Becca, who was the club treasurer, quickly realized there was $367 unaccounted for. Matt tried to explain there were fees for processing the transactions.

Becca asked Matt: "Why didn't you go to the stores that agreed to waive the fees for the disaster relief recovery?"

"Becca, they waived most of the fees but the remaining fees totaled $400. I donated $33 to cover the balance."

"Do you have receipts for the balance?"

"Becca, don't you trust me?"

"Matt, do you recall what our Auditing professor said yesterday? Trust but verify? I need the receipt for the gift cards."

"Ok, Becca. I'll find it and get it to you soon."

Shortly after the meeting ended, Becca hears Matt telling another member about a trip he planned to see his girlfriend.

"Matt, last week you told me you had no money to go. How did you get it?"

"It's not such an expensive trip. It should cost about $400," Matt told David.

David was surprised to hear the amount was the same as the credit card fees but said nothing. Becca happened to overhear the conversation and immediately realized that 4 more victims could have been helped. She was suspicious of Matt's explanation, to say the least.

Becca knew she had to do something but wasn't sure of the approach she should take. She also knows Matt is a former president of the club, is graduating this year, and has a position with a Big Four accounting firm.

Answer the following questions to develop a script for Becca assuming she has decided to approach Matt about the $400.

Discussion Questions (brief talking points are provided for Becca).

1.   **What are the main arguments you are trying to counter? That is, what are the reasons and rationalizations you need to address?**

- *Matt created a trust and loyalty defense (Locus of Loyalty).*
- *Matt is graduating and doesn't want anything to affect his position with the firm.*
- *Matt may say the $400 is a small amount and not worth arguing over (Materiality).*
- *Matt may say it was a one-time event and won't happen again (Isolated Incident).*

2.   **What's at stake for the key parties, including those with whom you disagree?**

- *Matt's reputation is on the line.*
- *Becca may be concerned other club members would not support her and suggest she should let it go, given Matt's situation. (They might approach the dilemma from an egoistic point of view; Becca needs to emphasize enlightened egoism/Rights).*
- *Becca needs to consider what would happen if the club faculty advisor found out or members of the community become aware of the situation (Kidder's front page test).*

3.   What levers can you use to influence those with whom you disagree?

- *Becca could speak to David who also attended the meeting and develop a plan to approach Matt.*

- *Becca could tell Matt that she will go to the faculty advisor if he doesn't repay the $367.*

- *Becca could emphasize to Matt he is jeopardizing the respect that others have for him.*

4.   What is your most powerful and persuasive response to the reasons and rationalizations you need to address?

- *Becca could explain to Matt he is cheating the victims out of money that is rightly theirs. She could emphasize the lack of ethical standards in his action.*

- *Becca could explain to Matt if he had acted similarly while working for the Big Four firm, he would have violated the profession's ethical standards including due care and integrity.*

- *Becca could explain that her loyalty obligation is to the club and victims of the disaster.*

- *Becca could emphasize to Matt that he doesn't want to implicate David in any cover-up and needs to do the right thing.*

Students should think about other points they might make if faced with a similar ethical dilemma.

Ace Manufacturing: GVV Analysis

Building on the Ace Manufacturing case discussed earlier on, once Davis has decided what to do, which is to give Paul a chance to explain, he needs to consider how best to express his point of view; act on his beliefs; and convince Paul to take corrective action. He needs to anticipate the reasons and rationalizations Paul may provide and how to counter them. Using the GVV framework, what follows is a brief explanation of how such a meeting with Paul might go.

What are the main arguments you are trying to counter? That is, what are the reasons and rationalizations you need to address?

These could be addressed from the perspective of Paul trying to convince Davis to remain silent about the apparent misappropriation of company cash and/or offering to pay back the money.

- Davis was told to put bank statements aside and not to do reconciliations.

- Paul may explain that, because the company is privately owned, no one gets hurt by what he did.

- He may try to convince Davis that the use of company cash for personal purposes is a common practice in the company because it's not publicly owned. (*Expected or Standard Practice*)

- Paul may play the sympathy card and explain that he needed the money to pay for hospitalization costs.

- He may argue that the amount of money involved is not significant. (*Materiality*)

- He may rationalize that the reason for withdrawing cash is the low monthly salary for someone in his position; he's not being compensated adequately.

- He may explain it was a one-time event and won't happen again. (*Isolated Incident*)

- Paul may pressure Davis into staying silent by implying his dad knows about it and has approved the withdrawals.

- He may promise to pay the money back as soon as he gets out of the hospital (no harm, no foul).

What is at stake for the key parties, including those who disagree with you? (Moral intensity issues exist here.)

- Paul's reputation is on the line because he committed a fraud on the company.

- Jack Jones will feel embarrassed for himself and his son if Davis discloses what Paul has done to the other owners.

- The other owners have a right to know what has happened.

- Davis may lose his job if he confronts Paul even if he drops the matter later on.

- The ability of the company to secure the $100,000 loan is at stake.

- Davis' reputation for integrity is at stake.

What levers can you use to influence those who disagree with you?

- Davis can ask Paul for supporting documentation to back up the coding of expenses to different accounts; he can share with Paul his analysis of the bank statements. When faced with the evidence, Paul may agree to repay the amount and not do it again.

- Davis can try to convince Paul that his actions are harmful to the company and potentially very embarrassing for his dad; he needs to come forward sooner rather than later and correct the "mistake."

- He can try to convince Paul that he needs to look at the long-term effects of taking money from the company that has not been properly authorized, rather than focus on short-term gain.

- Davis can use the leverage of threatening to go to all the owners if Paul doesn't admit the mistake and take corrective action; his loyalty obligation is to the three owners, not Paul. They are the ones with the most at stake.

- Davis has an ethical responsibility to inform the owners; Smith and Williams might serve as supporters to help counteract the reasons and rationalizations provided by Paul for his actions.

- Davis' reputation is at stake. As a CPA, he cannot violate the ethics of the profession; the accounting is wrong and needs to be corrected; he needs to explain about his integrity obligation.

What is your most powerful and persuasive response to the reasons and rationalizations you need to address? To whom should the argument be made? When and in what context?

- Davis should explain to Paul that he was acting diligently when he looked at the bank statements because he didn't want to pay the same vendor twice and needed to see whether the first check had cleared the bank statement.

- He should explain that using company cash for personal purposes is never acceptable unless Paul can demonstrate that the other owners knew about it and approved it.

- He should stress to Paul that taking company funds without approval is wrong regardless of the amount involved; it violates ethical norms; there are no good reasons for doing so.

- Davis should challenge Paul's statement that his dad knows about it and approved it by suggesting they both go to Jack Jones and discuss the matter; he is calling Paul's bluff. Paul may back off at this point, which confirms the asset misappropriation.

- He should explain to Paul that it is not enough to simply pay the money back. Davis doesn't want to get caught up in a cover-up. He should ask himself: What if Paul persists in his actions even after repaying the $30,000? If he doesn't inform the owners now, he could be accused of being part of the problem, dismissed from his job, and the oversight authorities in the accounting profession may be contacted. While this may seem remote at the time, Davis should be skeptical of anything Paul tells him.

Responses to Reasons and Rationalizations: Ace Manufacturing Case

Assume that Larry Davis calls Paul Jones and they set a 2:00 p.m. meeting at Paul's home where he is convalescing. The meeting goes like this:

"Paul, how are you feeling?"

"OK, Larry. What's happening at work?"

"That's why I wanted to see you."

"Yeah, why's that?"

"I noticed $10,000 payments to you each month for the first three months of the year. I can't find any supporting documentation for these amounts."

Paul immediately becomes indignant. "I told you not to look at the bank statements. You ignored my orders and disrespected my position. Your job is on the line here."

Davis is taken aback. He hesitates at first but explains about the vendor billing and tells Paul he saved the company $40,000 by detecting the duplicate billing. Paul starts to get tired and stressed out so they agree to meet in Paul's office the following week when he returns to work.

Paul's final comment is, "Tell no one about this meeting!" Davis returns to the office and starts to reflect on the meeting. He is not sure what to do at this point. He is thinking about his options, including not waiting for the meeting with Paul before acting.

Based on the meeting between Paul and Davis and earlier considerations, what are the most powerful and persuasive responses to the reasons and rationalizations given by Paul in his defense that Davis needs to address?

Davis might seek out some advice at this point. Perhaps he has a trusted friend or adviser who can bring a fresh perspective to the situation? Davis has to be be true to his values, have the courage to act on his beliefs, and meet his ethical and professional obligations.

What would you do at this point if you were in Larry's position?

Concluding Thoughts

In this chapter we have progressed from describing Kohlberg's model of moral development to Rest's model of ethical decision making and considered issues of moral intensity and virtue in developing an Integrated Ethical Decision-Making Model. We intend the model to be used as a framework to guide ethical analysis by students and frame the debate in the classroom when ethical dilemmas are discussed. It is not necessary to consider every element of the model in every case. Instead, it should serve as a reminder to students of some of the most important points to consider when making ethical decisions.

Ethical decisions are not made in a vacuum. Pressures exist in the real world of business and accounting; cultures may support or work against ethical behavior; and individuals react differently to the reasons and rationalizations given for not taking the ethical path. Therefore, it is important to understand how best to make your case when faced with an ethical dilemma. As we have learned, knowing what to do is not the same as doing it. We need a way to overcome obstacles and deal with those who would distract us from our goal to be the best person we can be; to make the ethical choice; and to follow through with ethical action. This is where the GVV framework is most valuable.

The tendency when a book on ethics is written is to focus on negative behaviors whether by a CEO, CFO, or accounting professional who does not live up to her values. But we should not loose sight of the many heroes we have in accounting, some of which were named in our concluding thoughts to Chapter 1. There are many such people who on a daily basis stand up to their supervisors and clients who pressure them to go along with financial wrongdoing; clients want to tell their own story about the company's success rather than a truthful one. New whistleblowing laws and protections in SOX and the Dodd-Frank Financial Reform Act that will be discussed in Chapter 3 provide a mechanism for accounting professionals to speak out after they have made a good faith effort to change things albeit to no avail. However, application of the GVV methodology in the real world may serve to negate the need for whistleblowing. The protagonist may be successful in voicing her values in an effective manner and changing the ethical landscape.

The field of behavioral ethics holds great promise for helping students to better understand their motivations for action and learn how to speak up when wrongdoing exists. Speaking up when things go wrong and voicing one's beliefs is something that takes practice, which is why we discussed the GVV methodology in this chapter. We follow through with additional discussions in the rest of the book.

You will face dilemmas in the workplace; all of us do. You may make some mistakes, but in truth the only mistake is not trying to correct wrongdoing. Perhaps the least likely person to choose for our final inspirational quote in this chapter is Kristi Loucks, a cake designer and pastry chef who also writes books. Loucks famously said, "The road to success is littered with failures, but the lessons learned are crucial in plotting your course to success!"

Discussion Questions

Sometimes in life things happen that seem to defy logic, yet that may be a sign of the times we are living in today. The following story applies to questions 1 and 2:

On October 15, 2009, in Fort Collins, Colorado, the parents of a six-year-old boy, Falcon Heene, claimed that he had floated away in a homemade helium balloon that was shaped to resemble a silver flying saucer. Some in the media referred to the incident as "Balloon Boy." The authorities closed down Denver International Airport, called in the National Guard, and a police pursuit ensued. After an hour-long flight that covered more than 50 miles across three counties, the empty balloon was found near the airport. It was later determined that the boy was hiding in the house all along in an incident that was a hoax and motivated by publicity that might lead to a reality television show. The authorities blamed the father, Richard, for the incident and decided to prosecute him. Richard Heene pleaded guilty on November 13, 2009, to the felony count of falsely influencing authorities. He pleaded to protect his wife, Mayumi, a Japanese citizen, whom he believed may have been deported if Richard was convicted of a more serious crime. Richard also agreed to pay $36,000 in restitution.

1. Identify the stakeholders and how they were affected by Heene's actions using ethical reasoning. What stage of moral reasoning in Kohlberg's model is exhibited by Richard Heene's actions? Do you believe the punishment fit the crime? In other words, was justice done in this case? Why or why not?

2. In an example of art imitating life, 16-year-old playwright Billy Reece was inspired by the Balloon Boy incident to write a play that was first performed at the Thespian Festival at the University of Nebraska–Lincoln in 2014. *Balloon Boy: The Musical* was presented in the 2015 New York Musical Theater Festival Developmental Reading Series. It has been said that, "Art has the power to evoke the same emotions, thoughts, moral and ethical controversies, and conflicts that we experience in life." Plato was certain that art was nothing but a dangerous and shallow imitation of life that served only to draw humans far away from the Truth. Discuss these thoughts from your own perspective of emotions, thoughts, moral considerations, and what "truth" means to you.

3. In the debate over why good people do bad things, Tenbrunsel suggests that people are often blind to the ethical dimensions of a situation, a concept he refers to as "bounded ethicality." Craig Johnson addresses moral disengagement by saying: When others try to encourage you to bad behavior ("the dark side") realize that you are an independent agent, and that you have a personal responsibility to behave morally. Discuss what this means to you.

4. One reason otherwise good people may do bad things is what psychologists call scripts. This term refers to the procedures that experience tells us to use in specific situations. Unlike other forms of experience, scripts are stored in memory in a mechanical or rote fashion. Explain why a System 1 approach to decision making might create a script that leads us to make a questionable or unethical decision.

5. How do you assess at what stage of moral development in Kohlberg's model you reason at in making decisions? Do you believe your level of reasoning is consistent with what is expected of an accounting professional? How does the stage you indicate relate to the findings of research studies discussed in this chapter about moral reasoning in accounting?

6. Using the child abuse scandal at Penn State discussed in Chapter 1, explain the actions that would have been taken by Joe Paterno if he had been reasoning at each stage in Kohlberg's model and why.

7. In his research into the components of ethical decision making, Rest raised the following issue: Assuming someone possesses sound moral reasoning skills, "Why would they ever chose the moral alternative, especially if it involves sacrificing some personal value or suffering some hardship? What motivates the selection of moral values over other values?" How does Rest's model deal with such a question? How would you answer it from the point of view of an accounting professional?

8. In the text, we point out that Rest's model is not linear in nature. An individual who demonstrates adequacy in one component may not necessarily be adequate in another, and moral failure can occur when there is a deficiency in any one component. Give an example in accounting when ethical intent may not be sufficient to produce ethical behavior and explain why that is the case.

9. In teaching about moral development, instructors often point out the threefold nature of morality: It depends on emotional development (in the form of the ability to feel guilt or shame), social development (manifested by the recognition of the group and the importance of moral behavior for the group's existence), and cognitive development (especially the ability to adopt another's perspective). How does this perspective of morality relate to ethical reasoning by accountants and auditors?

10. Do you believe that our beliefs trigger our actions, or do we act and then justify our actions by changing our beliefs? Explain.

11. Do you believe that a person's stage of moral development and personal moral philosophy play a role in how values and actions are shaped in the workplace? Explain.

12. Explain why moral problems may be of greater intensity than nonmoral problems.

13. Michael just graduated with a degree in Accounting from State University. He worked hard in school but could only achieve a 2.95 GPA because he worked 40 hours a week to pay his own way through college. Unfortunately, Michael was unable to get a job because the recruiters all had a 3.0 GPA cut-off point. Michael stayed with his college job for another year but is anxious to start his public accounting career. One day he reads about a job opening with a local CPA firm. The entry-level position pays little but it's a way for Michael to get his foot in the door. However, he knows there will be candidates for the position with a higher GPA than his so he is thinking about using his overall GPA, which was 3.25 including two years of community college studies, rather than his major GPA and the GPA at State, even though the advertisement asks for these two GPAs. Michael asks for your opinion before sending in the resume. What would you say to Michael and why?

14. In this chapter, we discuss the study by Libby and Thorne of the association between auditors' virtue and professional judgment, done by asking members of the Canadian Institute of Chartered Accountants to rate the importance of a variety of virtues. The most important virtues identified were truthful, independent, objective, and having integrity. The authors note that the inclusion of these virtues in professional codes of conduct (such as the Principles of the AICPA Code of Professional Conduct) may account for their perceived importance. Explain how these virtues relate to an auditor's intention to make ethical decisions.

15. You are in charge of the checking account for a small business. One morning, your accounting supervisor enters your office and asks you for a check for $150 for expenses that he tells you he incurred entertaining a client last night. He submits receipts from a restaurant and lounge. Later, your supervisor's girlfriend stops by to pick him up for lunch, and you overhear her telling the receptionist what a great time she had at dinner and dancing with your supervisor the night before. What would you do and why?

16. According to a survey reported by the *Daily Mail* in the United Kingdom, one in eight women has bought expensive clothes, worn them on a night out, and then returned them the next day. Nearly half of those who did confess said they were motivated by money because they couldn't afford to keep the clothes given their current economic condition. But 18 percent said they did it because they enjoyed the "buzz." Those most likely to do it were 18- to 24-year-olds, 16 percent of whom admitted to returning worn clothes (http://www.dailymail.co.uk/femail/article-2157430 /How-women-wear-expensive-new-frock-shop.html#ixzz3ea5m2mo).

Assume you are best friends with one such woman. She asks you to go shopping with her for a dress for the Senior Prom. She says the dress will be returned after the prom. You know what she does is wrong, but she is your best friend and don't want her to get in trouble. What would you do and why? How might you counter the likely reasons and rationalizations she will give for her actions?

17. Sharon is an intern with a local CPA firm. Prior to returning to school, her supervisor goes on sick leave and asks her to do some complicated reconciliation work for him. She is given what seems to her to be an unrealistic deadline. Sharon looks at the workpapers and supporting documentation and realizes she doesn't have the skills to complete the work without help. She contacts her supervisor who tells her to talk to Holly, a good friend of Sharon and former intern at the firm, for help. Holly returned to school one semester ago. What ethical considerations do you have in this matter? What would you do and why?

18. Identify the ethical issues in each of the following situations and what your ethical obligations are, assuming you are faced with the dilemma.

a. A consultant for a CPA firm is ordered by her superior to downgrade the ratings of one company's software package being considered for a client and increase the ratings for another company, which is run by the superior's wife. What would you do and why?

b. A tax accountant is told by his superior to take a position on a tax matter that is not supportable by the facts in order to make the client happy. This is a common practice in the firm and the likelihood of the IRS questioning it is remote. Would you go along with your supervisor?

c. An auditor for a governmental agency concluded a contractor's accounting system was inadequate; her supervisor changed the opinion to adequate in order to minimize the audit hours on the job and make the process seem more efficient. Would you go above your supervisor in this matter and bring your concerns to high-ups in the agency?

19. In a June 1997 paper published in the *Journal of Business Ethics,* Sharon Green and James Weber reported the results of a study of moral reasoning of accounting students prior to and after taking an auditing course. The study also compared the results between accounting and nonaccounting students prior to the auditing course. The authors found that (1) accounting students, after taking an auditing course that emphasized the AICPA Code, reasoned at higher levels than students who had not taken the course; (2) there were no differences in moral reasoning levels when accounting and nonaccounting majors were compared prior to an auditing course; and (3) there was a significant relationship between the students' levels of ethical development and the choice of an ethical versus unethical action.[66] Do you think that taking an Accounting Ethics course would affect your level of moral development and ability to reason through ethical issues? Why or why not?

20. Explain why the process of ethical decision making depends on a number of moral, social, psychological, and organizational factors.

21. Emotional self-awareness refers to understanding your own feelings, what causes them, and how they impact your thoughts and actions. It is widely known that ethical dilemmas involving other employees/managers are inherently emotional. Researchers have found that such strong negative emotions as sadness and anger influenced individuals to make less ethical decisions, and that emotional intelligent individuals were able to make ethical decisions against the biasing influence of those negative emotions. Explain how moods could influence the thought process and ethical decision making. Have you made a decision you later regretted based on your emotional response?

22. Windsor and Kavanagh propose in a research study that client management economic pressure is a situation of high moral intensity that sensitizes auditors' emotions and thus motivates their moral reasoning to make deliberative decisions either to resist or accede to client management wishes. Explain how you think such a process might work.

23. The nature of accountants' work puts them in a special position of trust in relation to their clients, employers, and the general public, who rely on their professional judgment and guidance in making decisions. Explain the link between professional judgment and ethical decision making in accounting.

24. Explain what you think each of the following statements means in the context of moral development.

a. How far are you willing to go to do the right thing?

b. How much are you willing to give up to do what you believe is right?

c. We may say that we would do the right thing, but when it requires sacrifice, how much are we willing to give up?

25. A major theme of this chapter is that our cognitive processes influence ethical decision making. Use the theme to comment on the following statement, which various religions claim as their own and has been attributed to Lao Tzu and some say the Dalai Lama:

"Watch your thoughts; they become your words.

Watch your words; they become your actions.

Watch your actions; they become your habits.

Watch your habits; they become your character.

Watch your character; it becomes your destiny."

Endnotes

1. Max H. Bazerman and Ann E. Trebrunsel, *Blind Spots: Why We Fail to Do What's Right and What to Do About It* (Princeton, NJ: Princeton University Press, 2011).

2. Wendy Zellner, "The Fall of Enron," *BusinessWeek,* December 17, 2001, p. 30.

3. Barbara Ley Toffler with Jennifer Reingold, *Final Accounting: Ambition, Greed, and the Fall of Arthur Andersen* (New York: Broadway Books, 2003), p. 217.

4. Bethany McLean and Peter Elkind, *The Smartest Guys in the Room: The Amazing Rise and Scandalous Fall of Enron* (New York: Penguin Group, 2003).

5. Paul M. Clikeman, *Called to Account: Fourteen Financial Frauds That Shaped the American Accounting Profession* (New York: Routledge, 2009).

6. Daniel Edelman and Ashley Nicholson, "Arthur Andersen Auditors and Enron: What Happened to Their Texas CPA Licenses?" *Journal of Finance and Accountancy,* http://www.aabri.com /manuscripts/11899.pdf.

7. Lawrence Kohlberg, "Stage and Sequence: The Cognitive Developmental Approach to Socialization," in *Handbook of Socialization Theory and Research,* ed. D. A. Goslin (Chicago: Rand McNally, 1969), pp. 347–480.

8. Carol Gilligan, *In a Different Voice: Psychological Theory and Womens Development* (Cambridge, MA: Harvard University Press, 1982).

9. James R. Rest and Darcia Narvaez, eds., *Moral Development in the Professions: Psychology and Applied Ethics* (New York: Psychology Press, 1994), p. 4.

10. Rest and Narvaez.

11. Rest and Narvaez.

12. Muriel J. Bebeau and S. J. Thoma, "Intermediate Concepts and the Connection to Moral Education," *Educational Psychology Review* 11, no. 4 (1999), p. 345.

13. O. C. Ferrell, John Fraedrich, and Linda Ferrell, *Business Ethics: Ethical Decision Making and Cases* (Mason, OH: South-Western, Cengage Learning, 2009 Update), pp. 162–163.

14. Clare M. Pennino, "Is Decision Style Related to Moral Development Among Managers in the U.S.?" *Journal of Business Ethics* 41 (December 2002), pp. 337–347.

15. William Crain, *Theories of Development: Concepts and Applications,* 6th ed. (Upper Saddle River, NJ, 2010).

16. Kay Plummer, "Improving Ethical Judgment through Deep Learning," in *Ethics and Auditing,* eds. Tom Campbell and Keith Houghton (Canberra, Australia: ANU-E Press, 2010).

17. Milton Snoeyenbos, Robert F. Almeder, and James M. Humber, *Business Ethics, Corporate Values and Society* (Buffalo, NY: Prometheus Books, 1983), pp. 239–264.

18. Lawrence A. Ponemon and David R. L. Gabhart, "Ethical Reasoning Research in the Accounting and Auditing Professions," in *Moral Development in the Professions: Psychology and Applied Ethics,* eds. James R. Rest and Darcia Narvaez (New York: Psychology Press, 1994), pp. 101–120.

19. See Michael K. Shaub, "An Analysis of the Association of Traditional Demographic Variables with the Moral Reasoning of Auditing Students and Auditors," *Journal of Accounting Education* (Winter 1994), pp. 1–26; and Lawrence A. Ponemon, "Ethical Reasoning and Selection Socialization in Accounting," *Accounting, Organizations, and Society* 17 (1992), pp. 239–258.

20. David Arnold and Larry Ponemon, "Internal Auditors' Perceptions of Whistle-Blowing and the Influence of Moral Reasoning: An Experiment," *Auditing: A Journal of Practice and Theory* (Fall 1991), pp. 1–15.

21. Larry Ponemon and David Gabhart, "Auditor Independence Judgments: A Cognitive Developmental Model and Experimental Evidence," *Contemporary Accounting Research* (1990), pp. 227–251.

22. Larry Ponemon, "Auditor Underreporting of Time and Moral Reasoning: An Experimental-Lab Study," *Contemporary Accounting Research* (1993), pp. 1–29.

23. Ponemon and Gabhart, 1994, p. 108.

24. Plummer, p. 244.

25. Lawrence Kohlberg, *Essays on Moral Development: Vol. II: The Psychology of Moral Development: The Nature and Validity of Moral Stages* (San Francisco: Harper & Row, 1984).

26. Mary Louise Arnold, "Stage, Sequence, and Sequels: Changing Conceptions of Morality, Post-Kohlberg," *Educational Psychology Review,* Vol. 12, No. 4, 2000, pp. 365–383.

27. James R. Rest, Darcia Narvaez, Muriel J. Bebeau, and Stephen J. Thoma, *Postconventional Moral Thinking: A Neo-Kohlbergian Approach* (Mahwah, NJ: Lawrence Erlbaum, 1999).

28. M. L. Arnold, pp. 367–368.

29. John C. Gibbs, "Toward an Integration of Kohlberg's and Hoffman's Moral Development Theories," *Human Development* 34, 1991, pp. 88–104.

30. Richard S. Peters, *Moral Development and Moral Education* (London: George Allen & Unwin, 1982).

31. Augusto Blasi, "Bridging Moral Cognition and Moral Action: A Critical Review of the Literature," *Psychological Bulletin,* Vol. 88, No. 1, 1980, pp. 1–45.

32. William Damon and Anne Colby, "Education and Moral Commitment," *Journal of Moral Education,* Vol. 25, No. 1, 1996, pp. 31–37.

33. Craig E. Johnson, *Organizational Ethics: A Practical Approach,* 3rd ed. (NY: Sage Publications, Inc., 2015).

34. Plummer, pp. 242–244.

35. James R. Rest, "Morality," in *Handbook of Child Psychology: Cognitive Development,* Vol. 3, series ed. P. H. Mussen and vol. ed. J. Flavell (New York: Wiley, 1983), pp. 556–629.

36. Lawrence Kohlberg, *The Meaning and Measurement of Moral Development* (Worcester, MA: Clark University Press, 1979).

37. Rest and Narvaez, p. 24.

38. Jeremy I. M. Carpendale, "Kohlberg and Piaget on Stages and Moral Reasoning," *Developmental Review,* Vol. 20, Issue 2, 2000, pp. 181–205.

39. Craig E. Johnson, *Meeting the Ethical Challenges of Leadership* (New York: Sage Publications, 2011).

40. Steven Dellaportas, Beverly Jackling, Philomena Leung, Barry J. Cooper, "Developing an Ethics Education Framework for Accounting," *Journal of Business Ethics Education*, 8, no.1 (2011), pp. 63–82.

41. Thomas Jones, "Ethical Decision Making by Individuals in Organizations: An Issue-Contingent Model," *Academy of Management Review* 16, pp. 366–395.

42. Jones, p. 379.

43. Sarah Hope Lincoln and Elizabeth K. Holmes, "Ethical Decision Making: A Process Influenced by Moral Intensity," *Journal of Healthcare, Science and the Humanities,* Vol. 1, No. 1, 2011, pp. 55–69.

44. Johnson.

45. Theresa Libby and Linda Thorne, "Virtuous Auditors: While Virtue Is Back in Fashion, How Do You Define It and Measure Its Importance to an Auditor's Role?" *CA Magazine,* November 2003, Available at: www.camagazine.com/archives/print-edition/2003/nov/regulars/camagazine24374.aspx.

46. Libby and Thorne.

47. Linda Thorne, "The Role of Virtue in Auditors' Ethical Decision Making: An Integration of Cognitive-Developmental and Virtue Ethics Perspectives," *Research on Accounting Ethics,* no. 4 (1998), pp. 293–294.

48. Mary Beth Armstrong, J. Edward Ketz, and Dwight Owsen, "Ethics Education in Accounting: Moving Toward Ethical Motivation and Ethical Behavior," *Journal of Accounting Education* 21 (2003), pp. 1–16.

49. Manuel Velasquez, Claire Andre, Thomas Shanks, and Michael J. Meyer, "Thinking Ethically: A Framework for Moral Decision Making," Available at: http://www.scu.edu/ethics/practicing /decision/thinking.html#sthash.zMGI3C7i.dpuf.

50. Rushworth M. Kidder, *How Good People Make Tough Choices* (NY: Simon & Schuster, 1995).

51. Johnson, 2011, pp. 249–250.

52. Richard F. West and Keith Stanovich, "Individual Differences in Reasoning: Implications for the Rationality Debate," *Behavioral & Brain Sciences* (2000), 23, pp. 645–665.

53. Daniel Kahneman, "A Perspective on Judgment and Choice: Mapping Bounded Rationality," *American Psychologist* (2003), 58, pp. 697–720.

54. Leon Festinger, *A Theory of Cognitive Dissonance* (Evanston, IL: Row & Peterson, 1957).

55. Penny Tompkins and James Lawley, "Cognitive Dissonance and Creative Tension—The Same or Different?" from presentation at The Developing Group, October 3, 2009, Available at: http://www.cleanlanguage.co.uk/articles/articles/262/0/Cognitive-Dissonance-and-Creative-Tension/ Page0.html.

56. Festinger.

57. Max H. Bazerman and Francesca Gino, "Behavioral Ethics: Toward a Deeper Understanding of Moral Judgment and Dishonesty," *Annual Review of Law and Social Science* 8 (December 2012), pp. 85–104.

58. Dennis P. Wittmer, "Behavioral Ethics in Business Organizations: What the Research Teaches Us," in *Encyclopedia of Business Ethics and Society*, ed. Robert W. Kolb (NY: Sage Publications, 2008).

59. Wittmer, p. 62.

60. Bazerman and Gino.

61. The University of Texas uses a program, "Ethics Unwrapped," to teach GVV to its students. Videos are available on the following Web site: http://ethicsunwrapped.utexas.edu/

62. Materials to teach GVV and cases are available on the GVV Web site: http://www.babson.edu /Academics/teaching-research/gvv/Pages/curriculum.aspx

63. M.C. Gentile, *Giving Voice to Values: How to Speak Your Mind When You Know What's Right.* (New Haven, CT: Yale University Press, 2010).

64. Gentile.

65. Gentile.

66. Sharon Green and James Weber, "Influencing Ethical Development: Exposing Students to the AICPA Code of Conduct," *Journal of Business Ethics* 16, no. 8 (June 1997), pp. 777–790.

Chapter 2 Cases

Case 2-1 A Team Player? (a GVV case)

Barbara is working on the audit of a client with a group of five other staff-level employees. During the audit, Diane, a member of the group, points out that she identified a deficiency in the client's inventory system that she did not discover during the physical observation of the client's inventory. The deficiency was relatively minor, and perhaps that is why it was not detected at the time. Barbara suggests to Diane that they bring the matter to Jessica, the senior in charge of the engagement. Diane does not want to do it because she is the one who identified the deficiency and she is the one who should have detected it at the time of the observation. Three of the other four staff members agree with Diane. Haley is the only one, along with Barbara, who wants to inform Jessica.

After an extended discussion of the matter, the group votes and decides not to inform Jessica. Still, Barbara does not feel right about it. She wonders: What if Jessica finds out another way? What if the deficiency is more serious than Diane has said? What if it portends other problems with the client? She decides to raise all these issues but is rebuked by the others who remind her that the team is already behind on its work and any additional audit procedures would increase the time spent on the audit and make them all look incompetent. They remind Barbara that Jessica is a stickler for keeping to the budget and any overages cannot be billed to the client.

Questions

1. Discuss these issues from the perspective of Kohlberg's model of moral development. How does this relate to the established norms of the work group as you see it?

2. Assume you are in Barbara's position. What would you do and why? Consider the following in answering the question:

- How can you best express your point of view effectively?

- What do you need to say, to whom, and in what sequence?

- What do you expect the objections or pushback will be and, then, what would you say next?

Case 2-2 FDA Liability Concerns (a GVV case)

Gregory and Alex started a small business based on a secret-recipe salad dressing that got rave reviews. Gregory runs the business end and makes all final operational decisions. Alex runs the creative side of the business.

Alex's salad dressing was a jalapeno vinaigrette that went great with barbeque or burgers. He got so many requests for the recipe and a local restaurant asked to use it as the house special, that Alex decided to bottle and market the dressing to the big box stores. Whole Foods and Trader Joe's carried the dressing; sales were increasing every month. As the business grew, Gregory and Alex hired Michael, a college friend and CPA, to be the CFO of the company.

Michael's first suggestion was to do a five-year strategic plan with expanding product lines and taking the company public or selling it within five to seven years. Gregory and Alex weren't sure about wanting to go public and losing control, but expanding the product lines was appealing. Michael also wanted to contain costs and increase profit margins.

At Alex's insistence, they called a meeting with Michael to discuss his plans. "Michael, we hired you to take care of the accounting and the financial details," Alex said. "We don't understand profit margins. On containing costs, the best ingredients must be used to ensure the quality of the dressing. We must meet all FDA requirements for food safety and containment of food borne bacteria, such as listeria or e coli, as you develop cost systems."

"Of course," Michael responded. "I will put processes in place to meet the FDA requirements."

At the next quarterly meeting of the officers, Alex wanted an update on the FDA processes and the latest inspection. He was concerned whether Michael understood the importance of full compliance.

"Michael," Alex said, "the FDA inspector and I had a discussion while he was here. He wanted to make sure I understood the processes and the liabilities of the company if foodborne bacteria are traced to our products. Are we doing everything by the book and reserving some liabilities for any future recalls?"

Michael assured Alex and Gregory that everything was being done by the book and the accounting was following standard practices. Over the next 18 months, the FDA inspectors came and Michael reported everything was fine.

After the next inspection, there was some listeria found in the product. The FDA insisted on a recall of batch 57839. Alex wanted to recall all the product to make sure that all batches were safe.

"A total recall is too expensive and would mean that the product could be off the shelves for three to four weeks. It would be hard to regain our shelf advantage and we would lose market share," Michael explained.

Alex seemed irritated and turned to Gregory for support, but he was silent. He then walked over to where Michael was sitting and said, "Michael, nothing is more important than our reputation. Our promise and mission is to provide great-tasting dressing made with the freshest, best, organic products. A total recall will show that we stand by our mission and promise. I know we would have some losses, but don't we have a liability reserve for recall, like a warranty reserve?"

"The reserve will not cover the entire expense of a recall," Michael said. "It will be too expensive to do a total recall and will cause a huge loss for the quarter. In the next six months, we will need to renew a bank loan; a loss will hurt our renewal loan rate and terms. You know I have been working to get the company primed to go public as well."

Alex offered that he didn't care about going public. He didn't start the business to be profitable. Gregory, on the other hand, indicated he thought going public was a great idea and would provide needed funds on a continuous basis.

Alex told Michael that he needed to see all the FDA inspection reports. He asked, "What is the FDA requiring to be done to address the issue of listeria?"

"I'm handling it, Alex," Michael said. "Don't worry about it. Just keep making new salad dressings so that we can stay competitive."

"Well, Michael, just answer what the FDA is asking for."

"Just to sterilize some of our equipment, but it shouldn't be too bad."

"Michael, it's more than that," Alex responded. "The FDA contacted me directly and asked me to meet with them in three days to discuss our plans to meet the FDA requirements and standards. We will be fined for not addressing issues found in prior inspections. I want to see the past inspection reports so I can better understand the scope of the problem."

"Listen, Alex," Michael said. "I just completed a cost–benefit analysis of fixing all the problems identified by the FDA and found the costs outweighed the benefits. We're better off paying whatever fines they impose and move on."

"Michael, I don't care about cost–benefit analysis. I care about my reputation and that of the company. Bring me all the inspection reports tomorrow."

The three of them met the following day. As Alex reviewed the past inspection reports, he realized that he had relied on Michael too much and his assurances that all was well with the FDA. In fact, the FDA had repeatedly noted that more sterilization of the equipment was needed and that storage of the products and ingredients needed additional care. Alex began to wonder whether Michael should stay on with the company. He also was concerned about the fact that Gregory had been largely silent during the discussions. He wondered whether Gregory was putting profits ahead of safety and the reputation of the company.

Questions

Alex knows what the right thing to do is. As Alex prepares for a meeting on the inspection reports the next day, he focuses on influencing the positions of Michael and Gregory, both of whom will be involved in the meeting. Put yourself in Alex's position and answer the following questions.

1. What are the main arguments you are trying to counter? That is, what are the reasons and rationalizations you need to address?
2. What is at stake for the key parties, including those who disagree with you?
3. What levers can you use to influence those who disagree with you?
4. What is your most powerful and persuasive response to the reasons and rationalizations you need to address? To whom should the argument be made? When and in what context?

Case 2-3 The Tax Return (a GVV case)

Brenda Sells sent the tax return that she prepared for the president of Purple Industries, Inc., Harry Kohn, to Vincent Dim, the manager of the tax department at her accounting firm. Dim asked Sells to come to his office at 9 a.m. on Friday, April 12, 2016. Sells was not sure why Dim wanted to speak to her. The only reason she could come up with was the tax return for Kohn.

"Brenda, come in," Vincent said.

"Thank you, Vincent," Brenda responded.

"Do you know why I asked to see you?"

"I'm not sure. Does it have something to do with the tax return for Mr. Kohn?" asked Brenda.

"That's right," answered Vincent.

"Is there a problem?" Brenda asked.

"I just spoke with Kohn. I told him that you want to report his winnings from the lottery. He was incensed."

"Why?" Brenda asked. "You and I both know that the tax law is quite clear on this matter. When a taxpayer wins money by playing the lottery, then that amount must be reported as revenue. The taxpayer can offset lottery gains with lottery losses, if those are supportable. Of course, the losses cannot be higher than the amount of the gains. In the case of Mr. Kohn, the losses exceed the gains, so there is no net tax effect. I don't see the problem."

"You're missing the basic point that the deduction for losses is only available if you itemize deductions," Vincent said. "Kohn is not doing that. He's using the standard deduction."

Brenda realized she had blown it by not knowing that.

Brenda didn't know what to say. Vincent seemed to be telling her the lottery amounts shouldn't be reported. But that was against the law. She asked, "Are you telling me to forget about the lottery amounts on Mr. Kohn's tax return?"

"I want you to go back to your office and think carefully about the situation. Consider that this is a one-time request and we value our staff members who are willing to be flexible in such situations. And, I'll tell you, other staff in the same situation have been loyal to the firm. Let's meet again in my office tomorrow at 9 a.m."

Questions

1. Analyze the alternatives available to Brenda using Kohlberg's six stages of moral development. Assume that Brenda has no reason to doubt Vincent's veracity with respect to the statement that it is "a one-time request." Should that make a difference in what Brenda decides to do? Why or why not?

2. Assume you have decided what your position will be in the meeting with Vincent but are not quite sure how to respond to the reasons and rationalizations provided by him to ignore the lottery losses. How might you counter those arguments? What would be your most powerful and persuasive responses?

3. Assume that Brenda decides to go along with Vincent and omits the lottery losses and gains. Next year a similar situation arises with winnings from a local poker tournament. Kohn now trusts Brenda and shared with her that he won $4,950 from that event. He tells you to not report it because it was below the $5,000 threshold for the payer to issue a form W-2G. If you were Brenda, and Vincent asked you to do the same thing you did last year regarding omitting the lottery losses and gains, what would you do this second year and why?

Case 2-4 A Faulty Budget (a GVV Case)

Jackson Daniels graduated from Lynchberg State College two years ago. Since graduating from college, he has worked in the accounting department of Lynchberg Manufacturing. Daniels was recently asked to prepare a sales budget for the year 2016. He conducted a thorough analysis and came out with projected sales of 250,000 units of product. That represents a 25 percent increase over 2015.

Daniels went to lunch with his best friend, Jonathan Walker, to celebrate the completion of his first solo job. Walker noticed Daniels seemed very distant. He asked what the matter was. Daniels stroked his chin, ran his hand through his bushy, black hair, took another drink of scotch, and looked straight into the eyes of his friend of 20 years. "Jon, I think I made a mistake with the budget."

"What do you mean?" Walker answered.

"You know how we developed a new process to manufacture soaking tanks to keep the ingredients fresh?"

"Yes," Walker answered.

"Well, I projected twice the level of sales for that product than will likely occur."

"Are you sure?" Walker asked.

"I checked my numbers. I'm sure. It was just a mistake on my part."

Walker asked Daniels what he planned to do about it.

"I think I should report it to Pete. He's the one who acted on the numbers to hire additional workers to produce the soaking tanks," Daniels said.

"Wait a second, Jack. How do you know there won't be extra demand for the product? You and I both know demand is a tricky number to project, especially when a new product comes on the market. Why don't you sit back and wait to see what happens?"

"Jon, I owe it to Pete to be honest. He hired me."

"You know Pete is always pressuring us to 'make the numbers.' Also, Pete has a zero tolerance for employees who make mistakes. That's why it's standard practice around here to sweep things under the rug. Besides, it's a one-time event—right?"

"But what happens if I'm right and the sales numbers were wrong? What happens if the demand does not increase beyond what I now know to be the correct projected level?"

"Well, you can tell Pete about it at that time. Why raise a red flag now when there may be no need?"

As the lunch comes to a conclusion, Walker pulls Daniels aside and says, "Jack, this could mean your job. If I were in your position, I'd protect my own interests first."

Jimmy (Pete) Beam is the vice president of production. Jackson Daniels had referred to him in his conversation with Jonathan Walker. After several days of reflection on his friend's comments, Daniels decided to approach Pete and tell him about the mistake. He knew there might be consequences, but his sense of right and wrong ruled the day. What transpired next surprised Daniels.

"Come in, Jack" Pete said.

"Thanks, Pete. I asked to see you on a sensitive matter."

"I'm listening."

"There is no easy way to say this so I'll just tell you the truth. I made a mistake in my sales budget. The projected increase of 25 percent was wrong. I checked my numbers and it should have been 12.5 percent. I'm deeply sorry; want to correct the error; and promise never to do it again."

Pete's face became beet red. He said, "Jack, you know I hired 20 new people based on your budget."

"Yes, I know."

"That means ten have to be laid off or fired. They won't be happy and once word filters through the company, other employees may wonder if they are next."

"I hadn't thought about it that way."

"Well, you should have." Here's what we are going to do…and this is between you and me. Don't tell anyone about this conversation."

"You mean not even tell my boss?"

"No, Pete said." Cwervo can't know about it because he's all about correcting errors and moving on. Look, Jack, it's my reputation at stake here as well."

Daniels hesitated but reluctantly agreed not to tell the controller, Jose Cwervo, his boss. The meeting ended with Daniels feeling sick to his stomach and guilty for not taking any action.

Questions

1. What are Daniels's options in this situation? Use ethical reasoning to identify the best alternative. What would you do if you were in Daniels' position?

2. Given that you have decided to take some action even though you had agreed not to do so, who would you approach to express your point of view and why?

3. What is at stake for the key parties?

4. What are the main arguments you are likely to encounter in making the strongest case possible?

5. What is your most powerful and persuasive response to the reasons and rationalizations you may need to address? To whom should the argument be made? When and in what context?

Case 2-5 Gateway Hospital (a GVV case)

Troy just returned from a business trip for health-care administrators in Orlando. Kristen, a relatively new employee who reports to him, also attended the conference. They both work for Gateway Hospital, a for-profit hospital in the St. Louis area. The Orlando conference included training in the newest reporting requirements in the health-care industry, networking with other hospital administrators, reports on upcoming legislation in health care, and the current status of regulations related to the Affordable Care Act. The conference was in late March and coincided with Troy's kids' spring break, so the entire family traveled to Orlando to check out Walt Disney World and SeaWorld.

The hospital's expense reimbursement policy is very clear on the need for receipts for all reimbursements. Meals are covered for those not provided as part of the conference registration fee, but only within a preset range. Troy has never had a problem following those guidelines. However, the trip to Orlando was more expensive than Troy expected. He did not attend all sessions of the conference, to enjoy time with his family. Upon their return to St. Louis, Troy's wife suggested that Troy submit three meals and one extra night at the hotel as business expenses, even though they were personal expenses. Her rationale was that the hospital policies would not totally cover the business costs of the trip. Troy often has to travel and misses family time that cannot be recovered or replaced. Troy also knows that his boss has a reputation of signing forms without reading or careful examination. He realizes the amount involved is not material and probably won't be detected.

Kristen is approached by Joyce, the head of the accounting department, about Troy's expenses, which seem high and not quite right. Kristen is asked about the extra night because she did not ask for reimbursement for that time. Kristen knows it can be easily explained by saying Troy had to stay an extra day for additional meetings, a common occurrence for administrators, although that was not the case. She also knows that the hospital has poor controls and a culture of "not rocking the boat," and that other employees have routinely inflated expense reports in the past.

Assume you, as Kristen, have decided the best approach, at least in the short run, is to put off responding to Joyce so that you can discuss the matter with Troy. Answer the following questions.

Questions

1. What are the main arguments you feel Troy will make and reasons and rationalizations you need to address?

2. What is at stake for the key parties in this situation?

3. What levers can you use to influence how Troy reacts to your position in this matter?

4. What is your most powerful and persuasive response to the reasons and rationalizations you need to address? To whom should the argument be made? When and in what context?

Case 2-6 LinkedIn and Shut Out

The facts of this case are fictional. Any resemblance to real persons, living or dead, is purely coincidental.

Kenny is always looking to make contacts in the business world and enhance his networking experiences. He knows how important it is to drive customers to his sports memorabilia business. He's just a small seller in the Mall of America in Bloomington, Minnesota.

Kenny decided to go on LinkedIn. Within the first few weeks, he received a number of requests that said, "I'd like to add you to my professional network." At first almost all of such requests came from friends and associates he knew quite well. After a while, however, he started to receive similar requests from people he didn't know. He would click on the "view profile" button, but that didn't provide much useful information so he no longer looked at profiles for every request. He simply clicked the "accept" button and the "You are now connected" message appeared.

One day Kenny received the following message with a request to "connect":

"I plan to come to your sports memorabilia store in the future so I thought I'd introduce myself first. I am a financial planner and have helped small business owners like yourself to develop financial plans that provide returns on their investments three times the average rate received for conventional investments. I'm confident I can do the same for you. As a qualified professional, you can trust my services."

Kenny didn't think much about it. It certainly sounded legitimate. Besides, he would meet the financial planner soon and could judge the type of person he was. So, Kenny linked with the planner.

A week later, the financial planner dropped by Kenny's store and provided lots of data to show that he had successfully increased returns for dozens of people. He even had testimonials with him. Kenny agreed to meet with him in his St. Paul office later that week to discuss financial planning.

The meeting took place and Kenny gave the financial planner a check for $30,000, which was most of Kenny's liquid assets. At first the returns looked amazing. Each of the first two quarterly statements he received from the planner indicated that he had already earned $5,000; a total of $10,000 in six months. Three months later Kenny did not receive a statement. He called the planner and the phone had been disconnected. He sent e-mails but they were returned as not valid. No luck with text messages.

Kenny started to worry whether he ever would see his money—at least the $30,000. He was at a loss what to do. A friend suggested he contact LinkedIn and see if it could help. His online contact led to the following response in an e-mail:

> As per our agreement with you, we are not liable to you or others for any indirect, incidental, special, consequential, or punitive damages, or any loss of data, opportunities, reputation, profits or revenues, related to the services of LinkedIn. In no event shall the liability of LinkedIn exceed, in the aggregate for all claims against us, an amount that is the lesser of (a) five times the most recent monthly or yearly fee that you paid for a premium service, if any, or (b) $1,000. This limitation of liability is part of the basis of the bargain between you and LinkedIn and shall apply to all claims of liability (e.g., warranty, tort, negligence, contract, law) and even if LinkedIn has been told of the possibility of any such damage, and even if these remedies fail their essential purpose. If disputes arise relating to this Agreement and/or the Services, both parties agree that all of these claims can only be litigated in the federal or state courts of Santa Clara County, California, USA, and we each agree to personal jurisdiction in those courts.

To say Kenny was distraught is an understatement. He felt like he had been shut out. While he did he not understand all the legalese, he knew enough that he would have to hire an attorney if he wanted to pursue the matter.

Questions

1. How would you characterize Kenny's thought process in the way he responded to requests to connect on LinkedIn?

2. Who is to blame for what happened to Kenny and why?

3. What would you do at this point if you were in Kenny's position and why?

Case 2-7 Milton Manufacturing Company

Milton Manufacturing Company produces a variety of textiles for distribution to wholesale manufacturers of clothing products. The company's primary operations are located in Long Island City, New York, with branch factories and warehouses in several surrounding cities. Milton Manufacturing is a closely held company, and Irv Milton is the president. He started the business in 2005, and it grew in revenue from $500,000 to $5 million in 10 years. However, the revenues declined to $4.5 million in 2015. Net cash flows from all activities also were declining. The company was concerned because it planned to borrow $20 million from the credit markets in the fourth quarter of 2016.

Irv Milton met with Ann Plotkin, the chief accounting officer (CAO), on January 15, 2016, to discuss a proposal by Plotkin to control cash outflows. He was not overly concerned about the recent decline in net cash flows from operating activities because these amounts were expected to increase in 2016 as a result of projected higher levels of revenue and cash collections. However, that was not Plotkin's view.

Plotkin knew that if overall negative capital expenditures continued to increase at the rate of 40 percent per year, Milton Manufacturing probably would not be able to borrow the $20 million. Therefore, she suggested establishing a new policy to be instituted on a temporary basis. Each plant's capital expenditures for 2016 for investing activities would be limited to the level of those capital expenditures in 2013, the last year of an overall positive cash flow. Operating activity cash flows had no such restrictions. Irv Milton pointedly asked Plotkin about the possible negative effects of such a policy, but in the end, he was convinced that it was necessary to initiate the policy immediately to stem the tide of increases in capital expenditures. A summary of cash flows appears in Exhibit 1.

EXHIBIT 1	Milton Manufacturing Company

Summary of Cash Flows
For the Years Ended December 31, 2015 and 2014 (000 omitted)

	December 31, 2015	December 31, 2014
Cash Flows from Operating Activities		
Net income	$ 372	$ 542
Adjustments to reconcile net income to net cash provided by operating activities	(2,350)	(2,383)
Net cash provided by operating activities	$ (1,978)	$ (1,841)
Cash Flows from Investing Activities		
Capital expenditures	$ (1,420)	$ (1,918)
Other investing inflows (outflows)	176	84
Net cash used in investing activities	$ (1,244)	$ (1,834)
Cash Flows from Financing Activities		
Net cash provided (used in) financing activities	$ 168	$ 1,476
Increase (decrease) in cash and cash equivalents	$ (3,054)	$ (2,199)
Cash and cash equivalents—beginning of the year	$ 3,191	$ 5,390
Cash and cash equivalents—end of the year	$ 147	$ 3,191

Sammie Markowicz is the plant manager at the headquarters in Long Island City. He was informed of the new capital expenditure policy by Ira Sugofsky, the vice president for operations. Markowicz told Sugofsky that the new policy could negatively affect plant operations because certain machinery and equipment, essential to the production process, had been breaking down more frequently during the past two years. The problem was primarily with the motors. New and better models with more efficient motors had been developed by an overseas supplier. These were expected to be available by April 2016. Markowicz planned to order 1,000 of these new motors for the Long Island City operation, and he expected that other plant managers would do the same. Sugofsky told Markowicz to delay the acquisition of new motors for one year, after which time the restrictive capital expenditure policy would be lifted. Markowicz reluctantly agreed.

Milton Manufacturing operated profitably during the first six months of 2016. Net cash inflows from operating activities exceeded outflows by $1,250,000 during this time period. It was the first time in two years that there was a positive cash flow from operating activities. Production operations accelerated during the third quarter as a result of increased demand for Milton's textiles. An aggressive advertising campaign initiated in late 2015 seemed to bear fruit for the company. Unfortunately, the increased level of production put pressure on the machines, and the degree of breakdown was increasing. A big problem was that the motors wore out prematurely.

Markowicz was concerned about the machine breakdown and increasing delays in meeting customer demands for the shipment of the textile products. He met with the other branch plant managers, who complained bitterly to him about not being able to spend the money to acquire new motors. Markowicz was very sensitive to their needs. He informed them that the company's regular supplier had recently announced a 25 percent price increase for the motors. Other suppliers followed suit, and Markowicz saw no choice but to buy the motors from the overseas supplier. That supplier's price was lower, and the quality of the motors would significantly enhance the machines' operating efficiency. However, the company's restrictions on capital expenditures stood in the way of making the purchase.

Markowicz approached Sugofsky and told him about the machine breakdowns and the concerns of other plant managers. Sugofsky seemed indifferent but reminded Markowicz of the capital expenditure restrictions in place and that the Long Island City plant was committed to keeping expenditures at the same level as it had in 2014. Markowicz argued that he was faced with an unusual situation and he had to act now. Sugofsky hurriedly left, but not before he said to Markowicz, "You and I may not agree with it, but a policy is a policy."

Markowicz reflected on his obligations to Milton Manufacturing. He was conflicted because he viewed his primary responsibility and that of the other plant managers to ensure that the production process operated smoothly. The last thing the workers needed right now was a stoppage of production because of machine failure.

At this time, Markowicz learned of a 30-day promotional price offered by the overseas supplier to gain new customers by lowering the price for all motors by 25 percent. Coupled with the 25 percent increase in price by the company's supplier, Markowicz knew he could save the company $1,500, or 50 percent of cost, on each motor purchased from the overseas supplier.

After carefully considering the implications of his intended action, Markowicz contacted the other plant managers and informed them that while they were not obligated to follow his lead because of the capital expenditure policy, he planned to purchase 1,000 motors from the overseas supplier for the headquarters plant in Long Island City.

Markowicz made the purchase at the beginning of the fourth quarter of 2016 without informing Sugofsky. He convinced the plant accountant to record the $1.5 million expenditure as an operating (not capital) expenditure because he knew that the higher level of operating cash inflows resulting from increased revenues would mask the effect of his expenditure. In fact, Markowicz was proud that he had "saved" the company $1.5 million, and he did what was necessary to ensure that the Long Island City plant continued to operate.

The acquisitions by Markowicz and the other plant managers enabled the company to keep up with the growing demand for textiles, and the company finished the year with record high levels of profit and net cash inflows from all activities. Markowicz was lauded by his team for his leadership. The company successfully executed a loan agreement with Second Bankers Hours & Trust Co. The $20 million borrowed was received on October 3, 2016.

During the course of an internal audit of the 2016 financial statements, Beverly Wald, the chief internal auditor (and also a CPA), discovered that there was an unusually high number of motors in inventory. A complete check of the inventory determined that $1 million worth of motors remained on hand.

Wald reported her findings to Ann Plotkin, and together they went to see Irv Milton. After being informed of the situation, Milton called in Sugofsky. When Wald told him about her findings, Sugofsky's face turned beet red. He told Wald that he had instructed Markowicz *not* to make the purchase. He also inquired about the accounting since Wald had said it was wrong.

Wald explained to Sugofsky that the $1 million should be accounted for as inventory, not as an operating cash outflow: "What we do in this case is transfer the motors out of inventory and into the machinery account once they are placed into operation because, according to the documentation, the motors added significant value to the asset."

Sugofsky had a perplexed look on his face. Finally, Irv Milton took control of the accounting lesson by asking, "What's the difference? Isn't the main issue that Markowicz did not follow company policy?" The three officers in the room nodded their heads simultaneously, perhaps in gratitude for being saved the additional lecturing. Milton then said he wanted the three of them to brainstorm some alternatives on how best to deal with the Markowicz situation and present the choices to him in one week.

Questions

Use the Integrated Ethical Decision-Making Process discussed in the chapter to help you assess the following:

1. Identify the ethical and professional issues of concern to Beverly Wald as the chief internal auditor and a CPA.
2. Who are the stakeholders in this case and what are their interests?

3. Identify alternative courses of action for Wald, Plotkin, and Sugofsky to present in their meeting with Milton. How might these alternatives affect the stakeholder interests?

4. If you were in Milton's place, which of the alternatives would you choose and why?

Case 2-8 Juggyfroot

"I'm sorry, Lucy. That's the way it is," Ricardo said. The client wants it that way.

"I just don't know if I can go along with it, Ricardo," Lucy replied.

"I know. I agree with you. But, Juggyfroot is our biggest client, Lucy. They've warned us that they will put the engagement up for bid if we refuse to go along with the reclassification of marketable securities," Ricardo explained.

"Have you spoken to Fred and Ethel about this?" Lucy asked.

"Are you kidding? They're the ones who made the decision to go along with Juggyfroot," Ricardo responded.

"I don't care, Ricardo. I expect more from you. I didn't join this firm to compromise my values."

The previous scene took place in the office of Deziloo LLP, a large CPA firm in Beverly Hills, California. Lucy Spheroid is the partner on the engagement of Juggyfroot, a publicly owned global manufacturer of pots and pans and other household items. Ricardo Rikey is the managing partner of the office. Fred and Ethel are the engagement review partners that make final judgments on difficult accounting issues, especially when there is a difference of opinion with the client. All four are CPAs.

Ricardo Rikey is preparing for a meeting with Norman Baitz, the CEO of Juggyfroot. Ricardo knows that the company expects to borrow $5 million next quarter and it wants to put the best possible face on its financial statements to impress the banks. That would explain why the company reclassified a $2 million market loss on a trading investment to the available-for-sale category so that the "loss" would now show up in stockholder's equity, not as a charge against current income. The result was to increase earnings in 2015 by 8 percent. Ricardo knows that without the change, the earnings would have declined by 2 percent and the company's stock price would have taken a hit. However, he is also very aware of his ethical and professional responsibilities.

In the meeting, Ricardo decides to overlook the recommendation by Fred and Ethel. Ricardo points out to Baitz that the investment in question was marketable, and in the past, the company had sold similar investments in less than one year. Ricardo adds there is no justification under generally accepted accounting principles (GAAP) to change the classification from trading to available-for-sale.

What happened next shocked Ricardo back to reality. The conversation between Baitz and Ricardo went this way.

"I hate to bring it up, Ricardo, but do you recall what happened last year at about the same time?"

"What do you mean?"

"You agreed that we could record $1 million as revenue for 2014 based on a sale of our product that we held at an off-site distribution warehouse until the client asked for delivery, which occurred in 2015."

Ricardo remembered all too well. It almost cost the firm the Juggyfroot account. "Are you going to throw that in my face?"

"No, Ricardo. Just a gentle reminder that you had agreed to go along with what we had asked at that time. We expect you to be loyal to our interests here as well."

The meeting broke up when Baitz received a confidential phone call. They agreed to continue it first thing in the morning.

Questions

1. Should Ricardo let what happened last year affect how he approaches the issue of the improper recording of marketable securities when he resumes his discussion with Baitz in the morning? Why or why not?

2. How would you handle the issue if you were in Ricardo's position? Develop an action plan to get your point of view across. What would you say? What do you expect the objections or pushback will be? How would you convince Baitz of the rightness of your position?

Case 2-9 Phar-Mor

The Dilemma

The story of Phar-Mor shows how quickly a company that built its earnings on fraudulent transactions can dissolve like an Alka-Seltzer.

One day, Stan Cherelstein, the controller of Phar-Mor, discovered cabinets stuffed with held checks totaling $10 million. Phar-Mor couldn't release the checks to vendors because it did not have enough cash in the bank to cover the amount. Cherelstein wondered what he should do.

Background

Phar-Mor was a chain of discount drugstores, based in Youngstown, Ohio, and founded in 1982 by Michael Monus and David Shapira. In less than 10 years, the company grew from 15 to 310 stores and had 25,000 employees. According to Litigation Release No. 14716 issued by the SEC,[1] Phar-Mor had cumulatively overstated income by $290 million between 1987 and 1991. In 1992, prior to disclosure of the fraud, the company overstated income by an additional $238 million.

The Cast of Characters

Mickey Monus personifies the hard-driving entrepreneur who is bound and determined to make it big whatever the cost. He served as the president and chief operating officer (COO) of Phar-Mor from its inception until a corporate restructuring was announced on July 28, 1992.

David Shapira was the CEO of both Phar-Mor and Giant Eagle, Phar-Mor's parent company and majority stockholder. Giant Eagle also owned Tamco, which was one of Phar-Mor's major suppliers. Shapira left day-to-day operations of Phar-Mor to Monus until the fraud became too large and persistent to ignore.

Patrick Finn was the CFO of Phar-Mor from 1988 to 1992. He brought Monus the bad news that, following a number of years of eroding profits, the company faced millions in losses in 1989.

John Anderson was the accounting manager at Phar-Mor. Hired after completing a college degree in accounting at Youngstown State University, Anderson became a part of the fraud.

Coopers & Lybrand, prior to its merger with Price Waterhouse, were the auditors of Phar-Mor. The firm failed to detect the fraud as it was unfolding.

How It Started

The facts of this case are taken from the SEC filing and a PBS *Frontline* episode called "How to Steal $500 Million." The interpretation of the facts is consistent with reports, but some literary license has been taken to add intrigue to the case.

Finn approached Monus with the bad news. Monus took out his pen, crossed off the losses, and then wrote in higher numbers to show a profit. Monus couldn't bear the thought of his hot growth company that had been sizzling for five years suddenly flaming out. In the beginning, it was to be a short-term fix to buy time while the company improved efficiency, put the heat on suppliers for lower prices, and turned a profit. Finn believed in Monus's ability to turn things around, so he went along with the fraud. Also, he thought of himself as a team player. Finn prepared the reports, and Monus changed the numbers for four months before turning the task over to Finn. These reports with the false numbers were faxed to Shapira and given to Phar-Mor's board. Basically, the company was lying to its owners.

The fraud occurred by dumping the losses into a "bucket account" and then reallocating the sums to one of the company's hundreds of stores in the form of increases in inventory amounts. Phar-Mor issued fake invoices for merchandise purchases and made phony journal entries to increase inventory and decrease cost of sales. The company overcounted and double-counted merchandise in inventory.

The fraud was helped by the fact that the auditors from Coopers observed inventory in only 4 out of 300 stores, and that allowed the finance department at Phar-Mor to conceal the shortages. Moreover, Coopers informed Phar-Mor in advance which stores they would visit. Phar-Mor executives fully stocked the 4 selected stores but allocated the phony inventory increases to the other 296 stores. Regardless of the accounting tricks, Phar-Mor was heading for collapse and its suppliers threatened to cut off the company for nonpayment of bills.

Stan Cherelstein's Role

Cherelstein, a CPA, was hired to be the controller of Phar-Mor in 1991, long after the fraud had begun. One day, Anderson called Cherelstein into his office and explained that the company had been keeping two sets of books—one that showed the true state of the company with the losses and the other, called the "subledger," that showed the falsified numbers that were presented to the auditors.

Cherelstein and Anderson discussed what to do about the fraud. Cherelstein asked Anderson why he hadn't done something about it. Anderson asked how could he? He was the new kid on the block. Besides, Pat (Finn) seemed to be disinterested in confronting Monus.

Cherelstein was not happy about the situation and felt like he had a higher responsibility. He demanded to meet with Monus. Cherelstein did get Monus to agree to repay the company for the losses from Monus's (personal) investment of company funds into the World Basketball League (WBL). But Monus never kept his word. In the beginning, Cherelstein felt compelled to give Monus some time to turn things around through increased efficiencies and by using a device called "exclusivity fees," which vendors paid to get Phar-Mor to stock their products. Over time, Cherelstein became more and more uncomfortable as the suppliers called more and more frequently, demanding payment on their invoices.

Accounting Fraud

Misappropriation of Assets

The unfortunate reality of the Phar-Mor saga was that it involved not only bogus inventory but also the diversion of company funds to feed Monus's personal habits. One example was the movement of $10 million in company funds to help start the WBL.

False Financial Statements

According to the ruling by the U.S. Court of Appeals that heard Monus's appeal of his conviction on all 109 counts of fraud, the company submitted false financial statements to Pittsburgh National Bank, which increased a revolving credit line for Phar-Mor from $435 million to $600 million in March 1992. It also defrauded Corporate Partners, an investment group that bought $200 million in Phar-Mor stock in June 1991. The list goes on, including the defrauding of Chemical Bank, which served as the placing agent for $155 million in 10-year senior secured notes issued to Phar-Mor; Westinghouse Credit Corporation, which had executed a $50 million loan commitment to Phar-Mor in 1987; and Westminster National Bank, which served as the placing agent for $112 million in Phar-Mor stock sold to various financial institutions in 1991.

Tamco Relationship

The early financial troubles experienced by Phar-Mor in 1988 can be attributed to at least two transactions. The first was that the company provided deep discounts to retailers to stock its stores with product. There was concern early on that the margins were too thin. The second was that its supplier, Tamco, was shipping partial orders to Phar-Mor while billing for full orders. Phar-Mor had no way of knowing this because it was not logging in shipments from Tamco.

After the deficiency was discovered, Giant Eagle agreed to pay Phar-Mor $7 million in 1988 on behalf of Tamco. Phar-Mor later bought Tamco from Giant Eagle in an additional effort to solve the inventory and billing problems. However, the losses just kept on coming.

Back to the Dilemma

Cherelstein looked out the window at the driving rain. He thought about the fact that he didn't start the fraud or engage in the cover-up. Still, he knew about it now and felt compelled to do something. Cherelstein thought about the persistent complaints by vendors that they were not being paid and their threats to cut off shipments to Phar-Mor. Cherelstein knew that, without any product in Phar-Mor stores, the company could not last much longer.

Questions

1. Evaluate the role of each of the stakeholders in this case from an ethical perspective. How do you assess blame for the Phar-Mor fraud?

2. Assume you are in Stan Cherelstein's position. Evaluate the moral intensity issues in the case. How do these issues relate to Rest's Four-Component Model of Ethical Decision Making? What are the challenges for Cherelstein in that regard?

3. Assume you decide to confront Monus. How would you counter the likely reasons and rationalizations you will hear from Monus? What levers do you have to influence Monus's behavior?

4. What is the ethical message of Phar-Mor? That is, explain what you think the moral of this story is.

Case 2-10   WorldCom

The WorldCom fraud was the largest in U.S. history, surpassing even that of Enron. Beginning modestly during mid-year 1999 and continuing at an accelerated pace through May 2002, the company—under the direction of Bernie Ebbers, the CEO; Scott Sullivan, the CFO; David Myers, the controller; and Buford Yates, the director of accounting—"cooked the books" to the tune of about $11 billion of misstated earnings. Investors collectively lost $30 billion as a result of the fraud.

The fraud was accomplished primarily in two ways:

1. Booking "line costs" for interconnectivity with other telecommunications companies as capital expenditures rather than operating expenses.

2. Inflating revenues with bogus accounting entries from "corporate unallocated revenue accounts."

During 2002, Cynthia Cooper, the vice president of internal auditing, responded to a tip about improper accounting by having her team do an exhaustive hunt for the improperly recorded line costs that were also known as "prepaid capacity." That name was designed to mask the true nature of the costs and treat them as capitalizable costs rather than as operating expenses. The team worked tirelessly, often at night and secretly, to investigate and reveal $3.8 billion worth of fraud.

Soon thereafter, Cooper notified the company's audit committee and board of directors of the fraud. The initial response was not to take action, but to look for explanations from Sullivan. Over time, Cooper realized that she needed to be persistent and not give in to pressure that Sullivan was putting on her to back off. Cooper even approached KPMG, the auditors that had replaced Arthur Andersen, to support her in the matter. Ultimately, Sullivan was dismissed, Myers resigned, Andersen withdrew its audit opinion for 2001, and the Securities and Exchange Commission (SEC) began an investigation into the fraud on June 26, 2002.

In an interview with David Katz and Julia Homer for *CFO Magazine* on February 1, 2008, Cynthia Cooper was asked about her whistleblower role in the WorldCom fraud. When asked when she first suspected something was amiss, Cooper said: "It was a process. My feelings changed from curiosity to discomfort to suspicion based on some of the accounting entries my team and I had identified, and also on the odd reactions I was getting from some of the finance executives."[1]

---

[1]David K. Katz and Julia Homer, "WorldCom Whistle-blower Cynthia Cooper," *CFO Magazine*, February 1, 2008. Available at: www.cfo.com/article.cfm/10590507.

Cooper did exactly what is expected of a good auditor. She approached the investigation of line-cost accounting with a healthy dose of skepticism and maintained her integrity throughout, even as Sullivan was trying to bully her into dropping the investigation.

When asked whether there was anything about the culture of WorldCom that contributed to the scandal, Cooper laid blame on Bernie Ebbers for his risk-taking approach that led to loading up the company with $40 billion in debt to fund one acquisition after another. He followed the same reckless strategy with his own investments, taking out loans and using his WorldCom stock as collateral. Cooper believed that Ebbers's personal decisions then affected his business decisions; he ultimately saw his net worth disappear, and he was left owing WorldCom some $400 million for loans approved by the board. Ebbers was sentenced to 25 years in jail for his offenses.

Betty Vinson, the company's former director of corporate reporting, was one of five former WorldCom executives who pleaded guilty to fraud. At the trial of Ebbers, Vinson said she was told to make improper accounting entries because Ebbers did not want to disappoint Wall Street. "I felt like if I didn't make the entries, I wouldn't be working there," Vinson testified. She said that she even drafted a resignation letter in 2000, but ultimately she stayed with the company. It was clear she felt uneasy with the accounting at WorldCom.

Vinson said that she took her concerns to Sullivan, who told her that Ebbers did not want to lower Wall Street expectations. Asked how she chose which accounts to alter, Vinson testified, "I just really pulled some out of the air. I used some spreadsheets."[2]

Her lawyer urged the judge to sentence Vinson to probation, citing the pressure placed on her by Ebbers and Sullivan. "She expressed her concern about what she was being directed to do to upper management, and to Sullivan and Ebbers, who assured her and lulled her into believing that all was well," he said. In the end, Vinson was sentenced to five months in prison and five months of house arrest.

Questions

1. Identify the stakeholders in the WorldCom case and how their interests were affected by the financial fraud.
2. Do you think Betty Vinson was a victim of "motivated blindness"? Are there steps should could have taken to stand up for what she believed? Explain.
3. In a presentation at James Madison University in November 2013, Cynthia Cooper said, "You don't have to be a bad person to make bad decisions." Discuss what you think Cooper meant and how it relates to our discussion of ethical and moral development in the chapter.

---

[2]Susan Pulliam, "Ordered to Commit Fraud, a Staffer Balked, Then Caved: Accountant Betty Vinson Helped Cook the Books at WorldCom," *The Wall Street Journal*, June 23, 2003. Available at: www.people.tamu.edu/~jstrawser/acct229h/Current%20 Readings/E.%20WSJ.com%20-%20A%20Staffer%20 Ordered%20to%20Commit%20Fraud,%20Balked.pdf.

Chapter

3

Organizational Ethics and Corporate Governance

Learning Objectives

After studying Chapter 3, you should be able to:

LO 3-1 Describe the link between organizational climate and ethical leadership.

LO 3-2 Explain the link between organizational ethics, individual ethics, and corporate culture.

LO 3-3 Analyze why and how organizational culture is formed.

LO 3-4 Discuss the views of employees about ethics in their organizations.

LO 3-5 Describe the causes of fraud, detection methods, and preventative controls.

LO 3-6 Explain the components of corporate governance and their relationship to corporate culture.

LO 3-7 Analyze the moral basis for whistleblowing and accountants' obligations to whistle blow.

Ethics Reflection

Satyam: India's Enron

Corporate governance failures marked the business and accounting frauds of the early 2000s. The United States was not alone. Enron and WorldCom had their counterparts in the global arena. Italy had a massive fraud at Parmalat, and Satyam, sometimes referred to India's Enron, was a $1.4 billion fraud that triggered a reduction in share price of almost 99 percent.

Satyam Computer Services was the fourth-largest software exporter in India until January 2009, when the CEO and cofounder, Ramalinga Raju, confessed to inflating the company's profits and cash reserves over an eight-year period. The accounting fraud at Satyam involved dual accounting books, more than 7,000 forged invoices, and dozens of fake bank statements. The total amount of losses was 50 billion Rs (rupees) (equal to about $1.40 billion). This represented about 94 percent of the company's cash and cash equivalents. Raju stepped down in early January 2009. In April 2015, he was convicted of forging documents and falsifying accounts. He is currently serving a seven-year prison term.

The Satyam incident was investigated by India's "Serious Frauds" (seems a redundancy) Office that coordinated the investigations and the diversion of funds by promoters within and outside India and corporate governance failings.

Corporate Governance Failings

The legal complaints alleged that members of the audit committee of the Satyam board of directors—who were responsible for overseeing the integrity of the company's financial statements, the performance and compensation of the outside auditors from PricewaterhouseCoopers (PwC) India firms, and the adequacy and effectiveness of internal accounting and financial controls—were responsible for the publication of false and misleading public statements due to their extreme recklessness in discharging their duties and their resulting failure to discover and prevent the massive accounting fraud.

Effective corporate governance was missing at Satyam at all levels including:

- Lack of independent members of the board of directors; those not beholden to management.
- Audit committee failings to properly oversee financial reporting and internal controls.
- Questionable "ethical" tone at the top that worked against promoting ethical and competent behavior throughout the organization.
- External audits that were heavily influenced by conflicts of interest between PwC and management.

A unique aspect of the corporate governance system in India is the ownership of shares by outside promoters, multinational blockholder companies, and the state. Unlike in the United States where public ownership is high and transparency is key, the more closed system in India leads to a relative lack of full and fair disclosure.

Audit Failures by PwC and Resulting Legal Actions

The complaint asserted claims against PwC and its Indian partners and affiliates. Satyam's outside auditors from the PwC India firms allegedly were aware of the fraud but still certified the company's financial statements as accurate. The company's financial statements were signed off on by PwC on March 31, 2008.

PwC and its Indian affiliates initially hid behind "client confidentiality" and stated that it was "examining the contents of the statement." Realizing that this was not enough, PwC came up with a second statement claiming that "the audits were conducted in accordance with applicable auditing standards and were supported by appropriate audit evidence." This is somewhat troublesome because an audit in accordance with generally accepted auditing standards (GAAS) calls for examining the contents of the financial statements. Given that the firm did not identify the financial wrongdoing at Satyam, it would appear that the firm, at the very least, was guilty of professional negligence. At a minimum, the firm missed or failed to do the following:

- Fictitious invoices with customers were recorded as genuine.

- Raju recorded a fictional interest credit as income.

- The auditors didn't ask for a statement of confirmation of balance from banks (for cash balances) and debtors (for receivables), a basic procedure in an audit.

One ironic note about the Satyam fraud is in September 2008 the World Council for Corporate Governance honored the company with a "Golden Peacock Award" for global excellence in corporate governance. Once news of the fraud broke, the council rescinded the award, stating that the company failed to disclose material information.

As you read this chapter, reflect on the following questions: (1) What systems are necessary to ensure that a company runs efficiently and ethically? (2) What role does corporate culture and ethical leadership play in creating an ethical organization? (3) What are the components of an ethical control environment from an accounting and auditing perspective? (4) How do whistleblowing obligations of accounting professionals influence ethical behavior?

The thing I have learned at IBM is that culture is everything. Underneath all the sophisticated processes, there is always the company's sense of values and identity.

Louis V. Gerstner, Jr., former CEO, IBM

This statement by former IBM chief executive officer (CEO) Louis Gerstner highlights one of the themes of this chapter: The culture of an organization establishes the boundaries within which ethical decisions must be made. As we learned from previous chapters, it is one thing to know that you should behave in a certain way, but it is quite another to do it (or even want to do it) given the pressures that may exist from within the organization.

Organizational Ethics and Leadership

LO 3-1
Describe the link between organizational climate and ethical leadership.

Organizational ethics can be thought of as the generally accepted principles and standards that guide behavior in business and other organizational contexts. High ethical standards require both organizations and individuals to conform to sound moral principles. In organizations, a critical component of creating an ethical organization environment is the culture that includes shared values, beliefs, goals, norms, and problem solving mechanisms. The ethical climate of an organization plays an important role in organizational culture. Whereas an organization's overall culture establishes ideals that guide a wide variety of member behaviors, the ethical climate focuses specifically on issues of right and wrong.

Organizational ethical climate refers to the moral atmosphere of the work environment and the level of ethics practiced within a company. Leaders determine organizational climate and establish character and define norms. Character plays an important role in leadership. Leaders of good character have integrity, courage, and compassion. They are careful and prudent. Their decisions and actions inspire employees to think and act in a way that enhances the well-being of the organization, its people, and society in general. Ralph Waldo Emerson, the American essayist, poet, and philosopher, said, "Our chief want is someone who will inspire us to be what we know we could be."

Johnson points out that virtues are woven into the inner lives of leaders, shape the way they see and behave, operate independent of the situation, and help leaders to live more fulfilling lives. He identifies courage, temperance, wisdom, justice, optimism, integrity, humility, reverence, and compassion as underlying traits of character of effective leaders. Ethical leaders recognize that moral action is risky but continue to model ethical behavior despite the danger. They refuse to set their values aside to go along with the group, to keep silent when customers may be hurt, or to lie to investors. They strive to create ethical environments even when faced with opposition from their superiors and subordinates. Ethical leaders serve as role models for those within the organization and stakeholders that rely on it.[1]

There is no one size fits all for ethical climates. Johnson believes that an organization must first identify principles and practices that characterize positive ethical climates and then adapt them to a particular organization setting. He identifies key markers of highly ethical organizations including humility, zero tolerance for individual and collective destructive behaviors, justice, integrity, trust, a focus on process, structural reinforcement, and social responsibility. We add that an ethical climate is enhanced through a values-driven organization that encourages openness and transparency, and provides a supportive environment to voice matters of concern without fear of retribution or retaliation.[2]

Is there a difference between ethical decision making in general, as we discussed in Chapter 2, and ethical decision making in an organizational setting? We believe there are important differences that incorporate both individual and organizational factors into the process. Ferrell et al. describes a process that is depicted in Exhibit 3.1.[3] What follows is a brief explanation of the components of the framework.

Ethical Issue Intensity

Recall our previous discussion of Rest's Model and the first step of recognizing that an ethical issue exists. Ethical awareness requires that an individual or work group choose among several actions that various stakeholders inside or outside the firm will ultimately evaluate as right or wrong. The relative importance of the issue to the individual, work group and/or organization (intensity) is based on the values, beliefs, and norms involved and situational pressures in the workplace.

EXHIBIT 3.1   Framework for Understanding Ethical Decision Making in Business

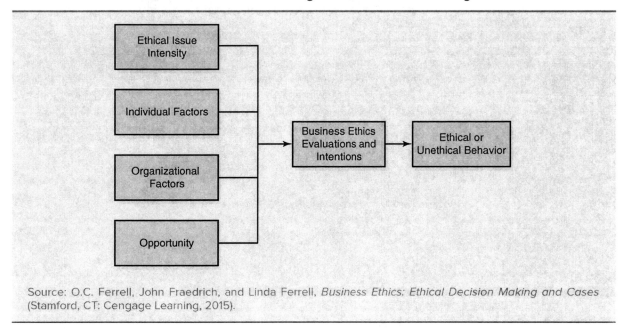

Source: O.C. Ferrell, John Fraedrich, and Linda Ferrell, *Business Ethics: Ethical Decision Making and Cases* (Stamford, CT: Cengage Learning, 2015).

Individual Factors

Values of individuals can be derived from moral philosophies, such as those discussed in Chapter 1. These provide principles or rules people use to decide what is right or wrong from a moral and personal perspective. Although an individual's intention to engage in ethical behavior relates to individual values, organizational and social forces also play an important role by shaping behavioral intentions and decision making.[4]

Organizational Factors

Research has established that in the workplace, the organization's values often have a greater influence on decisions than a person's own values.[5] Ethical decisions in the workplace are made jointly, in work groups or other organizational settings. The strength of personal values, the opportunities to behave unethically, and the exposure to others who behave ethically or unethically influence decision making. An alignment between an individual's own values and the values of the organization help create positive work environments and organizational outcomes.

Opportunity

Ferrell points out that opportunity describes the conditions in an organization that limit or permit ethical or unethical behavior.[6] Opportunity results from conditions that either provide internal or external rewards, or fail to erect barriers against unethical behavior. The opportunities that employees have for unethical behavior in an organization can be reduced or eliminated with aggressive enforcement of rules and codes of ethics.

Business Ethics Evaluations and Intentions

Ethical dilemmas involve problem-solving situations when the rules governing decisions are often vague or in conflict. The results of an ethical decision are often uncertain: It is not always immediately clear whether or not we made the right decision. Moreover, the decision we make may not always comport with the one we intended to make because of pressures within the organization. As discussed in Chapter 2, this is where giving voice to one's values becomes a critical component of taking ethical action.

Ethical or Unethical Behavior

The resulting ethical or unethical behavior is greatly influenced by the decision maker's ability to express one's values; be supported by the norms, standards, and rules of conduct in the organization; and find a way to be true to these guidelines even in the face of opposing points of view. An organizational ethical culture is shaped by effective leadership. Without top management support for ethical behavior, the opportunity for employees to engage in their own personal approaches to decision making will evolve.

Organizational Influences on Ethical Decision Making

LO 3-2
Explain the link between organizational ethics, individuals ethics, and corporate culture.

Organizational factors can impede ethical decision making. Smith and Carroll presented a detailed argument that organizational factors such as socialization processes, environmental influences, and hierarchical relationships collectively constitute a "stacked deck," which impedes moral behavior.[7] Organizational factors are likely to play a role in moral decision making and behavior at two points: establishing moral intent and engaging in moral behavior. Explicit organizational behaviors may cause unethical (or ethical) behavior to result despite good (or bad) intention.

Thomas Jones developed an explanatory model[8] that merged Rest's four-step moral reasoning model with Fiske and Taylor's work on social cognition to illustrate the ethical decision-making process of an individual who encounters an ethical dilemma within the context of work.[9] Of particular importance is the role that moral intensity plays in recognizing moral issues. Moral issues of high intensity will be more salient because the magnitude of consequences is greater, their effects stand out, and their effects involve significant others (greater social, cultural, psychological, or physical proximity).

While Jones's model illustrates the impact that moral intensity has on ethical choices and behavior and acknowledges that organizational factors influence the establishment of moral intent and behavior—the last two steps in Rest's model—the model fails to address what Burchard calls the cyclical, ongoing dynamic exchange between the individual and organization, which affects the development and sustaining of one's code of conduct in the organizational context.[10] It was left to Jones and Hiltebeitel to fill the gap when they conducted a study of organizational influence on moral decisions and proposed a model that demonstrated organizational influence on the moral decision-making process.[11] As Jones had done with his previous model, Jones and Hiltebeitel based their model on Rest's moral reasoning and Kohlberg's moral development theory.

The Jones-Hiltebeitel model looks at the role of one's personal code of conduct in ethical behavior within an organization. When an employee was called upon to perform routine tasks—those with no internal conflict or cognitive dissonance—the actions taken were almost automatic. However, when those tasks diverged from the routine, the employee would refer to her personal code of conduct for ethical cues. The implications for ethical behavior within the organization are significant because an unethical individual might act dishonestly in one case, while a virtuous person would act in a truthful, trustworthy manner.

According to the model, when one's personal code is insufficient to make the necessary moral decision, the individual will look at the factors that influenced the formation of the code, including professional and organizational influences to resolve the conflict. The influences that are strongest are the ones that determine the reformation of the individual's code of conduct. The implications for the culture of an organization are significant because an organization that values profits above all else might elicit one kind of response, such as to go along with improper accounting, while an organization that values integrity above all else might lead to questioning improper accounting and doing what one can to reverse false and misleading financial results.[12]

Ethical Dissonance Model

Burchard points out that the Jones-Hiltebeitel model and others like it pay too little attention to the examination of ethical person-organization fit upon the person-organization exchange, within each of the four potential fit options. Burchard presents what she calls the Ethical Dissonance Cycle Model to illustrate the interaction between the individual and the organization, based on the person-organization ethical fit at various stages of the contractual relationship in each potential ethical fit scenario.[13] The model is complex, so we restrict our coverage to the basics of the person-organization interchange and its implications for ethical behavior within organizations. This is an important consideration because the ethics of an individual influences the values that one brings to the workplace and decision making, while the ethics (through its culture) of an organization influences that behavior. To keep it simple, we adopt the idea that there can be a dissonance between what is considered ethical and what may actually be "best" for the subject inviting ethical consideration.

Of the four potential fit options, two possess high person-organization fit: (1) high organizational ethics, high individual ethics (High-High), and (2) low organizational ethics, low individual ethics (Low-Low); and two possess low person-organization fit: (1) high organizational ethics, low individual ethics (High-Low) and (2) low organizational ethics, high individual ethics (Low-High).[14]

Let's pause for a moment and consider the practical implications of this model. Imagine that you are interviewing for a position with a mid-sized company in your town. You can easily find out information about the company on the Internet to prepare for the interview, such as the scope of its operations, products and services, customer base, and geographical locations. However, it is less easy to find out about its reputation for ethics, although reports in the media about specific events might be of some use. Now, let's assume that you knew (and understood) what is meant by organizational fit and in this case the fit is Low-High. Would that affect whether you interview with the company? Might you ask questions to better understand why that fit exists? Would it affect your final decision whether to work for the company? The information you might gather during the process could be invaluable when you face ethical dilemmas in the workplace.

In two of the fit options (High-High and Low-Low), no ethical dissonance exists. Person-organization fit is optimal, and the organization is highly effective, either to constructive or destructive ends. The other two (High-Low and Low-High) demonstrate a lack of person-organization fit in the realm of ethics and values.[15]

High Organizational Ethics, High Individual Ethics (High-High)[16]

Assume that you know your values and beliefs are an ethical match for the company you work for. You are likely to continue to stay employed in the organization. The issue for us is how you might assess organizational ethics. Koh and Boo identified three distinct measures of organizational ethics: support for ethical behavior from top management, the ethical climate of the organization, and the connection between career success and ethical behavior.[17] These three factors relate to the culture of the organization and may have implications for actions such as whistleblowing, as discussed later on. Koh and Boo found that positive ethical culture and climate produces favorable organizational outcomes by setting down the ethical philosophy and rules of conduct and practices (i.e., code of ethics).

Low Organizational Ethics, Low Individual Ethics (Low-Low)[18]

When both the individual and organization possess low moral and ethical development, the fit is there, but it is turns in a negative direction. A culture of corruption is difficult to change, and for the employee, it takes more conscious effort to stop the corruption than to participate in it. You might say that the employee adopts the attitude of going along to get along. Padilla et al. contends that "dysfunctional leader behaviors and susceptible followers interacting in the context of a contributing environment produce negative organizational outcomes in which 'followers must consent to, or be unable to resist, a destructive leader.' "[19]

High Organizational Ethics, Low Individual Ethics (High-Low)[20]

According to Hamilton and Kelman, if the individual possesses lower ethics than that which is held by the organization, the discovery of an individual's lack of person-organization fit is often pointed out by socialized members within the ethical organization.[21] Those assimilated members of the organization may attempt to socialize the individual to the ways of the organization to alleviate the ethical dissonance. Once this dissonance is discovered, the likelihood that the mismatched employee will leave the company rises. The more the individual's personal decisions are seen to be in conflict with the ethical decisions that are perceived to be encouraged by the organization, the greater the discomfort of the individual. Imagine, for example, a newly hired employee thought there was nothing wrong with accepting free gifts from contractors doing business with one's employer, but the employer has a code of ethics forbidding such practices. The culture of the organization conflicts with the individual's low ethical standards in this instance, and others in the organization that identify with organizational values may attempt to resolve the dissonance and alter the employee's behavior. If the employee's behavior does not change, the employee may be let go for cause or insubordination.

Low Organizational Ethics, High Individual Ethics (Low-High)[22]

A reduction in job satisfaction is likely if an employee striving to be ethical perceives little top management support for ethical behavior, an unfavorable ethical climate in the organization, and/or little association between ethical behavior and job success.[23] Once this ethical dissonance is discovered, the likelihood of employee turnover rises. Sims and Keon found a significant relationship between the ethical rift between one's personal decisions and the perceived unwritten/informal policies of the organization, and the individual's level of comfort within the organization. The greater the difference between the decisions that the individual made and the decisions perceived as expected and reinforced by the organization, the greater levels of discomfort the individual would feel, and the more likely the individual would be to report these feelings of discomfort.[24] The case of Cynthia Cooper, discussed in Chapter 1, illustrates the low organizational, high individual ethics environment. Cooper reported her concerns to top management, and once she was convinced that nothing would be done to address the improper accounting for capitalized costs, she blew the whistle by going to the audit committee and external auditors.

Seven Signs of Ethical Collapse

In her book *The Seven Signs of Ethical Collapse*, Marianne Jennings analyzes the indicators of possible ethical collapse in companies and provides advice how to avoid impending disaster. She starts with a description of ethical collapse, saying that it "occurs when any organization has drifted from the basic principles of right and wrong," and she uses financial reporting standards and accounting rules as one area where this might occur. She points out that "not all companies that have drifted ethically have violated any laws."[25] Enron did not necessarily violate generally accepted accounting principles (GAAP) in treating the effects of *some* of its transactions with special-purpose entities off-balance-sheet. However, the company ignored conflicts of interest of Andy Fastow who managed some of the entities while wearing a second hat as CFO of Enron during the time the two entities had mutual dealings.

According to Jennings, "When an organization collapses ethically, it means that those in the organization have drifted into rationalizations and legalisms, and all for the purpose of getting the results they want and need at almost any cost." A good example is Dennis Kozlowski at Tyco International who misappropriated company resources for personal purposes without the approval of the board of directors and rationalized that he was just doing what those before him had done. Thus, he invoked one of the reasons and rationalizations that we discussed in giving voice to values—Expected or Standard Practice. Jennings links the rationalizations and legalisms to a culture that leads to behavior based on the notion "It's not a question of should we do it." It is a culture of "Can we do it legally?" This mentality occurs because of the combination of the seven factors working together to cloud judgment.[26]

Jennings identifies seven common ethical signs of moral meltdowns in companies that have experienced ethical collapse. The common threads she found that make good people at companies do really dumb things include (1) pressure to maintain numbers; (2) fear and silence; (3) young 'uns and a bigger-than-life CEO (i.e., loyalty to the boss); (4) weak board of directors; (5) conflicts of interest overlooked or unaddressed; (6) innovation like no other company; and (7) goodness in some areas atones for evil in others.[27] We briefly address four of the seven signs.

Pressure to Maintain the Numbers

Jennings points out that the tension between ethics and the bottom line will always be present. The first sign of a culture at risk for ethical collapse occurs when there is not just a focus on numbers and results, but an unreasonable and unrealistic obsession with meeting quantitative goals. This "financial results at all costs" approach was a common ethical problem at both Enron and WorldCom. At WorldCom, the mantra was that financial results had to improve in every quarter, and the shifting of operating expenses to capitalized costs was used to accomplish the goal regardless of the propriety of the accounting treatment. It was an "ends justifies means" culture that sanctioned wrongdoing in the name of earnings. Accountants like Betty Vinson got caught up in the culture and did not know how to extricate themselves from the situation.

Fear of Reprisals

Fear and silence characterizes a culture where employees are reluctant to raise issues of ethical concern because they may be ignored, treated badly, transferred, or worse. It underlies the whistleblowing process in many organizations where ethical employees want to blow the whistle but fear reprisals, so they stay silent. One aspect of such a culture is a "kill the messenger syndrome," whereby an employee brings bad news to higher-ups with the best intentions of having the organization correct the matter, but instead the messenger is treated as an outcast.

Loyalty to the Boss

Dennis Kozlowski, the dominant, larger-then-life CEO of Tyco, had an appetite for a lavish style of living. He surrounded himself with young people who were taken by his stature and would not question his actions. Kozlowski, who once spent $6,000 on a shower curtain for an apartment paid for by the company, made sure these "young 'uns" received all the trappings of success so they would be reluctant to speak up when ethical and legal issues existed for fear of losing their expensive homes, boats, and

cars and the prestige that comes along with financial success at a young age. They were selected by the CEO for their positions based on their inexperience, possible conflicts of interest, and unlikelihood to question the boss's decisions. Of course, not all bigger-than-life CEOs are unethical (e.g., Steve Jobs and Warren Buffett).

Weak Board of Directors

A weak board of directors characterizes virtually all the companies with major accounting frauds in the early part of the 2000s. One example is HealthSouth, one of the largest healthcare providers in the United States specializing in patient rehabilitation services. Richard Scrushy surrounded himself with a weak board so that when he made decisions as CEO at HealthSouth that contributed to an accounting scandal where the company's earnings were falsely inflated by $1.4 billion, the board would go along, in part because of their interrelationships with Scrushy and HealthSouth that created conflicts of interest. Jennings identifies the following conflicts of interest:[28]

- One director earned $250,000 per year from a consulting contract with HealthSouth over a seven-year period.
- Another director had a joint investment venture with Scrushy on a $395,000 investment property.
- Another director's company was awarded a $5.6 million contract to install glass at a hospital being built by HealthSouth.
- MedCenter District, a hospital-supply company that was run online, did business with HealthSouth and was owned by Scrushy, six directors, and the wife of one of those directors.
- The same three directors had served on both the audit committee and the compensation committee for several years.
- Two of the directors had served on the board for 18 years.
- One director received a $425,000 donation to his favorite charity from HealthSouth just prior to his going on the board.

Stakeholder Orientation

In a business context, investors and shareholders, creditors, employees, customers, suppliers, governmental agencies, communities, and many others who have a "stake" or a claim in some aspect of a company's products, operations, markets, industry, and outcome are known as *stakeholders*. Business influences these groups, but these groups also have the ability to influence business; therefore, the relationship between companies and their stakeholders is a two-way street.

The well-known ethicist Archie Carroll points out that questions of right, wrong, fairness, and justice permeate an organization's activities as it attempts to interact successfully with major stakeholder groups. He believes that the principal task of management is not only to deal with the various stakeholder groups in an ethical fashion, but also to reconcile the conflicts of interest that occur between the organization and the stakeholder groups.[29]

Ferrell states that the degree to which an organization understands and addresses stakeholder demands can be referred to as a *stakeholder orientation*.[30] This orientation comprises three sets of activities: (1) the organization-wide generation of data about stakeholder groups and assessment of the firm's effects on these groups, (2) the distribution of this information throughout the firms, and (3) the responsiveness of the organization as a whole to this information.[31]

Generating data about stakeholders begins with identifying the stakeholders that are relevant to the firm followed by the concerns about the organization's conduct that each relevant stakeholder group shares. At this stage, the values and standards of behavior are used to evaluate stakeholder interests and concerns from an ethical perspective. The ethical reasoning methods previously discussed help to make the necessary judgments.

Stakeholder management requires that an individual consider issues from a variety of perspectives other than one's own or that of the organization. The case of the Ford Pinto illustrates how important stakeholder concerns can be left out of the decision-making process.

The Case of the Ford Pinto

The case of the Ford Pinto illustrates a classic example of how a company can make a fatal mistake in its decision making by failing to consider the interests of the stakeholders adequately. The failure was due to total reliance on utilitarian thinking instead of the universality perspective of rights theory, to the detriment of the driving public and society in general.

The Pinto was Ford Motor Company's first domestic North American subcompact automobile, marketed beginning on September 11, 1970. It competed with the AMC Gremlin and Chevrolet Vega, along with imports from makes such as Volkswagen, Datsun, and Toyota. The Pinto was popular in sales, with 100,000 units delivered by January 1971, and was also offered as a wagon and Runabout hatchback. Its reputation suffered over time, however, especially from a controversy surrounding the safety of its gas tank.

The public was shocked to find out that if the Pinto cars experienced an impact at speeds of only 30 miles per hour or less, they might become engulfed in flames, and passengers could be burned or even die. Ford faced an ethical dilemma: what to do about the apparently unsafe gas tanks that seemed to be the cause of these incidents. At the time, the gas tanks were routinely placed behind the license plate, so a rear-end collision was more likely to cause an explosion (whereas today's gas tanks are placed on the side of the vehicle). However, the federal safety standards at the time did not address this issue, so Ford was in compliance with the law. Ford's initial response was based on ethical legalism—the company complied with all the laws and safety problems, so it was under no obligation to take any action.

Eventually, Ford did use ethical analysis to develop a response. It used a risk–benefit analysis to aid decision making. This was done because the National Highway Traffic Safety Administration (NHTSA) excused a defendant from being penalized if the monetary costs of making a production change were greater than the "societal benefit" of that change. The analysis followed the same approach modeled after Judge Learned Hand's ruling in *United States v. Carroll Towing* in 1947 that boiled the theory of negligence down to the following: If the expected harm exceeded the cost to prevent it, the defendant was obligated to take the precaution, and if he (or it, in the case of a company) did not, liability would result. But if the cost was larger than the expected harm, the defendant was not expected to take the precaution. If there was an accident, the defendant would not be found guilty.[32] A summary of the Ford analysis follows.

Ford's Risk-Benefit Analysis[33]

Benefits of Fixing the Pintos

> *Savings:* 180 burn deaths, 180 serious burn injuries, 2,100 burned vehicles
>
> *Unit cost:* $200,000 per death (figure provided by the government); $67,000 per burn injury and $700 to repair a burned vehicle (company estimates)
>
> *Total benefits:* 180 × ($200,000) + 180 × ($67,000) + 2,100 × ($700) = **$49.5 million**

Costs of Fixing the Pintos

Sales: 11 million cars, 1.5 million light trucks

Unit cost: $11 per car, $11 per light truck

Total cost: $11,000,000 \times (\$11) + 1,500,000 \times (\$11) = \mathbf{\$137\ million}$

Based on this analysis and other considerations, including not being required by law to change its product design, Ford decided not to change the placement of the fuel tank.

Ford's risk–benefit analysis relied only on act-utilitarian reasoning, an approach that ignores the rights of various stakeholders. A rule-utilitarian approach might have led Ford to follow the rule "Never sacrifice public safety." A rights theory approach would have led to the same conclusion, based on the reasoning that the driving public has an ethical right to expect that their cars will not blow up if there is a crash at low speeds.

The other danger of utilitarian reasoning is that an important factor may be omitted from the analysis. Ford did not include as a potential cost the lawsuit judgments that might be awarded to the plaintiffs and against the company. For example, in May 1972, Lily Gray was traveling with 13-year-old Richard Grimshaw when their Pinto was struck by another car traveling approximately 30 miles per hour. The impact ignited a fire in the Pinto, which killed Gray and left Grimshaw with devastating injuries. A judgment was rendered against Ford, and the jury awarded the Gray family $560,000 and Matthew Grimshaw, the father of Richard Grimshaw, $2.5 million in compensatory damages. The surprise came when the jury also awarded $125 million in punitive damages. This was subsequently reduced to $3.5 million.[34]

In the aftermath of the scandal, it is interesting to consider whether any of the Ford executives who were involved in the decision-making process would have predicted in advance that they would have made such an unethical choice. Dennis Gioia, who was in charge of recalling defective automobiles at Ford, did not advocate ordering a recall. Gioia eventually came to view his decision not to recall the Pinto as a moral failure—what De Cremer and Tenbrunsel call a failure to think outside his prevailing background narrative or script at the point of decision. "My own schematized (scripted) knowledge influenced me to perceive recall issues in terms of the prevailing decision environment and to unconsciously overlook key features of the Pinto case . . . mainly because they did not fit an existing script." While personal morality was very important to Gioia, he admits that the framing narrative of his workplace "did not include ethical dimension."[35] The moral mistake was that there were other, better choices that he could have made—albeit ones outside the purview of Gioia's framing narrative.

Lessons Learned?

Has the automobile industry learned a lesson from Ford's experience with the Pinto? Some observers thought not when, in February 1993, an Atlanta jury held the General Motors Corporation responsible for the death of a Georgia teenager in the fiery crash of one of its pickup trucks. At the trial, General Motors contended in its defense that when a drunk driver struck seventeen-year-old Shannon Moseley's truck in the side, it was the impact of the high-speed crash that killed Moseley. However, the jury was persuaded that Moseley survived the collision only to be consumed by a fire caused by his truck's defective fuel-tank design. Finding that the company had known that its "side-saddle" gas tanks which are mounted outside the rails of the truck's frame, are dangerously prone to rupture, the jury awarded $4.2 million in actual damages and $101 million in punitive damages to Moseley's parents.

What undoubtedly swayed the jury was the testimony of former GM safety engineer Ronald E. Elwell. Although Elwell had testified in more than 15 previous cases that the pickups were safe, this time he switched sides and told the jury that the company had known for years that the side-saddle design was defective but had intentionally hidden its knowledge and had not attempted to correct the problem. At the trial, company officials attempted to paint Elwell as a disgruntled employee, but his testimony was supported by videotapes of General Motors' own crash tests. After the verdict, General Motors said that it still stood behind the safety of its trucks and contended "that a full examination by the National Highway Traffic Safety Administration of the technical issues in this matter will bear out our contention that the 1973–1987 full-size pickup trucks do not have a safety-related defect."[36] Of course, that wasn't to be.

A stakeholder orientation adds to a corporation's reputation for being trustworthy. Many parties rely on the considerate, fair-minded, and ethical treatment of stakeholders. Gone are the days when only shareholder interests mattered. Too many groups rely on a corporation today for too many things for an ethical company to ignore those interests.

Establishing an Ethical Culture

LO 3-3
Analyze why and how organizational culture is formed.

Corporate culture is the shared beliefs of top managers in a company about how they should manage themselves and other employees, and how they should conduct their business(es). Southwest Airlines promotes a culture of a: (1) warrior spirit; (2) servant's heart; and (3) (fun-loving attitude). Most people who fly on Southwest see it as caring about the customer.[37]

An important element of ethical culture is the tone at the top. Tone at the top refers to the ethical environment that is created in the workplace by the organization's leadership. An ethical tone creates the basis for standards of behavior that become part of the code of ethics.

The tone set by managers influences how employees respond to ethical challenges and is enhanced by ethical leadership. When leaders are perceived as trustworthy, employee trust increases; leaders are seen as ethical and as honoring a higher level of duties. Employees identify with the organization's values and the likely outcome is high individual ethics; high organization ethics; and a lack of dissonance.[38]

If the tone set by management upholds ethics and integrity, employees will be more inclined to uphold those same values. However, if top management appears unconcerned about ethics and focuses solely on the bottom line, employees will be more prone to commit fraud, whether occupational (i.e., job-related), or participation in fraudulent financial reporting as occurred with Betty Vinson.

The culture at Tyco can be characterized as laissez-faire because Dennis Kozlowski was too preoccupied with his personal affairs to pay much attention to the company. Consequently, there was an absence of directions, standards, and expectations. With an absence of effective leadership, each department, in fact, each individual did whatever they wanted.

Corporate culture starts with an explicit statement of values, beliefs, and customs from top management. A code of ethics serves as a guide to support ethical decision making. It clarifies an organization's mission, values, and principles, linking them with standards of professional conduct.

Trust in Business

Trust in business is the cornerstone of relationships with customers, suppliers, employees, and others who have dealings with an organization. Trust means to be reliable and carry through words with deeds. Looking back at Rest's model, trust is gained when an employee follows through ethical intent with ethical action. Trust becomes pervasive only if the organization's values are followed and supported by top management. By modeling the organization's values, senior leaders provide a benchmark for all employees.

A good example of building trust in an organization is from Paul O'Neill, former CEO at Alcoa Inc., the world's third-largest producer of aluminum. O'Neill created a reputation for trust among his employees by setting strict ethical standards and carrying through with them. In an interview with "PBS Newshour" on July 9, 2002, O'Neill was asked by reporter Jim Lehrer why Alcoa was able to avoid the accounting scandals that infected so many companies in the late 1990s and early 2000s. He responded with the following statement: "When I went there [to Alcoa], I called the chief financial officer and the controller and I said to them, 'I don't want to ever be accused of or guilty of managing earnings,' that is to say making earnings that really aren't as a consequence of operations." O'Neill went on to express in the interview his dismay at the number of cases where employees of a company were told that these are the company's values, and then senior management totally ignored those same values.

Trust can be lost, even if once gained in the eyes of the public, if an organization no longer follows the guiding principles that helped to create its reputation for trust. A good example is what has happened with Johnson & Johnson. The company was a model of ethical behavior during the Tylenol incident but has come under intense scrutiny lately over questions about the safety of its other products.

Johnson & Johnson: Trust Gained

In addition to a statements of values, standards of business practices, and a code of ethics, some companies use a credo to instill virtue. A credo is an aspirational statement that encourages employees to internalize the values of the company. A good example of a corporate credo is that of Johnson & Johnson, which appears in Exhibit 3.2.

EXHIBIT 3.2   Johnson & Johnson Credo

We believe our first responsibility is to the doctors, nurses, and patients, to mothers and fathers and all others who use our products and services. In meeting their needs, everything we do must be of high quality. We must constantly strive to reduce our costs in order to maintain reasonable prices. Customers' orders must be serviced promptly and accurately. Our suppliers and distributors must have an opportunity to make a fair profit.

We are responsible to our employees, the men and women who work with us throughout the world. Everyone must be considered as an individual. We must respect their dignity and recognize their merit. They must have a sense of security in their jobs. Compensation must be fair and adequate, and working conditions clean, orderly, and safe. We must be mindful of ways to help our employees fulfill their family responsibilities. Employees must feel free to make suggestions and complaints. There must be equal opportunity for employment, development, and advancement for those qualified. We must provide competent management, and their actions must be just and ethical.

We are responsible to the communities in which we live and work, and to the world community as well. We must be good citizens—support good works and charities and bear our fair share of

(Continued)

taxes. We must encourage civic improvements and better health and education. We must maintain in good order the property we are privileged to use, protecting the environment and natural resources.

Our final responsibility is to our stockholders. Business must make a sound profit. We must experiment with new ideas. Research must be carried on, innovative programs developed, and mistakes paid for. New equipment must be purchased, new facilities provided, and new products launched. Reserves must be created to provide for adverse times. When we operate according to these principles, the stockholders should realize a fair return.

Source: *Johnson & Johnson Credo,* http://www.jnj.com/sites/default/files /pdf/jnj_ourcredo_english_us_8.5x11_cmyk.pdf.

The Johnson & Johnson credo clearly sets a positive tone. Notice how it emphasizes the company's primary obligations to those who use and rely on the safety of its products. The Johnson & Johnson credo implies that shareholders will earn a fair return if the company operates in accordance with its ethical values. Johnson & Johnson was credited with being an ethical organization in part because of the way it handled the Tylenol poisoning incidents in 1982. However, more recent events bring into question whether the company is suffering from a "Dr. Jekyll and Mr. Hyde" syndrome.

Tylenol Poisoning

In the fall of 1982, seven people in the Chicago area collapsed suddenly and died after taking Tylenol capsules that had been laced with cyanide. These five women and two men became the first victims ever to die from what came to be known as "product tampering."

McNeil Consumer Products, a subsidiary of Johnson & Johnson, was confronted with a crisis when it was determined that each of the seven people had ingested an Extra-Strength Tylenol capsule laced with cyanide. The news of this incident traveled quickly and was the cause of a massive, nationwide panic.

Tamara Kaplan, a professor at Penn State University, contends that Johnson & Johnson used the Tylenol poisonings to launch a public relations program immediately to preserve the integrity of both their product and their corporation as a whole. We find this to be a vacuous position, however. By Kaplan's own admission, "Johnson & Johnson's top management put customer safety first, before they worried about their company's profit and other financial concerns."[39] This hardly sounds like a company that used a catastrophic event to boost its image in the eyes of the public.

Johnson & Johnson's stock price dropped precipitously after the initial incident was made public. In the end, the stock price recovered because the company's actions gained the support and confidence of the public. Johnson & Johnson acted swiftly to remove all the product from the shelves of supermarkets, provide free replacements of Tylenol capsules with the tablet form of the product, and make public statements of assurance that the company would not sell an unsafe product. To claim that the company was motivated by a public relations agenda (even though in the end, its actions did provide a public relations boon for the company) is to ignore a basic point that Johnson & Johnson's management may have known all along: that is, good ethics is good business. But don't be fooled by this expression. It is good for the company if it benefits as a result of an ethical action. However, the main reason to make ethical decisions, as Johnson & Johnson did, is that it is the proper way to act. Much like Alcoa, Johnson & Johnson's credo instills a sense of pride for what the company stands for.

Johnson & Johnson: Trust Deficit

Johnson & Johnson learned the hard way that trust gained can easily be lost simply with one or two bad acts. The company learned that losing sight of one's values can cost. Johnson & Johnson announced in January 2012 that it recorded pretax charges and special items totaling $3.3 billion for the fourth quarter of 2011 in order to provide a reserve for probable losses from product liability lawsuits. The pending lawsuits are attributable to misleading marketing practices and manufacturing-quality lapses.

On November 4, 2013, Johnson & Johnson agreed to pay more than $2.2 billion in criminal and civil fines to settle accusations that it improperly promoted the antipsychotic drug Risperdal to older adults, children and people with developmental disabilities. The agreement is the third-largest pharmaceutical settlement in U.S. history and the largest in a string of recent cases involving the marketing of antipsychotic and anti-seizure drugs to older dementia patients. It is part of a decade-long effort by the federal government to hold the health care giant — and other pharmaceutical companies — accountable for illegally marketing the drugs as a way to control patients with dementia in nursing homes and children with certain behavioral disabilities, despite the health risks of the drugs.[40]

In another setback for the company, on February 24, 2015, a Philadelphia jury decided J&J must pay $2.5 million in damages for failing to warn that its Risperdal antipsychotic could cause gynecomastia, which is abnormal development of breasts in males. The lawsuit was brought by the family of an autistic boy who took the drug in 2002 and later developed size 46 DD breasts, according to a lawyer for the family. The case has drawn attention for a few reasons. For one, this was the first lawsuit claiming J&J hid the risks of gynecomastia to go to trial after a handful of cases were settled in recent years. The trial also served as a reminder that J&J had already paid $2.2 billion two years prior to resolve criminal and civil allegations of illegally marketing Risperdal to children and the elderly.[41]

Unfortunately, the problems for Johnson & Johnson go further back. Exhibit 3.3 provides a brief summary of the investigations against the company:

EXHIBIT 3.3   Johnson & Johnson's Product Liabilities

- On December 21, 2011, it was announced that Johnson & Johnson must defend a lawsuit claiming that it misled investors about quality control failures at manufacturing plants that led to recalls of the popular over-the-counter drug Motrin. Allegedly, top executives made misleading statements about details of the recalls, leading to stock losses after the true reasons for the recalls became public.

- Earlier in 2011, a lawsuit filed by a group of consumers alleging that Johnson & Johnson's baby shampoo includes potentially cancer-causing chemicals was allowed to go forward after evidence came out that the product contained a chemical ingredient called methylene chloride, which is banned by the U.S. Food and Drug Administration (FDA) for use in cosmetics.

- In January 2011, it was announced that Johnson & Johnson might have to pay up to $1 billion for lawsuits concerning its subsidiary DePuy Orthopaedics, which sold metal-on-metal hip implants that were found to shed minute metal particles into a patient's bloodstream over time. Lawsuits over the implants have piled up across the country, accusing DePuy of manufacturing a defective product, failing to warn patients and doctors of problems with the implant, and negligence in designing, manufacturing, and selling the product.

  It is worth noting that Johnson & Johnson raised its product-liability reserves to $570 million at the end of 2010 and allotted $280 million for medical costs of patients directly affected by the recalled hip implants. In November 2013, it was announced that Johnson & Johnson agreed to a settlement that could reach up to $4 billion to resolve thousands of lawsuits filed by patients injured by a flawed all-metal replacement hip.

- Women who have suffered serious injury and disfiguration filed lawsuits in 2012 against Johnson & Johnson subsidiary Ethicon, claiming that vaginal mesh manufactured by Ethicon caused them life-altering complications. Upon investigation, a number of doctors and scientists concluded that the Ethicon vaginal mesh and bladder slings did not meet reasonable safety standards. The FDA issued Public Health Notifications regarding the use of vaginal mesh products to treat pelvic organ prolapse and stress urinary incontinence in October 2008, in February 2009, and in July 2011.

(Continued)

In March 2015, The Lawsuit Settlement Funding Company announced that Johnson & Johnson's Ethicon subsidiary reached a settlement in their transvaginal mesh devices. The settlement came just one day after a $5.7 million verdict was reached against Johnson & Johnson's Ethicon by a California jury over their Gynecare TVT Abbrevo vaginal mesh device. Details of the latest settlement have not been disclosed.

Some might say that Johnson & Johnson made withdrawals from its "trust" bank in recent years. The company reacted slowly to a variety of crises, at first failing to admit any culpability and disclaiming financial liability. We can't escape the logical conclusion that "where there is smoke, there is fire." The disappointing fact is that these instances occurred as a result of management and internal actions and reflect a culture that has changed dramatically from the days of the Tylenol poisoning. Perhaps Johnson & Johnson is learning the hard way that it takes a long time to build a reputation for trust, but not very long to tear it down.

Ethics in the Workplace

LO 3-4
Discuss the views of employees about ethics in their organizations.

When we think about workplace ethics, the first thing that comes to mind is a code of conduct that influences the development of an ethical culture in the workplace. A code goes beyond what is legal for an organization and provides normative guidelines for ethical conduct. Support for ethical behavior from top management is a critical component of fostering an ethical climate. Employees who sense that top managers act unethically quickly lose trust in those managers. The result can be to become disillusioned with the goals of the organization and question whether the corporate culture is one that is consistent with individual, personal values and beliefs.

An ethical organization is one in which top managers establish a tone at the top that promotes ethical behavior including to raise questions when questionable behavior occurs. Here is a list of measures that should be taken to establish an ethical culture:

1. Establish clear policies on ethical conduct including a code of ethics.
2. Develop an ethics training program that instills a commitment to act ethically and explains code provisions.
3. Assign a top-level officer (i.e., Chief Ethics and Compliance Officer) to oversee compliance with ethics policies.
4. Use the internal auditors to investigate whether ethics policies have been followed in practice.
5. Establish strong internal controls to prevent and detect unethical behaviors, such as fraud.
6. Establish whistleblowing policies including reporting outlets.
7. Establish an ethics hotline where employees can discuss questionable behavior on an anonymous basis.
8. Have employees sign a statement that they have complied with ethics policies.
9. Enforce ethics policies fairly and take immediate action against those who violate the policies.
10. Reward ethical behavior by including it in the performance evaluation system.

Character and Leadership in the Workplace

"Character Counts" is the mantra of the Josephson Institute of Ethics whose Six Pillars of Character were discussed in Chapter 1. Characteristics of ethical behavior in leaders include: compassion, courage, diligence, fairness, honesty, inclusiveness, initiative, integrity, optimism, respect, responsibility, and trustworthiness. Good leaders have strong character and have a moral imperative underwrite their actions. Management guru, Warren Bennis, is quoted as saying, "Managers are people who do things right, and leaders are people who do the right thing."

Good character can be developed through experience and learning. Each situation we encounter presents a different experience and opportunity to learn and deepen character. Character becomes critical when managing a crisis, such as an ethical dilemma where stakeholder interests conflict.

Managers can set the right tone at the top and foster ethical leadership, both of which are necessary for ethical decision making, by following four simple rules:

1. *Consider how your actions affect others.* How will the stakeholders be affected by my intended actions? Here, a utilitarian analysis might help.
2. *Do no harm.* Your actions and decisions should not harm others. One exception is whistleblowing because of the need to emphasize "the greater good," which means the public interest in accounting.
3. *Make decisions that are universal.* Consistent with the categorical imperative, ask yourself whether you would want others to resolve the conflict by taking the same or similar action you are about to take. Universal decisions are those that respect the rights of others.
4. *Reflect before deciding.* As a final step, think about how you would feel if your actions and decisions appear on the front pages of the local newspaper. Would you be proud to defend them and comfortable explaining them?

Integrity: The Basis for Trust in the Workplace

Albert Camus, the French Nobel Prize winning author, journalist, and philosopher, said, "Integrity has no need of rules." People of integrity are self-driven to do the right thing. Leaders of integrity act on the knowledge that their actions are ethical and provide the basis for others in the workplace to follow their lead.

KPMG's *Integrity Survey 2013* provides an inside look at organizational misconduct based upon responses from more than 3,500 U.S. working adults. Key findings from the report include:[42]

- Nearly three out of four employees reported that they had observed misconduct within their organizations in the previous 12 months.
- More than half of employees reported that what they observed could potentially cause a significant loss of public trust if discovered.
- Some of the driving forces behind fraud and misconduct in the corporate environment include pressure to do "whatever it takes" to meet targets, not taking the code of conduct seriously, believing employees will be rewarded based upon results and not the means used to achieve them, and fear of losing one's job for not meeting performance targets.
- Nearly half of employees were uncertain that they would be protected from retaliation if they reported concerns to management. And more than half suggested a lack of confidence that they would be satisfied with the outcome.

- Ethics and compliance programs continue to have a favorable impact on employee perceptions and behaviors.

Employees were asked what they would do if they observed a violation of their organization's standards of conduct. The results were: 78 percent would notify their supervisor or another manager; 54 percent would try resolving the matter directly; 53 percent would call the ethics or compliance hotline; 26 percent would notify someone outside the organization; and 23 percent would look the other way or do nothing.

It's encouraging to learn that over three-fourths would inform their supervisor, in part because it is the generally recognized initial step in considering whether to blow the whistle. It is somewhat troubling that almost one-quarter of the workers would look the other way or do nothing. Perhaps they have not been given an opportunity to voice their values or have not discovered an effective means to do so.

The tone at the top set by top management is a determining factor in creating organizational commitment to high ethics and integrity. Employees were asked whether the chief executive officer and other senior executives exhibited characteristics attributable to personal integrity and ethical leadership. Approximately two-thirds of the employees agreed that their leaders set the right tone regarding the importance of ethics and integrity and served as positive role models for their organization, leaving one-third unsure or in disagreement.

Perhaps not surprisingly, a large percentage (64 percent) indicated that the root cause of misconduct was pressure to do "whatever it takes" to meet business objectives, while 59 percent said they believed they would be rewarded for results, not the means used to achieve them. In such instances, the corporate culture does not foster integrity or ethical behavior; instead, expedience and self-interest drive workplace behavior.

Employees Perceptions of Ethics in the Workplace

Going beyond the Integrity Survey, it is important to understand how employees view the ethics of the organizations they work for, in part to better understand corporate governance systems and whistleblowing. The *2013 National Business Ethics Survey* (NBES) conducted by the Ethics Resource Center provides interesting data about ethics in the workplace. The report is the eighth in a series. The 2013 survey provides information on the views of 6,579 respondents that represent a broad array of employees in the for-profit sector.[43] Exhibit 3.4 summarizes observed misconduct. It is encouraging that all such instances have declined between 2011 and 2013.

EXHIBIT 3.4   2013 NBES Survey of Reporting of Observed Misconduct

Type of Misconduct	2013	2011
Stealing or theft	64%	69%
Falsifying time reports or hours worked	49%	61%
Falsifying expense reports	48%	66%
Falsifying and/or manipulating financial reporting information	45%	62%
Falsifying invoices, books, and/or records	40%	N/A
Accepting inappropriate gifts or kickbacks from suppliers or vendors	36%	52%

The results of the NBES survey depicted in Exhibit 3.5, indicate a lessening of observed misconduct, virtually no change in reporting it, and a decline in pressure to compromise ethical standards from 2011 to 2013, which may reflect an improving corporate culture. This seems to be the case since the "weak-leaning" culture response went down by 6 points in the same time period. The results also show an increase in ethics training programs and the use of ethical conduct as a performance measure in employee evaluations.

EXHIBIT 3.5   Views of Employees on Ethics in the Workplace from the 2011 National Business Ethics Survey

Item	2013	2011	2009
Pressure to compromise ethical standards	9%	13%	8%
Weak/weak-leaning ethical culture	34%	40%	35%
Observed misconduct	41%	45%	55%
Reported observed misconduct	63%	65%	63%
Experienced retaliation after reporting (i.e., whistleblowing)	21%	22%	15%

The percentage of employees experiencing retaliation is up, indicating it still remains a problem in corporate America. Perhaps the new protections under SOX and Dodd-Frank will help to stem the rising tide.

One concern is that, while misconduct is down overall, a relatively high percentage of misconduct is committed by managers—the very people who should be establishing an ethical culture and providing ethical leadership. Workers reported that 60 percent of misconduct involved someone with managerial authority from the supervisory level up to top management. Nearly a quarter (24 percent) of observed misdeeds involved senior managers. Also, workers said that 26 percent of misconduct is ongoing within their organizations and about 12 percent of wrongdoing was reported to take place company-wide.

Perhaps not surprising, the results indicate that occupational fraud and financial statement fraud are of greatest concern because of their effects on the accuracy and reliability of the financial statements.

Fraud in Organizations

LO 3-5
Describe the causes of fraud, detection methods, and preventative controls.

Fraud can be defined as a deliberate misrepresentation to gain an advantage over another party. Fraud comes in many different forms, including fraud in financial statements, the misappropriation of assets (theft) and subsequent cover-up, and disclosure fraud. We introduce the concept of fraudulent financial statements in this chapter and discuss it more fully in Chapter 5. In this chapter, we will look at the results of the *2014 Global Fraud Survey: Report to the Nations on Occupational Fraud and Abuse,* conducted by the Association of Certified Fraud Examiners (ACFE).

Occupational Fraud

The 2014 ACFE survey is a follow-up to its *2012 Global Fraud Study.* The 2014 survey reports on 1,483 cases of occupational fraud that were reported by the Certified Fraud Examiners (CFEs) who investigated them. These offenses occurred in nearly 100 countries on six continents.[44]

The ACFE report focuses on *occupational fraud* schemes in which an employee abuses the trust placed in him by an employer for personal gain. The ACFE defines occupational fraud as "the use of one's occupation for personal enrichment through the deliberate misuse or misapplication of the employing organization's resources or assets."[45] A summary of the findings follows:

- Survey participants estimated that the typical organization loses 5 percent of its revenues to fraud each year. If applied to the 2013 estimated Gross World Product, this translates into a potential projected global fraud loss of nearly $3.7 trillion.

- The median loss caused by the occupational fraud cases studied was $145,000. Additionally, 22 percent of the cases involved losses of at least $1 million.

- The frauds reported lasted a median of 18 months before being detected.

- Asset misappropriation schemes were the most common type of occupational fraud, comprising 85 percent of the reported cases.

- Financial statement fraud schemes made up just 9 percent of the cases, but caused the greatest median loss at $1 million.

- Occupational fraud is more likely to be detected by a tip than by any other method—more than twice the rate of any other detection method. Employees accounted for nearly half of all the tips that led to the discovery of fraud.

- Organizations with hotlines were much more likely to catch fraud by a tip. These organizations also experienced frauds that were 41 percent less costly, and they detected frauds 50 percent more quickly.

- Corruption and billing schemes pose the greatest risks to organizations throughout the world.

- The presence of anti-fraud controls is correlated with significant decreases in the cost and duration of occupational fraud schemes.

- Perpetrators with higher levels of authority tend to cause much larger losses. Owners/executives only accounted for 19 percent of all cases, but they caused a median loss of $500,000. Employees, conversely, committed 42 percent of occupational frauds but only caused a median loss of $75,000. Managers ranked in the middle, committing 36 percent of frauds with a median loss of $130,000.

How Occupational Fraud Is Committed and Detected

Asset misappropriation schemes include when an employee steals or misuses resources, such as charging personal expenses to the company while traveling on business trips. Corruption schemes include misusing one's position or influence in an organization for personal gain, something that Dennis Kozlowski was known for doing. Kozlowski and chief financial officer (CFO) Mark Swartz were convicted on June 21, 2005, of taking bonuses worth more than $120 million without the approval of Tyco's directors, abusing an employee loan program, and misrepresenting the company's financial condition to investors to boost the stock price while selling $575 million in stock.

A surprising result is that a "tip" was the most common way of detecting fraud, at 42.2 percent in 2014. According to the ACFE report, detection by tip has been the most common method of initial detection since the first survey in 2002. It could be that tips are primarily provided by whistleblowers, but the study does not reach that conclusion. Exhibit 3.6 shows the frequency of detection methods as reported by survey respondents.

An important conclusion from these results is that controls such as management reviews and internal audits account for a significant percentage of detection methods (30 percent), and the external audit, at only 3 percent, does not seem to be a reliable method to detect fraud.

EXHIBIT 3.6   Initial Detection of Occupational Frauds from the *ACFE 2014 Global Survey: Report to the Nations on Occupational Fraud and Abuse*

Detection Method	Percentage Reported	Median Loss
Tip	42.2%	$149,000
Management Review	16.0%	$125,000
Internal Audit	14.1%	$100,000
By Accident	6.8%	$325,000
Account Reconciliation	6.6%	$75,000
Document Examination	4.2%	$220,000
External Audit	3.0%	$360,000
Surveillance/Monitoring	2.6%	$49,000
Notified by Law Enforcement	2.2%	$1,250,000
IT Controls	1.1%	$70,000
Confession	0.8%	$220,000
Other	0.5%	N/A

Frequency of Anti-Fraud Controls

The survey concludes that proactive fraud prevention and detection controls are a vital part in managing the risk of fraud. Respondents indicated that external audits were the most common control enacted by the victim organization, as they were present in 80 percent of the reported cases. It seems counterintuitive that only 3 percent of the frauds are detected by external audits. The answer lies in that an audit is not designed to detect fraud *per se;* instead it is to identify and detect risks of material misstatement of the financial statements due to error and fraud.

With more than 42 percent of frauds being detected by tips, hotlines should play an essential role in organizations' anti-fraud programs. However, only 54 percent had a hotline mechanism in place, and less than 11 percent provided rewards for whistleblowers. Exhibit 3.7 summarizes the frequency of anti-fraud controls.

EXHIBIT 3.7   Frequency of Anti-Fraud Controls: 2014 ACFE Global Fraud Survey

Anti-Fraud Control	Percentage Reported
External Audit of Financial Statements	81.4%
Code of Conduct	77.4%
Internal Audit Department	70.8%
Management Certification of Financial Statements	70.0%
External Audit of Internal Controls over Financial Reporting	65.2%
Management Review	62.6%
Independent Audit Committee	62.0%
Hotline	54.1%
Employee Support Programs	52.4%

(Continued)

Fraud Training for Managers/Executives	47.8%
Fraud Training for Employees	47.7%
Anti-Fraud Policy	45.4%
Dedicated Fraud Department, Function, or Team	38.6%
Proactive Data Monitoring/Analysis	34.8%
Formal Fraud Risk Assessments	33.5%
Surprise Audits	33.2%
Job Rotation/Mandatory Vacations	19.9%
Rewards for Whistleblowers	10.5%

Red-Flag Warnings of Fraud

The ACFE study found that most occupational fraudsters' crimes are motivated at least in part by some kind of financial pressure. In addition, while committing a fraud, an individual will frequently display certain behavioral traits associated with stress or a fear of being caught.[46] Overall, at least one red flag was identified in 92 percent of cases, and, in 64 percent of cases, the fraudster displayed two or more behavioral red flags. Approximately 44 percent of fraud perpetrators were living beyond their means while the fraud was ongoing, and 33 percent were experiencing known financial difficulties. These warning signs should alert internal auditors that trouble may lie ahead with respect to actual fraud. Exhibit 3.8 shows the fraud indicators identified in the study.

EXHIBIT 3.8   Behavioral Red Flags Displayed by Perpetrators: *ACFE 2014 Global Survey: Report to the Nations on Occupational Fraud and Abuse*

Behavioral Indicators of Fraud	Percentage Reported
Living Beyond Means	43.8%
Financial Difficulties	33.0%
Unusually Close Association with Vendor/Customer	21.8%
Control Issues, Unwillingness to Share Duties	21.1%
"Wheeler-Dealer" Attitude	18.4%
Divorce/Family Problems	16.8%
Instability, Suspiciousness, or Defensiveness	15.0%
Addiction Problems	11.8%
Complained about Inadequate Pay	9.4%
Past Employment-Related Problems	8.9%
Refusal to Take Vacations	8.8%
Excessive Pressure within Organization	8.4%
Social Isolation	7.4%
Complained about Lack of Authority	6.5%
Excessive Family/Peer Pressure for Success	6.0%
Instability in Life Circumstance	5.9%
Past Legal Problems	5.8%

The results of the survey clearly indicate that internal auditors should have their "eyes wide open" with respect to whether senior officers have adopted a lavish living style that creates the incentive to "cook the books" in a way that provides financial results to support their lifestyle. If earnings go up, stock prices often rise as well. Top managers typically own stock in their companies, so an incentive exists to boost earnings sometimes at any cost. A good example is the former CEO of HealthSouth, Richard Scrushy. Recall that we earlier identified the company as one that showed signs of ethical collapse because of its weak board of directors. Scrushy was behind the $2.7 billion earnings overstatement at HealthSouth.

Scrushy allegedly received $226 million in compensation over seven years, while HealthSouth was losing $1.8 billion during the same period. A skeptical auditor would have asked where all that money was going and would have looked for warnings that Scrushy might have been living beyond his means. Scrushy was charged with knowingly engaging in financial transactions using criminally derived property, including the purchase of land, aircraft, boats, cars, artwork, jewelry, and other items. At his trial, it become known that he had used money from his compensation for several residences in the state of Alabama and property in Palm Beach, Florida; a 92-foot Tarrab yacht called *Chez Soiree,* a 38-foot Intrepid Walkaround watercraft and a 42-foot Lightning boat; a 1998 Cessna Caravan 675, together with amphibious floats and other equipment, and a 2001 Cessna Citation 525 aircraft; diamond jewelry; several luxury automobiles, including a 2003 Lamborghini Murcielago, a 2000 Rolls Royce Corniche, and two 2002 Cadillac Escalades; and paintings by Pablo Picasso, Marc Chagall, Pierre-August Renoir, among others.

It is not just the internal auditors who wore blinders and the board that looked the other way. The external auditors did not detect the fraud either.

Internal Control Weaknesses

According to the Center for Audit Quality, internal control includes all of the processes and procedures that management puts in place to help make sure that its assets are protected and that company activities are conducted in accordance with the organization's policies and procedures.[47] For example, a bank reconciliation should be prepared regularly and by a person(s) with no responsibility for cash record keeping for the handling of cash. The bank reconciliation should be reviewed by an independent person and, in the case of a small business, by the owner. The ACFE survey found that cash-related fraud schemes accounted for almost 40 percent of all types of occupational fraud including skimming (14.1 percent)—the illegal practice of taking money from cash receipts for personal use; check tampering (13.7 percent); and cash larceny (10.7 percent)—the theft of cash after it has been recorded on the books.

An effective system of internal controls is critical to establish an ethical corporate culture that should be supported by the tone at the top. By examining Exhibit 3.7 we can see the importance of certain control mechanisms, including the external audit of financial statements (81.4 percent) and the external audit of the internal controls over financial reporting (65.2 percent). Also, the ACFE survey indicates that 32.2 percent of the internal control weaknesses are due to a lack of internal controls. While remaining at a high level, the 2014 results are 3.5 percent below the 2012 findings and 5.6 percent below 2010 findings. This may reflect a commitment by management to improve controls in view of the requirements in the Sarbanes-Oxley Act (SOX) of 2002.

As directed by Section 404 of SOX, the Securities Exchange Act of 1934 adopted a regulation that public companies have to include in their annual reports a report of management on the company's internal control over financial reporting. The internal control report must include a statement of management's responsibility for establishing and maintaining adequate internal control over financial reporting for the company; management's assessment of the effectiveness of the company's internal control over financial reporting as of the end of the company's most recent fiscal year; a statement identifying the framework used by management to evaluate the effectiveness of the company's internal control over financial reporting; and a statement that the registered public accounting firm that audited the company's financial statements included in the annual report has issued an attestation report on management's assessment of the company's internal control over financial reporting.

An internal control system, no matter how well conceived and operated, can provide only reasonable—not absolute—assurance to management and the board of directors regarding achievement of an entity's objectives. The likelihood of achievement is affected by a variety of factors including: judgments in decision making can be faulty; breakdowns can occur due to simple mistakes and errors in the application of controls; and controls can be circumvented by the collusion of two or more people. Management override of internal controls may be a problem as well similar to what happened at Enron and WorldCom. Indeed, 18.9 percent of respondents in the ACFE survey indicated that override of existing controls had occurred at victim organizations.

Example of Occupational Fraud

What follows is a description of a payroll fraud scheme. Payroll schemes accounted for 11.8 percent of of fraud techniques in the ACFE survey.

> The head of a department distributed paychecks to her employees on a weekly basis. Typically, the department head received the payroll checks each week from a payroll processing company and then distributed them to employees. One day another employee noticed the department head had locked his door after the checks were received and wondered about it. He became suspicious and reported it to his manager. A payroll audit discovered that several former employees were still receiving paychecks. It was discovered that the department head had the ability to access and edit electronic time keeping records for hourly employees and knew the passwords to the payroll system for their supervisors. He used this access to falsify hours, and thus paychecks, for previous employees. He then took the paychecks to check cashing companies to redeem them. The department head ultimately confessed to over 100 instances of payroll fraud over a 10-month period totaling almost $100,000.

In this case a lack of proper internal controls contributed to the fraud. The company lacked a proper separation of duties, did not regularly monitor payroll records for "ghost employees," did not require that employees regularly change their passwords, and allowed the department head who distributed the checks to also accept them from the payroll service. Perhaps a fraud hotline for employees to report suspicious behavior would have led to earlier reporting of the fraud.

Financial Statement Fraud

Financial statement fraud schemes occur because an employee—typically a member of top management—causes a misstatement or omission of material information in the organization's financial reports. Examples include recording fictitious revenues, understating reported expenses, artificially inflating reported assets, and failing to accrue expenses at the end of the year, such as what occurred in the DigitPrint case in Chapter 1.

A report by Ernst & Young, *Detecting Financial Statement Fraud: What Every Manager Needs to Know,*[48] provides examples of common methods to overstate revenue, understate expenses, and make improper asset valuations. Revenue overstatements include the following:

- Recording gross, rather than net, revenue.
- Recording revenues of other companies when acting as a "middleman."
- Recording sales that never took place.
- Recording future sales in the current period.

- Recording sales of products that are out on consignment.

Common methods of understating expenses include the following:

- Reporting cost of sales as a non-operating expense so that it does not negatively affect gross margin.
- Capitalizing operating costs, recording them as assets on the balance sheet instead of as expenses on the income statement (i.e., WorldCom).
- Not recording some expenses at all, or not recording expenses in the proper period.

Examples of improper asset valuations include the following:

- Manipulating reserves.
- Changing the useful lives of assets.
- Failing to take a write-down when needed.
- Manipulating estimates of fair market value.

One of the most bizarre examples of financial statement fraud involved Miniscribe, a manufacturer of computer hard drive disks that committed inventory fraud in the 1980s in the amount of $15 million. This was a mere pittance compared to the $11 billion fraud at WorldCom some 15 years later, but the efforts of Miniscribe's management to cover up the fraud were as audacious as any ever seen. Exhibit 3.9 summarizes this fraud.

EXHIBIT 3.9 Miniscribe Fraud

Miniscribe was a Colorado-based manufacturer of computer hard disk drives whose top officers were convicted of management fraud by covering up a multimillion-dollar inventory overstatement between December 1986 and January 1989, which falsely inflated Miniscribe's profits and accelerated its descent into bankruptcy.

Miniscribe went public in 1983, but it soon grew beyond its capacity. In 1985, a venture capital group, Hambrecht & Quist, invested $20 million in Miniscribe and gained control of its management.

Following its change in management, Quentin T. Wiles became the chair of the board and CEO. Wiles had a reputation as a successful, demanding executive who expected performance. Salaries and bonuses at Miniscribe often depended upon Miniscribe "making the numbers." Assisting Wiles was a management team consisting largely of CPAs. Patrick Schleibaum initially served as Miniscribe's CFO.

Despite reported growth and profitability, Miniscribe's financial position began to deteriorate early in 1987. In January 1987, Miniscribe conducted its annual inventory count to determine the value of inventory on hand. The accuracy of the inventory count was critical to the proper preparation of Miniscribe's 1986 year-end financial statements.

Management retained the independent accounting firm of Coopers & Lybrand (now PwC) to audit Miniscribe and verify the accuracy of its inventory count. The standard procedure for verifying a company's inventory count is through a test count—an inventory sampling deemed representative of the entire inventory. Problems arose when, unbeknownst to the auditors, management detected an inventory hole of between $2 million and $4 million. This inventory hole appeared because the actual inventory count, and thus dollar value of the inventory, was less than the value of the inventory recorded on Miniscribe's books. The overstatement of inventory led to the understatement of cost of goods sold and inflated earnings equal to the amount of the inventory overstatement.

(Continued)

At this point, Wiles was unaware of the inventory hole. Schleibaum properly decided to charge a portion of the hole against an emergency fund known as "inventory reserves." The remainder of the hole also should have been charged off or expensed as a cost of goods sold, with a corresponding reduction in profits. Schleibaum directed his subordinates to conceal the remainder of the inventory hole through improper means so that Miniscribe could continue to "make the numbers." This occurred by falsely inflating the inventory count. To hide the false count from the auditors, division managers broke into the auditors' work trunks at Miniscribe after business hours and altered the test count to match the inflated inventory count. The inflated numbers were then entered into Miniscribe's computer system and reflected as additional inventory. Schleibaum signed a management representation letter to the auditors indicating that Miniscribe's financial statements were accurate, including its inventory valuation. Miniscribe cleared the 1986 audit.

Miniscribe reported the false profits resulting from concealment of the inventory hole on its 1986 income statement and 1987 first-quarter earnings statement. Miniscribe disseminated this information to the public through its 1986 annual report and 1987 first-quarter financial report. Schleibaum signed the 1986 10-K report (annual report to the Securities and Exchange Commission) and 1987 first-quarter 10-Q report, which contained Miniscribe's false financial statements. Miniscribe filed the 10-K and 10-Q reports with the SEC as required by law. Miniscribe's reported success allowed the company to raise funds through a $97 million issue of debentures early in 1987.

In the spring of 1987, Wiles became concerned about Miniscribe's internal controls and financial strength. He worried that if an inventory problem actually existed, Miniscribe and its officers might be liable to those investors purchasing the debentures on the basis of the company's reported financial strength. Ultimately, a $15 million hole in inventory was discovered. Wiles had decided that Miniscribe could not afford to write off the inventory hole in 1987; instead, it had to cover it up to maintain investor confidence. Wiles planned to write off the inventory hole over six quarters, beginning with the first quarter of 1988.

In December 1987, independent auditors began preparing for Miniscribe's 1987 year-end audit. Miniscribe again faced the problem of clearing the independent audit. In mid-December, Miniscribe's management, with Wiles's approval and Schleibaum's assistance, engaged in an extensive cover-up, which included recording the shipment of bricks as in-transit inventory. To implement the plan, Miniscribe employees first rented an empty warehouse and procured 10 exclusive-use trailers. They then purchased 26,000 bricks.

On Saturday, December 18, 1987, Schleibaum and others gathered at the warehouse. Wiles did not attend. From early morning to late afternoon, those present loaded the bricks onto pallets, shrink-wrapped the pallets, and boxed them. The weight of each brick pallet approximated the weight of a pallet of disk drives. The brick pallets then were loaded onto the trailers and taken to a farm in Larimer County, Colorado.

Miniscribe's books, however, showed the bricks as in-transit inventory worth approximately $4 million. Employees at two of Miniscribe's buyers, CompuAdd and CalAbco, agreed to refuse fictitious inventory shipments from Miniscribe totaling $4 million. Miniscribe then added the fictitious inventory shipments to the company's inventory records.

Additionally, the officers employed other means to cover the inventory hole, including (1) recording the shipment of nonexistent inventory, (2) packaging scrap as inventory, (3) double-counting inventory, and (4) failing to record payables upon the receipt of materials. These various means distributed the inventory hole throughout Miniscribe's three facilities, making the problem more difficult for the independent auditors to detect.

Again, Schleibaum signed a management representation letter to the auditors stating that Miniscribe's 1987 financial reports were accurate and truthful, and Miniscribe cleared the independent audit. The result of the cover-up was that Miniscribe's book inventory and reported profits for 1987 were overstated by approximately $15 million and $22 million, respectively. These figures represented 17 percent of Miniscribe's inventory and 70 percent of its profits for the year.

(Continued)

> Eventually, Miniscribe got caught up in its own fraud, as it became more and more difficult to cover the inventory hole and questions were asked about its accounting. The sharp decline in the stock market in October 1987 hastened the day when the house of cards that was Miniscribe collapsed. The company finally declared bankruptcy in 1990.
>
> Source: *United States of America v. Quentin T. Wiles and Patrick J. Schleibaum*, Nos. 94-1592, 95-1022. United States Court of Appeals, Tenth Circuit, December 10, 1996 102 F.3d 1043.

Of particular note in the Miniscribe fraud is the unethical behavior at the highest levels of management that created a culture of blindness to what was right and wrong and led to the perpetuation of the fraud. It serves as an example of top management fraud, and an override of internal controls existed as well. The corporate governance system at Miniscribe failed because the company lacked independent members on its board of directors to serve as a check against excessive management behavior. To say the auditors were deficient in their procedures is an understatement. It is quite rare, to say the least, that auditors fail to adequately secure their working papers at the end of the day. These files should never be left at the client's office. Just imagine if electronic records were not password protected or flash drives were left on the premises.

Why Does Financial Statement Fraud Occur?

Why does financial statement fraud occur? This question has been examined since the 1980s when well-publicized financial statement frauds occurred at companies including ZZZZ Best, Miniscribe, Phar-Mor, Cendant, and Waste Management. Theoretically, there are three factors that appear to be present in every case of financial statement fraud that are addressed in auditing standards.[49] These are explored in detail in Chapter 5. We briefly summarize them here.

Situational pressure. Situational pressures may prompt an otherwise honest person to commit fraud. It typically occurs as a result of immediate pressure within either her internal or external environment. For example, financial analysts project earnings and companies feel the pressure to meet or exceed these amounts. An accountant may come to believe she has no option other than to go along with the fraud. The Betty Vinson situation at WorldCom is a case in point. She did not know how to effectively voice her values or where she could turn to for help.

Perceived opportunity. The opportunity to commit fraud and conceal it must exist. People do not normally commit fraud believing they will get caught. They do it because they believe they can get away with it (i.e., have access to the underlying financial information or override internal controls). The opportunity to commit fraud and conceal it often involves the absence of, or improper oversight by, the board of directors or audit committee, weak or nonexistent internal controls, unusual or complex transactions, accounting estimates that require sufficient subjective judgment by management, and ineffective internal audit staff.

Rationalization. People who commit financial statement fraud are able to rationalize the act. Being able to justify the act makes it possible. The individual must first convince herself that the behavior is temporary or is acceptable. She may believe it is in the best interest of the company to commit the fraud, perhaps because a needed loan will not be secured without financial statements to back it up. There is often the belief that everything will return to normal after the trigger event has passed.

Financial statement fraud does not occur in a vacuum. It is enabled by the absence of an ethical culture. Oftentimes, a culture is created and a tone at the top established that presents the image of a company willing to do whatever it takes to paint a rosy picture about financial results. Effective oversight and strong internal controls give way to greed, moral blindness, and inattentiveness to the important details that help to prevent and detect fraud. As with most situations in business, the desire to succeed crowds out ethical behavior. Those in the way are pressured to be team players; go along just this one time; and, in the end, compromise their values.

We end this section with a quote from Sophocles, the ancient Greek tragedian. He said, "I would prefer even to fail with honor than win by cheating." In other words, it is better to fail with one's morals and dignity intact than win by being dishonest.

Foundations of Corporate Governance Systems

An essential part of creating an ethical organization environment is to put in place effective corporate governance systems that establish control mechanisms to ensure that organizational values guide decision making and that ethical standards are being followed. The four pillars of corporate governance are accountability, fairness, transparency, and independence. *Accountability* means to ensure that management is accountable to the board and the board is accountable to the shareholders. *Fairness* means to protect shareholders rights, treat them equitably, and provide effective redress for violations. *Transparency* requires timely, accurate, disclosure on all material matters, including the financial situation, performance, ownership, and corporate governance. *Independence* means to have the procedures and structures in place to minimize, or avoid completely conflict of interest and to ensure that independent directors are free from the influence of others.[50]

Defining Corporate Governance

There is no single, accepted definition of *corporate governance*. A fairly narrow definition given by Shleifer and Vishny emphasizes the separation of ownership and control in corporations. They define corporate governance as dealing with "the ways in which the suppliers of finance to corporations assure themselves of getting a return on their investment."[51] Parkinson defines it as a process of supervision and control intended to ensure that the company's management acts in accordance with the interests of shareholders.[52]

The first corporate governance report, *Sir Adrian Cadbury's Report on the Financial Aspects of Corporate Governance* (1992), took a broader view in defining it as "the system by which companies are directed and controlled," and further explained that boards of directors are responsible for the governance of their companies, while the shareholders' role in governance is to appoint the directors and auditors, and to satisfy themselves that an appropriate governance structure is in place.[53]

The definition of corporate governance that we like the best is by Tricker, who says that governance is not concerned with running the business of the company *per se*, but with giving overall direction to the enterprise, with overseeing and controlling the executive actions of management, and with satisfying legitimate expectations of accountability and regulation by interests beyond the corporate boundaries.[54] In this regard, corporate governance can be seen as a set of rules that define the relationship between stakeholders, management, and board of directors of a company and influence how that company is operating. At its most basic level, corporate governance deals with issues that result from the separation of ownership and control. But corporate governance goes beyond simply establishing a clear relationship between shareholders and managers.

A corporate governance regime typically includes mechanisms to ensure that the agent (management) runs the firm for the benefit of one or more principals (shareholders, creditors, suppliers, clients, employees, and other parties with whom the firm conducts its business). The mechanisms include internal ones, such as the board of directors, its committees including the audit committee, executive compensation policies, and internal controls, and external measures, which include monitoring by large shareholders and creditors (in particular, banks), external auditors, and the regulatory framework of a securities exchange commission, the corporate law regime, and stock exchange listing requirements and oversight.

Views of Corporate Governance

Differences exist about the role of corporate governance in business. Some organizations take the view that as long as they are maximizing shareholder wealth and profitability, they are fulfilling their core responsibilities. Other firms take a broader view based on the stakeholder perspective.

The shareholder model of corporate governance is founded on classic economic precepts, including maximizing wealth for investors and creditors. In a public corporation, firm decisions should be oriented toward serving the best interests of investors. Underlying these decisions is a classic agency problem, in which ownership (investors) and control (managers) are separate. Managers act as the agents of the investors (principals), who expect those decisions to increase the value of the stock they own.[55] However, managers may have motivations beyond stockholder value such as increasing market share, or more personal ones including maximizing executive compensation. In these instances, decisions may be based on an egoist approach to ethical decision making that ignores the interests of others.

Because shareholder owners of public companies are not normally involved in the daily operations, the board of directors oversee the companies, and CEOs and other members of top management run them. Albrecht et al. points out that the principal-agent relationship involves a transfer of trust and duty to the agent, while also assuming that the agent is opportunistic and will pursue interests that are in conflict with those of the principal, thereby creating an "agency problem."[56] Because of these potential differences, corporate governance mechanisms are needed to align investor and management interests. A fundamental challenge underlying all corporate governance affairs dates back to the days of Adam Smith. In *The Wealth of Nations,* Smith said that "the directors of companies, being managers of other people's money, cannot be expected to watch over it with the same vigilance with which they watch over their own."

One traditional approach is for shareholders to give the CEO shares or options of stock that vest over time, thus inducing long-term behavior and deterring short-term actions that can harm future company value. When the interests of top management are brought in line with interests of shareholders, agency theory argues that management will fulfill its duty to shareholders, not so much out of any sense of moral duty to shareholders, but because doing what shareholders have provided incentives for maximizes their own utility.[57]

Jensen and Meckling demonstrate how investors in publicly traded corporations incur (agency) costs in monitoring managerial performance. In general, agency costs arise whenever there is an "information asymmetry" between the corporation and outsiders because insiders (the corporation) know more about a company and its future prospects than do outsiders (investors).[58]

Agency costs can occur if the board of directors fails to exercise due care in its oversight role of management. Enron's board of directors did not monitor the company's incentive compensation plans properly, thereby allowing top executives to "hype" the company's stock so that employees would add it to their 401(k) retirement plans. While the hyping occurred, often through positive statements about the company made by CEO Ken Lay, Lay himself sold about 2.3 million shares for $123.4 million.

The agency problem can never be perfectly solved, and shareholders may experience a loss of wealth due to divergent behavior of managers. Investigations by the SEC and U.S. Department of Justice of 20 corporate frauds during the Enron-WorldCom era indicate that $236 billion in shareholder value was lost between the time the public first learned of the first fraud and September 3, 2002, the measurement date.

An alternative to agency theory is stewardship theory. In this theory, managers are viewed as stewards of their companies, predominately motivated to act in the best interests of the shareholders. The theory holds that as stewards, managers will choose the interests of shareholders, perhaps psychologically identified as the best interests of "the company," over self-interests, regardless of personal motivations or incentives.[59]

Under stewardship theory, directors have a fiduciary duty to act as stewards of the shareholders' interest. Inherent in the concept of the company is the belief that directors can be trusted. Contrary to agency theory, stewardship theory believes that directors do not inevitably act in a way that maximizes their own personal interests: They can and do act responsibly with independence and integrity. Even though some will fail, it does not invalidate the theory.[60]

Stewardship advocates recognize that directors need to consider a broader range of interests, including employees, customers, suppliers, and other legitimate stakeholders, but under the law their first responsibility is to the shareholders. They argue that conflicts of interest between stakeholder groups and the company should be met by competitive pressures in free markets, backed by legislation and legal controls to protect various stakeholder interests (i.e., environmental law; health and safety law; employment discrimination law).

Other theories of management exist, including "resource dependency" and "managerial and class hegemony." However, our goal is not to address all such theories but to provide the framework within which control mechanisms exist to enhance behavior in accordance with laws and ethics.

Corporate Governance Regulation

Each state in the United States has its own companies law to regulate corporate activity within its boundaries. Federal laws are embodied in the SEC regulations. Over the years the SEC developed an extensive corporate governance regime for companies listed on stock exchanges, including the New York Stock Exchange (NYSE) and NASDAQ. The NYSE has issued extensive regulations as well.

Corporate governance regulation in the United States has been ratcheted up in the aftermath of passage of the Sarbanes-Oxley Act. SOX requires management certification of the internal controls over financial reporting (Section 302); that auditors attest to and report on management's assessment on the effectiveness of the internal control structure and procedures for financial reporting (Section 404); protections for whistleblowers (Section 806); and independent audit committees that oversee financial reporting.

One goal of SOX is to reduce the number of restatements of corporate financial reports, especially those that result from materially misleading financial statements. Have the corporate governance requirements of SOX made a differences in the level of financial statement restatements? After all, if this is not the case, then we must question the effectiveness of the act.

According to a study by Audit Analytics, the proportion of corporate financial restatements that had *no* impact on the bottom line was 59 percent in 2014. That brought the increase over the past four years to 22 percentage points, which suggests that the SOX corporate-governance law has succeeded in bolstering companies' internal controls over financial reporting. Among companies listed on major stock exchanges, there were 460 restatements in 2014 that had no effect on income statements, up slightly from a year earlier.[61]

KBR Inc. made the largest downward earnings restatement, with the engineering and construction company reducing its 2013 net income by $156 million. That was the smallest high for a downward adjustment since 2002; the largest during the period came in 2004, when Fannie Mae wiped $6.3 billion off its prior profits. The 2014 average downward net-income restatement was about $4.4 million, down from $6.6 million a year earlier.

These results are encouraging, although we are not convinced they will be sustained. The reason is, regardless of regulatory requirements under Section 404, the underlying consideration is good old-fashioned ethical behavior. Will egoistic CEOs and CFOs revert to self-interest–driven behavior, as occurred in the scandals of the early 2000s, or have they "seen the light"? If past history is used as a guide, we may be due for another round of corporate financial reporting scandals as seemingly have occurred every 10–15 years.

The takeaway from the results reported by Audit Analytics is it appears SOX is encouraging more ethical behavior on the part of top corporate executives, but the jury is still out whether it will have a long-lasting effect. Another concern is that, in accounting, it is only "material" restatements that are considered and the results of the study point to 59 percent as having "no impact" on the bottom line. What does that mean with respect to the size of the restatements and how was the materiality determined?

Executive Compensation

One of the most common approaches to the agency problem is to link managerial compensation to the financial performance of the corporation in general and the performance of the company's shares. Typically, this occurs by creating long-term compensation packages and stock option plans that tie executive wealth to an increase in the corporation's stock price. These incentives aim to encourage managers to maximize the market value of shares. One of the biggest issues that corporate boards of directors face is executive compensation. It has been found that most boards spend more time deciding how much to compensate top executives than they do ensuring the integrity of the company's financial reporting systems.[62]

Excessive Pay Packages

A problem arises when top management purposefully manipulates earnings amounts to drive up the price of stock so they can cash in more lucrative stock options. During the financial crisis of 2008–2009, Congress charged executives at some of the nation's largest companies with gaining pay packages in the millions while their companies suffered losses, and they may have even accepted funds from the government to keep them liquid. The Obama administration named a "compensation czar," Kenneth Feinberg, to set salaries and bonuses at some of the biggest firms at the heart of the economic crisis, as part of a broader government campaign to reshape pay practices across corporate America. The initiative reflected public uproar over executive compensation at companies such as American International Group (AIG), which received a $180 billion bailout from the government and decided to pay $165 million in bonuses to executives.

A 2014 study at the Harvard Business School found that Americans believe CEOs make roughly 30 times what the average worker makes in the United States, when in actuality they are making more than 340 times the average worker. On a global basis, this compares with a ratio of 148:1 in Switzerland, the nearest country, 84:1 in the United Kingdom, and 67:1 in Japan.

A troubling situation occurs when executives receive huge severance packages after leaving their organizations. The former CEO of CVS received a severance package worth $185 million when he left in early 2011, even though the company's net earnings had declined in the prior year. In 2014, the former chief operating officer of Yahoo, who was fired earlier in the year, received about $96 million in compensation for his 15 months on the job, including about $58 million in severance packages.

We do not know whether CEOs at top American companies are overpaid. After all, they have the daunting task of running multibillion-dollar companies in an increasingly globalized, competitive environment. However, it does give us pause when we read that, in 2013, the average CEO compensation was $15.2 million as compared with the average worker being paid about $52,100. From an ethical perspective, fairness issues do exist. Thomas Dunfee, a Wharton professor of legal studies and business ethics, puts it this way: Do executive compensation figures reflect an efficient market, or a failed one? Are pay levels adequately disclosed? Should shareholders have more say? Are there issues of fairness and justice?[63]

Backdating Stock Options

An executive compensation scandal erupted in 2006 when it was discovered that some companies had changed the grant dates of their options to coincide with a dip in the stock price, making the options worth more because less money would be needed to exercise them and buy stock. Although backdating was legal, it must be expensed and disclosed properly in the financial statements. Legalities aside, it is difficult to justify such a practice from an ethical perspective because it purposefully manipulates the option criteria that determine their value.

In the wake of this scandal, hundreds of companies conducted internal probes and the SEC launched investigations into more than 140 firms. The agency filed charges against 24 companies and 66 individuals for backdating-related offenses, and at least 15 people have been convicted of criminal conduct. An interesting case is that of Nancy Heinen, Apple Computer's general counsel until she left in 2006. She was investigated by the SEC for receiving backdated options and wound up agreeing to pay $2.2 million in disgorgement (return of ill-gotten gains), interest, and penalties. Steve Jobs, the former CEO of Apple, apologized on behalf of the company, stating that he did not understand the relevant accounting laws. Of course, ignorance of the law is no excuse for violating it—at least in spirit —especially by someone like Jobs, who presumably had dozens of accountants on staff to advise on these matters. Notably, SOX includes stricter reporting requirements that are supposed to cut down on such practices.

Clawbacks

The Dodd-Frank Wall Street Reform and Consumer Protection Act (H.R. 4173)[64] was signed into federal law by President Barack Obama on July 21, 2010. Passed as a response to the late-2000s recession, it brought the most significant changes to financial regulation in the United States since the regulatory reform that followed the Great Depression. Two areas where Dodd-Frank relates to corporate governance are in executive compensation and in whistleblowing procedures, which will be discussed later on.

Clawbacks have been on the regulatory radar screen in a big way since 2002, when SOX gave the SEC power to recover compensation and stock profits from CEOs and CFOs of public companies in the event of financial restatements caused by misconduct. Clawback policies among Fortune 100 companies were already on the rise before the financial crisis, jumping from 17.6 percent in 2006 to 42.1 percent in 2007. In 2010, the year Dodd-Frank was passed, 82.1 percent of the Fortune 100 had them. In 2012, 86.5 percent of the Fortune 100 firms had adopted publicly disclosed policies. Now, about 90 percent have such policies. The ethical justification for clawbacks is the breach of fiduciary duty owed by top management to shareholders and inequities when they benefit from their own wrongful acts.

On July 1, 2015, the SEC proposed rules directing U.S. stock exchanges to create listing standards requiring listed companies to implement policies to recover or "claw back" incentive-based compensation received by executive officers as a result of materially incorrect financial statements. These proposed rules are mandated by Section 954 of Dodd-Frank. Companies may need to comply with the proposed rules as early as the end of 2016, though this timing will depend on when the SEC's proposed rules are finalized, and will likely be in early 2017.

According to a PwC study, many companies have modified their clawback policies since enactment of SOX and Dodd-Frank, and others have indicated that their policies will likely change once the SEC issues its clawback rules. Of the 100 companies in the study, 90 percent have policies to recover compensation if there is a restatement of financial results. However, of those that claw back upon restatement, 73 percent require evidence that the employee caused or contributed to false or incorrect financial reporting, while 27 percent require repayment in the event of a restatement even without any personal accountability. In many cases, the clawback amount is only the excess of the amount paid over the payment determined based on the financial results after applying the restatement. We believe that, when designed properly, a policy allowing for clawback of pay from high-level executives is a significant mechanism for corporate accountability.

Say on Pay

Dodd-Frank includes "say-on-pay" provisions (Section 951) that require SEC-registered issuers to provide shareholders at least once every three calendar years a separate nonbinding say-on-pay vote regarding the compensation of the company's named executive officers (i.e., CEO and CFO) and the company's three other most highly compensated officers. Although the vote on compensation is nonbinding, the company must include a statement in the "Compensation Discussion and Analysis" of the proxy statement whether its compensation policies and decisions have taken into account the results of the shareholder-say-on-pay vote and, if so, how. The idea is for the vote of the shareholders to be taken seriously not only by the company, but also by other companies in the same marketplace.

In perhaps the most widely followed shareholder action, in April 2012, 55 percent of Citigroup's shareholders voted against CEO Vikram Pandit's $15 million compensation package for 2011, a year when the bank's stock tumbled. At the time of the vote, Pandit had received nearly $7 million in cash for 2011, with the remainder to be paid in restricted stock and cash over the next few years (and thus subject to possible restructuring by the board). Citigroup's shareholders expressed concerns that the compensation package lacked significant and important goals to provide incentives for improvement in the shareholder value of the institution. Soon after the vote, a shareholder filed a derivative lawsuit against the CEO, the board of directors, and other directors and executives for allegedly awarding excessive pay to its senior officers.

On April 29, 2015, the SEC proposed new rules requiring public companies to make it easier for investors to judge whether top executives' compensation is in step with the company's financial performance. The proposal aims to give investors greater clarity about the link between what corporate executives are paid each year and total shareholder return—the annual change in stock price plus reinvested dividends. If finalized, companies would have to include a new table in their annual proxy filings disclosing top executives' "actual pay." The new figure is based on the total compensation public companies already calculate for their five highest-paid executives, though it would exclude certain components of pay that officers do not actually take home, such as share grants that have yet to vest.

Questions raised by shareholders and others about the size of executive compensation packages and say-on-pay votes are designed to build equity into the compensation system. Issues with respect to whether CEOs are overpaid, as many have said, do bring up questions of fairness and justice. Without transparency, it is difficult to have accountability. Over the long haul, the question is whether these nonbinding referendums are likely to have any impact on the potential civil liability of directors for approving allegedly excessive executive compensation that the shareholders reject. According to Robert Scully, who analyzed the law in the January 2011 *The Federal Lawyer,* the answer is probably not. Scully maintains that Dodd-Frank does not preempt state fiduciary law or entirely occupy the field of director liability for excessive compensation. Instead, the act focuses on the process by which public company executive compensation is set, thereby enforcing the primacy of the business judgment rule in determining executive compensation.[65]

Corporate Governance Structures and Relationships

LO 3-6
Explain the components of corporate governance and their relationship to corporate culture.

In his book *Corporate Governance and Ethics,* Zabihollah Rezaee points out that corporate governance is shaped by internal and external mechanisms, as well as policy interventions through regulations. Internal mechanisms help manage, direct, and monitor corporate governance activities to create sustainable stakeholder value. Examples include the board of directors, particularly independent directors; the audit committee; management; internal controls; and the internal audit function. External mechanisms are intended to monitor the company's activities, affairs, and performance to ensure that the interests of insiders (management, directors, and officers) are aligned with the interests of outsiders (shareholders and other stakeholders). Examples of external mechanisms include the financial markets, state and federal statutes, court decisions, and shareholder proposals.[66] Three noteworthy points are: (1) independent directors enhance governance accountability; (2) separation of the duties of the CEO and board chair; and (3) separate meetings between the audit committee and external auditors strengthen control mechanisms.

Ethical and Legal Responsibilities of Officers and Directors

Duty of Care—Managers and Directors

Directors and officers are deemed fiduciaries of the corporation because their relationship with the corporation and its shareholders is one of trust and confidence. As fiduciaries, directors and officers owe ethical—and legal—duties to the corporation and to the shareholders. These fiduciary duties include the duty of care and the duty of loyalty.

The standard of *due care* provides that a director or officer act in good faith, exercise the care that an ordinarily prudent person would exercise in similar circumstances, and act in the way that she considers to be in the best interests of the corporation. Directors and officers who have not exercised the required duty of care can be held liable for the harms suffered by the corporation as a result of their negligence.

The duty of due care specifies the manner in which directors must discharge their legal responsibilities, not the substance of director decisions. Directors, due to their statutory responsibilities to direct the business and affairs of a corporation, also have a duty to monitor and oversee the business affairs of a corporation properly. Failure to do so may constitute a breach of the duty of care.

Duty of Loyalty

The duty of loyalty requires directors to act in the best interests of the corporation. *Loyalty* can be defined as faithfulness to one's obligations and duties. In the corporate context, the duty of loyalty requires directors and officers to subordinate their personal interests to the welfare of the organization. For example, directors must not use corporate funds or confidential corporate information for personal advantage. They must also refrain from self-dealing, such as when a director opposes a stock tender offer that is in the corporation's best interest simply because its acceptance may cost the director her position.

Duty of Good Faith

The obligation of good faith requires an honesty of purpose that leads to caring for the well-being of the constituents of the fiduciary. Vice Chancellor Leo Strine of the Delaware Chancery Court linked good faith to fiduciary analysis in the Enron fraud by suggesting that the Enron case might influence courts to look more carefully at whether directors have made a good faith effort to accomplish their duties. He connected good faith with directors' "state of mind." Strine identified certain kinds of director conduct that may call good faith into question. These include "a failure to monitor if [the directors'] laxity in oversight was so persistent and substantial that it evidences bad faith." It can also arise in situations where "committee members knew that their inadequate knowledge disabled them from discharging their responsibilities with fidelity."[67]

Business Judgment Rule

A corporate director or officer may be able to avoid liability to the corporation or to its shareholders for poor business judgments under the *business judgment rule.* Directors and officers are expected to exercise due care and to use their best judgment in guiding corporate management, but they are not insurers of business success. Honest mistakes of judgment and poor business decisions on their part do not make them liable to the corporation for resulting damages.

To obtain the business judgment rule's protection, directors must be independent and disinterested as to the matter acted upon. Directors must act with due care and good faith. The due care inquiry is process-oriented, and due care is measured by a standard of gross negligence, not simple negligence. The burden of proof is on the party challenging the board's decision, to establish facts rebutting the presumption in favor of upholding the decision. Unless a plaintiff succeeds in rebutting the rule, the court will not substitute its views for those of the board's if the latter's decision can be "attributed to any rational business purpose."

The business judgment rule generally immunizes directors and officers from liability for the consequences of a decision that is within managerial authority, as long as the decision complies with management's fiduciary duties and as long as acting on the decision is within the powers of the corporation. Therefore, if there is a reasonable basis for a business decision, it is unlikely that a court will interfere with that decision, even if the corporation suffers as a result.

Honest Services Fraud

Jeff Skilling, the former CEO of Enron, was originally sentenced to a 24-year jail sentence for fraud and insider trading. He has appealed the 19 out of 28 charges that he was sentenced for in 2006 all the way up to the U.S. Supreme Court. His lawyers challenged the ruling based on the instructions given to the jury, which asked them to consider whether he had deprived his company of "intangible honest services." The U.S. Supreme Court found on June 24, 2010, that he had not violated the honest services rule, as he had not solicited or accepted bribes or kickbacks; rather, he conspired to defraud Enron's shareholders by other means.

Honest services fraud refers to a ruling in *18 U.S.C. § 1346* that addresses any "scheme or artifice to defraud" designed to deprive another of the intangible right of honest services. The statute has been applied by federal prosecutors in cases of public corruption as well as in cases in which private individuals breached a fiduciary duty to another. In the former, the courts have been divided on the question of whether a state law violation is necessary for honest services fraud to have occurred. In the latter, the courts have taken differing approaches to determining whether a private individual has committed honest services fraud—a test based on reasonably foreseeable economic harm and a test based on materiality.

In *Skilling v. United States,* the U.S. Supreme Court said that one of Skilling's convictions was flawed when it sharply curtailed the use of the honest services fraud law. The high court ruled prosecutors can use the law only in cases where evidence shows the defendant accepted bribes or kickbacks, and because Skilling's misconduct entailed no such things, he did not conspire to commit honest services fraud. In the opinion, Justice Ginsburg wrote: "The Government charged Skilling with conspiring to defraud Enron's shareholders by misrepresenting the company's fiscal health to his own profit, but the Government never alleged that he solicited or accepted side payments from a third party in exchange for making these misrepresentations. Instead, he conspired to defraud Enron's shareholders by other means." The Supreme Court told a lower court to decide whether he deserved a new trial; the lower court said no.[68]

Perhaps the legal system is growing weary of dealing with Skilling's appeals because on May 8, 2013, it was announced by the U.S. Department of Justice that Skilling might be freed 10 years early. This means he would spend a total of 14 years in jail. In return for the lighter sentence, Skilling agreed to stop appealing his conviction. The agreement would also allow more than $40 million seized from him to be freed up for distribution to Enron fraud victims.

Relationships between Audit Committee, Internal Auditors, and External Auditors

Following the passage of SOX, the audit committee was seen as the one body that was (or at least should be) capable of preventing identified fraudulent financial reporting. The audit committee has an oversight responsibility for the financial statements. The internal auditors should have direct and unrestricted access to the audit committee so that they can take any matters of concern directly to that group without having to go through top management. The external auditors rely on the support and actions of the audit committee to resolve differences with management over proper financial reporting. The goal of such relationships should be to establish an ethical corporate culture that supports good corporate governance. **Exhibit 3.10** depicts the ideal relationship between the internal auditors and audit committee. The framework is identified in the Treadway Commission Report titled *Report of the National Commission on Fraudulent Financial Reporting.*

EXHIBIT 3.10   Internal Control Environment—"Corporate Culture"

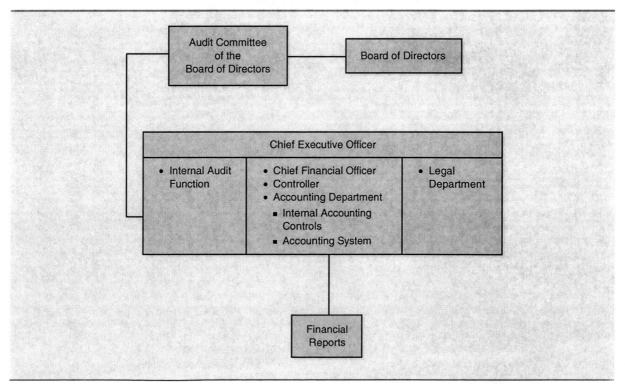

Audit Committee

In the accounting scandals of the early 2000s, the audit committee either didn't know about the fraud or chose to look the other way. A conscientious and diligent committee is an essential ingredient of an effective corporate governance system—one that takes its role in financial statement oversight to heart and follows basic principles of responsibility, accountability, and transparency. SOX requires that the audit committee of the board of directors should be completely independent of management and include at least three members, one of which should have "financial expertise."

An effective device to ensure audit committee independence is for the committee to meet separately with the senior executives, the internal auditors, and the external auditors. The perception of internal auditors as the "eyes and ears" of the audit committee suggests that the head of the internal audit department attend all audit committee meetings. Recall the role of Cynthia Cooper at WorldCom. She informed the audit committee every step of the way as her department uncovered the fraud, and ultimately she gained the support of the external auditors.

The audit committee's duties include: (1) monitor the integrity of the financial statements; (2) review any formal announcements relating to the company's financial performance; (3) review significant financial reporting judgments contained in the statements and performance statements; (4) review the company's internal financial controls and risk management procedures; (5) monitor the effectiveness of the company's internal audit function; (6) review the company's whistleblower processes and compliance program; and (7) review and monitor the external auditor's independence and objectivity and the effectiveness of the audit process.

The audit committee should also seek assurances from the CEO and CFO, as part of the CEO/CFO financial statement certification process under Section 302 of SOX, that they have put in place effective disclosure controls and procedures to ensure that all reports have been prepared and filed properly with the appropriate authorities in accordance with applicable requirements.

SOX calls on audit committees to create formal procedures to collect, track, and process hotline claims received by the issuer company related to accounting, internal controls, or auditing matters. Additionally, SOX holds audit committees responsible for establishing a channel for employees to submit confidential, anonymous concerns regarding questionable accounting or auditing matters through the whistleblower hotline. However, the legislation did not provide prescriptive guidance for establishing effective whistleblower programs. Because the SEC has not mandated specific processes and procedures, the audit committee plays a critical role in determining the processes appropriate for its organization.

Internal Auditors

Internal auditors interact with top management and, as such, should assist them to fulfill their role in developing accurate and reliable financial statements, ensure the effectiveness of internal control systems, and monitor compliance with laws and regulations. Specific obligations include: (1) monitor corporate governance activities and compliance with organization policies; (2) review effectiveness of the organization's code of ethics and whistleblower provisions; (3) assess audit committee effectiveness and compliance with regulations; and (4) oversee internal controls and risk management processes. Internal auditors should provide objective assurance on how effectively the organization assesses and manages its risks. A growing area of importance is to provide assurance with data security and privacy controls.

Internal auditors are part of the organization's culture and should operate in accordance with the ethical values embedded in that culture. They can serve as outlets for employees who face ethical dilemmas in the workplace but are not sure how best to handle them. They can support employees in conflict situations and enable them to voice their values.

External Auditors

External auditors have an obligation to the public interest that underlies their corporate governance responsibilities. One of the primary roles of external auditors in corporate governance is protecting the interests of shareholders. This is possible because external audits should be conducted independent of any influence of management or the board of directors of the company. External audits should be designed to introduce a measure of accountability into the financial reporting process.

Effective two-way communication between audit committees and external auditors is an integral part of the audit process. Such communications improve the ability of the audit committee to provide oversight and provide an opportunity for the auditors to discuss relevant matters with a forum other than management. These types of communications are essential to a high-quality audit.

The Public Company Accounting Oversight Board (PCAOB) has recognized the importance of this topic with the adoption of Auditing Standard No. 16, *Communications with Audit Committees* ("AS 16"). Required communications include:

- Matters relating to the company's accounting policies and practices including why certain accounting policies and practices are considered critical.
- Estimates made by management and the process used to develop these estimates including significant changes to the process used by management to develop estimates, reasons for the changes, and the effects on the financial statements.
- The auditor's judgment about the quality of the entity's financial reporting including the auditor's evaluation of and conclusions about the qualitative aspects of the company's significant accounting policies and practices. Auditors should also discuss significant unusual transactions and their opinion on the business rationale thereof.
- Whether the audit committee is aware of matters relevant to the audit including, but not limited to, violations or potential violations of laws or regulations including fraud risks.

While in the past communications between the external auditor and audit committee have been deemed an incidental part of the audit process, it is now recognized as an essential and required aspect of an effective and efficient audit. A company's audit committee is the primary link between the board of directors, management, and the independent auditors. Improving communication among these parties will play a vital role in improving the overall value of the audit for all stakeholders.

Internal Controls as a Monitoring Device

The internal controls that are established by management should help prevent and detect fraud, including materially false and misleading financial reports, asset misappropriations, and inadequate disclosures in the financial statements. These controls are designed to ensure that management policies are followed, laws are strictly adhered to, and ethical systems are built into corporate governance.

COSO Framework

The system of internal controls and whether it operates as intended enables the auditor to either gain confidence about the internal processing of transactions or create doubt for the auditor that should be pursued. *Internal Control—Integrated Framework,* published by the Committee of Sponsoring Organizations (COSO) of the Treadway Commission in 1992, establishes a framework that defines internal control as a process, effected by an entity's board of directors, management, and other personnel, designed to provide reasonable assurance regarding the achievement of the following objectives: (a) effectiveness and efficiency of operations; (b) reliability of financial reporting; and (c) compliance with applicable laws and regulations.[69]

The COSO report states that management should enact five components related to these objectives as part of the framework: (1) the control environment; (2) risk assessment; (3) control activities; (4) monitoring; and (5) information and communication.

1. The *control environment* sets the tone of an organization, influencing the control consciousness of its people. It is the foundation for all aspects of internal control, providing discipline and structure.
2. *Risk assessment* is the entity's identification and evaluation of how risk might affect the achievement of objectives.
3. *Control activities* are the strategic actions established by management to ensure that its directives are carried out.
4. *Monitoring* is a process that assesses the efficiency and effectiveness of internal controls over time.
5. *Information and communication* systems provide the information in a form and at a time that enables people to carry out their responsibilities.

The COSO framework emphasizes the roles and responsibilities of management, the board of directors, internal auditors, and other personnel in creating an environment that supports the objectives of internal control. One important contribution of COSO is in the area of corporate governance. COSO notes that if members of the board and audit committee do not take their responsibilities seriously, then the system will likely break down as occurred in Enron and WorldCom.

The results for a company can be devastating when internal controls fail or are overridden by management. A good example is what happened to Groupon after it announced a restatement in its financial statements on March 30, 2012, that resulted from a material weakness in its internal controls with respect to the inadequacy of its reserve for coupon returns. Exhibit 3.11 presents a summary of the facts surrounding the restatement. There can be no doubt that the company's fortunes changed on a dime after the announcement, as its IPO share price close of $26.11 on March 30, 2012, trended downward and continued going in the wrong direction declining to $4.14 as of November 30, 2012. The stock has not done much better since then, closing around the same level as recently as July 2015.

EXHIBIT 3.11   Internal Control Disaster at Groupon

Groupon, Inc., offers online retail services and provides daily deals on things to do, eat, see, and buy in more than 500 markets in 44 countries. It has offices across North America, Europe, Latin America, Asia, and other parts of the world.

On November 5, 2011, Groupon took its company public in an IPO with a buy-in price set at $20 per share. Groupon shares rose from their IPO price of $20 by 40 percent in early trading on NASDAQ and ended at the 4 p.m. market close at $26.11, up 31 percent. The closing price valued Groupon at $16.6 billion, making it more valuable than companies such as Adobe Systems and nearly the size of Yahoo.

Groupon employees broke out the champagne, as did Silicon Valley and Wall Street, as financial analysts took Groupon's stock market debut as a sign that investors are still willing to make risky bets on fast-growing but unprofitable young Internet companies, even as the IPO environment had shifted downward since the financial troubles that started in 2007.

At a size of up to $805 million, Groupon ranked as the third-largest Internet IPO sold in the United States in 2011, after a $1.4 billion issue by Russian search-engine operator Yandex NV in May and a $855 million issue by China social networking platform Renren, according to Dealogic. It was the ninth-largest ever, on a list topped by the $1.9 billion sale by Google in 2004.

Less than five months later, on March 30, 2012, Groupon announced that it had revised its financial results, an unexpected restatement that deepened losses and raised questions about its accounting practices. As part of the revision, Groupon disclosed a "material weakness" in its

(Continued)

internal controls, saying that it had failed to set aside enough money to cover customer refunds. The accounting issue increased the company's losses in the fourth quarter to $64.9 million from $42.3 million. The news that day sent shares of Groupon tumbling 6 percent, to $17.29. Shares of Groupon had fallen by 30 percent since it went public.

In its announcement of the restatement, Groupon explained that it had encountered problems related to certain assumptions and forecasts the company used to calculate its results. In particular, the company said that it underestimated customer refunds for higher-priced offers, such as laser eye surgery. Groupon collects more revenue on such deals, but it also sees a higher number of refunds. The company honors customer refunds for the life of its coupons, so these payments can affect its financials at various times. Groupon deducts refunds within 60 days from receiving revenue; after that, the company has to take an additional accounting charge related to the payments.

As Groupon prepared its financial statements for 2011, its independent auditor, Ernst & Young, determined that the company did not account accurately for the possibility of higher refunds. By the firm's assessment, that constituted a material weakness." Groupon said in its annual report, "We did not maintain effective controls to provide reasonable assurance that accounts were complete and accurate."

In an interesting twist, in response to the conclusion that the company's internal controls contained a material weakness, Groupon blamed Ernst & Young in part for not identifying the weakness. The auditors were at fault for not identifying problems with the financial controls earlier, said Herman Leung, a financial analyst at Susquehanna Financial Group in San Francisco. "This should have been highlighted by the auditors. The business is growing so fast that it sounds like they don't have the proper financial controls to deal with the growth."[70] In fact, it was management's assessment of the material weakness in internal controls over financial reporting that led to the disclosure. Ernst & Young had signed the fourth-quarter audit report included in Groupon's annual report, giving a clean (unmodified) opinion.

In a related issue, on April 3, 2012, a shareholder lawsuit was brought against Groupon, accusing the company of misleading investors about its financial prospects in its IPO and concealing weak internal controls. According to the complaint, the company overstated revenue, issued materially false and misleading financial results, and concealed how its business was not growing as fast and was not nearly as resistant to competition, such as from LivingSocial and Amazon, as it had suggested.

These claims bring up a gap in the sections of SOX that deal with companies' internal controls. There is no requirement to disclose a control weakness in a company's IPO prospectus. Groupon had no obligation to disclose the problem until it filed its first quarterly or annual report as a public company—which is what it did.

Liability for False Certifications

The SEC's increased focus on identifying and penalizing misstatements in public company financials came to light in April 2014 when Chairman Mary Jo White highlighted in prepared testimony before the U.S. House Financial Services Committee the SEC's new Financial Fraud Task Force and the strides it was taking to identify "both traditional and emerging financial fraud issues." The commission has been analyzing patterns of internal control problems even absent a restatement in the financials and holding "gatekeepers"—such as auditors and corporate officer—accountable for corporate misstatements.

The SEC's disclosure on July 30, 2014, of an enforcement action against two corporate executives of a small Florida-based computer equipment company exemplifies the type of emerging theory of fraud it is now pursuing. The commission went after both the CEO and CFO of Quality Services Group Inc. (QSGI) solely for alleged misrepresentations in public disclosures about the company's internal controls environment, which are required by SOX.

The SEC alleged that QSGI's CEO (Marc Sherman) and former CFO (Edward Cummings) knew of significant internal controls issues in the company's inventory practices that they failed to disclose to auditors and investors. Central to the SEC's theory of fraud is that Sherman and Cummings (1) signed Form 10-Ks with management reports on internal controls that falsely omitted issues and (2) signed certifications in which they falsely represented that they had evaluated the management report on internal controls and disclosed all significant deficiencies to auditors.[71]

What makes QSGI a unique case is that it did not arise from a restatement of the company's prior financial statements; indeed, there does not appear to have been any material mistakes in the company's reported financials. Here the SEC hinged its fraud claims on alleged unreported deficiencies in QSGI's internal controls over its accounting function.

From a legal perspective, this case may sound an end to the days where corporate officers may simply adopt a "no harm, no foul" approach to disclosure when a company identifies an immaterial accounting issue or otherwise fails to follow its accounting policies and practices.

The message of this case may be that transparency with the company's audit committee and with external auditors regarding evaluations of the company's internal controls will protect the company, its investors, and its officers.

Compliance Function

The Ethics and Compliance Officer Association (ECOA) has recognized its increased responsibilities resulting from SOX. The mission of ECOA is to promote "ethical business practices and [serve] as a global forum for the exchange of information and strategies among organizations and individuals responsible for ethics, compliance, and business conduct programs."[72] An important step in encouraging the reporting of wrongdoing is to appoint a trusted member of the management team to be the organization's ethics officer. This person should take the lead in ensuring that the organization is in compliance with the laws and regulations, including SEC securities laws, SOX, and Dodd-Frank. A chief compliance officer (CCO) should serve as a sounding board for management to try out new ideas to see if these ideas pass the ethics "smell" test. The ethics officer plays a critical role in helping create a positive ethical tone in organizations.

The 2012 State of Compliance study conducted by PwC found that oversight of the compliance function has been changing. Fewer compliance officers report to the general counsel on a daily basis (35 percent in 2012, compared to 41 percent in 2011), although the number reporting on a daily basis to the CEO held steady at 32 percent. On a formal basis, 32 percent of respondents report to the audit committee, almost as many as who report to the general counsel (33 percent).

Over the past decade, heightened regulations related to SOX and Dodd-Frank have elevated the importance and visibility of the chief compliance officer role. Now an official member of the C-suite, compliance leaders are tasked with building comprehensive and robust programs that not only address existing requirements, but also anticipate regulatory changes and their likely impact.

Has SOX Accomplished Its Intended Goal?

In virtually all the frauds of the late 1990s and early 2000s, the CEOs and CFOs knew about their companies' materially misstated financial statements. One important provision of SOX that helps protect the public against fraudulent financial statements is the requirement of Section 302 that the CEO and CFO must certify that to the best of their knowledge, there are no material misstatements in the financial statements.

A valid question, now that SOX is almost 15 years old, is whether its promise of holding CEOs and CFOs criminally responsible for fraud has been a success. The law states that, under Section 302, if top corporate executives knowingly sign off on a false financial report, they're subject to a prison term of up to 10 years and a fine of up to $1 million, with penalties escalating to 20 years and $5 million if their misconduct is willful. In practice, very few defendants have even been charged with false certification, and fewer still have been convicted.

Richard Scrushy, the former HealthSouth Corporation CEO, falsely certified the financial statements of the company but was not sent to jail for that crime. On the other hand, HealthSouth CFO Weston L. Smith was sentenced in 2005 to 27 months in prison for his role in the company's $2.7 billion accounting fraud. Smith had pleaded guilty to one count each of conspiracy to commit wire and securities fraud, falsely certifying a financial report, and falsifying a report to the SEC. In 2007, the former CFO of a medical equipment financing company called DVI pleaded guilty to mail fraud and false certification and was sentenced to 30 months in prison.

So, the question in the end is, why have there not been more prosecutions under Section 302? Frankel believes that the answer may lie partly in how corporations have responded to SOX. Most major corporations have implemented internal compliance systems that make it very difficult to show that the CEO or CFO knowingly signed a false certification. And when prosecutors have enough evidence to show that those internal systems failed and top executives knowingly engaged in wrongdoing, they often prefer, for strategic reasons, to charge crimes other than false certification.[73]

However, the tide may be turning against CFOs, who typically mastermind financial frauds. Emboldened by legislative expansions of liability for financial executives under SOX and Dodd-Frank, the SEC increasingly is pursuing claims against CFOs that do not allege actual wrongdoing. It does so by alleging that the CFO's subordinates violated securities laws and that the CFO either certified the resulting reports or failed to implement adequate internal safeguards.

Perhaps the most alarming of these cases was the prosecution of Craig Huff, CFO of Nature's Sunshine Products (NSP), in 2009. The SEC charged him as part of a Foreign Corrupt Practices Act allegation that a Brazilian subsidiary of the company bribed customs officials. The SEC alleged that a wholly owned Brazilian subsidiary of NSP made payments to customs agents to import unregistered products into Brazil.

Huff was not alleged to have participated in or even known about the bribery scheme, but he was charged under a theory of control-person liability for violations of the books-and-records and internal-controls provisions of the securities laws, because NSP did not disclose the payments to customs agents in its SEC filings. Huff paid a civil penalty of $25,000 to settle the case.

The SEC is also embracing its powers to seek disgorgement of bonuses and other compensation that CFOs received in years in which the company restated its financials. In 2007, the former CFO of Beazer Homes, James O'Leary, faced disgorgement of profits and bonuses from the SEC when Beazer Homes was found to have overstated its income while O'Leary was CFO. The SEC alleged that chief accounting officer Michael Rand directed the fraud by recording improper accounting reserves in order to decrease the company's net income and meet estimates of diluted earnings per share.

The SEC did not accuse O'Leary of any accounting misconduct, but it stated he received substantial compensation and stock-sale profits while Beazer was misleading investors and fraudulently overstating its income. He agreed to return $1.4 million in past bonuses and stock profits he received while the company was submitting false financial statements.

The jury is still out on whether SOX serves as an adequate deterrent to financial fraud. We should not be surprised if the answer is "no" because laws do not necessarily lead to ethical behavior. Any law—including SOX—establishes the rules of the game and how violators will be punished. As we have learned throughout these first three chapters, ethical behavior comes from within; it comes from a desire to do the right thing, not because we may be punished if we do not. In the end, it is a postconventional mindset that guides ethical reasoning when the chips are down, not a conventional one. Laws are needed, but they serve as only a minimum standard of ethical conduct. Codes of ethics are needed because they help to establish an ethical organization environment. But it is virtuous behavior that should guide corporate officers through the minefield of conflicts and pressures that exist in decision making.

Whistleblowing

LO 3-7
Analyze the moral basis for whistleblowing and accountants' obligations to whistle blow.

There is a symbiotic relationship between whistleblowing and an organization's culture. Effective internal whistleblowing processes are an important part of a healthy corporate culture. Internal auditors have a critical role to play in monitoring whistleblowing procedures, given the nature of internal control. The audit committee should ensure that matters of concern are raised through appropriate channels and promptly dealt with. Whistleblowing should be part of the internal control environment and an effective corporate governance system.

There is no one set definition of whistleblowing, although most definitions characterize the practice as disclosing to others in an organization an action that violates organizational norms or the law. Near and Miceli take a broad view of whistleblowing as "the disclosure by organization members (former or current) of illegal, immoral, or illegitimate practices under the control of their employers, to persons or organizations that may be able to effect action." This definition includes whistleblowers who use internal channels (e.g., a hotline or ombudsperson) or external channels (e.g., the external auditors or the SEC) to blow the whistle. They identify four elements of the whistleblowing process: the whistleblower, the whistleblowing act or complaint, the party to whom the complaint is made, and the organization against which the complaint is lodged. In discussing the act itself, they label it as an act of "dissidence" somewhat analogous to civil disobedience.[74] The term *organizational dissidence* fits in with our discussion of cognitive dissonance in Chapter 2, which emphasized the difference between our thoughts, beliefs or attitudes, and behavior.

Morality of Whistleblowing

Given that the act of whistleblowing is a personal choice, the key to whether an individual will blow the whistle on wrongdoing is whether the whistleblower perceives organizational policies are designed to encourage moral autonomy, individual responsibility, and organizational support for whistleblowers.

Moral agency is important for the determination of moral behavior and it enables the moral evaluation of the agent's behavior.[75] The basic characteristic of the philosophical concept of moral agency is autonomy and is viewed in the context of the ability or will to be one's own person. Autonomy plays an important role in conceptions of moral obligation and responsibility.[76]

Autonomous will means to act according to reasons and motives that are taken as one's own and not the product of organizational policies and external forces such as whistleblowing legislation. Autonomous will is the central value in the Kantian tradition of moral philosophy that moral requirements are based on the standard of rationality he called the Categorical Imperative.[77] The Categorical Imperative in Kant's ethical system is an unconditional moral law that applies to all rational beings and is independent of any personal motive or desire. Therefore, we could say that even if pressure exists in an organization to not report wrongdoing, a rational, moral person will withstand such pressure, regardless of perceived retaliation, because it is a moral requirement to do so. Kant argued that conformity to the Categorical Imperative, and hence to moral requirements themselves, is essential to rational agency.[78]

Rights and Duties

Researchers have posed the question of whether workplace whistleblowing is a right, and thus allows for responsible behavior, or whether it is an imposed corporate duty, thus resulting in liability of workers. If an organization institutes an internal whistleblowing policy, it is because it perceives moral autonomy to be weak. When businesses then implement the policy, it leads to the conclusion that moral autonomy is strong, and employees are expected to blow the whistle.[79] Therefore, if employees do not blow the whistle in accordance with corporate policy, they then become liable for not doing so, rendering the policy a tool that controls employee behavior. Responsibility for misdeeds then shifts from the organization to the individual, and employees are further stripped of the right to moral autonomy.[80]

Miceli and Near's research has shown that what whistleblowers hope and believe their speaking out will achieve is the correction of what they perceive as an organizational wrongdoing (e.g., fraudulent financial statements). This research also found that not everyone who perceives a wrongdoing acts upon that perception. In fact, only 42 percent stated they were ready to blow the whistle. Those who observe wrongdoing but would not do so identify a "retaliatory climate" in their organizations as the primary barrier to blowing the whistle on corporate wrongdoing, while those who say they would speak up about it were confident that they "would not experience managerial retaliation if they blew the whistle."[81] Recall that the National Business Ethics Survey found that 46 percent of employees did not blow the whistle for fear of retaliation, while 21 percent that reported misconduct said they faced some form of retribution.[82]

Whistleblowing regulations attempt to protect individuals when they behave responsibly toward society in light of irresponsible behavior by their organizations. This certainly is the motivation for the anti-retaliation provisions of both SOX and Dodd-Frank. The acknowledgement of the need for such protection, however, implies that moral agency, autonomy, and responsibility are problematic in organizations, or at the very least, that they do not come naturally and are not welcomed when they arrive. When organizations establish an ethical culture and anonymous channels to report wrongdoing, they create an environment that supports whistleblowing and whistleblowers while controlling for possible retaliation.[83]

Anthony Menendez v. Halliburton, Inc.[84]

Doing the right thing and blowing the whistle does not always pay off and can be an arduous task. A case in point is what happened to Anthony Menendez in his whistleblowing ordeal with Halliburton. One day in February 2006, he received an e-mail from Halliburton's chief accounting officer, Mark McCollum, that was addressed to much of the accounting department. It read, "The SEC has opened an inquiry into the allegations of Mr. Menendez." Everyone was told to retain their documents until further notice. Menendez had been outed. The facts of the case are summarized in Exhibit 3.12. (An expanded version of this case with multiple areas for discussion appears in Case 3-8).

EXHIBIT 3.12   Accountant Takes on Halliburton and Wins

The story begins less than one year earlier when Menendez was hired as the Director of Technical Accounting Research and Training at Halliburton. Only months before that, Halliburton had settled with the U.S. Securities and Exchange Commission (SEC) after a two-year accounting probe. It didn't take long for Menendez to realize the company was violating some very basic accounting revenue recognition rules.

Halliburton contracts with energy companies like Royal Dutch Shell and BP to find and exploit huge oil and gas fields. It sells services of its geologists and engineers who work intricate machinery that Halliburton built and sold to its customers. The company's accountants had been

(Continued)

allowing the company to count the full value of the equipment right away as revenue, sometimes even before it had assembled the equipment. But the customers could walk away in the middle of the contracts. Also, Menendez knew that if the equipment were damaged, Halliburton, not the customer, absorbed the loss.

Menendez recommended the company wait until the work was completed to record the equipment sales as revenue. Even though top Halliburton accounting executives, including Halliburton's chief accounting officer, Mark McCollum, agreed with Menendez's analysis, they didn't act to correct the accounting because of concern about its impact in slowing revenue growth. Later, an outside expert, Doug Carmichael, the former chief accountant of the Public Company Accounting Oversight Board (PCAOB), would agree with Menendez.

In meetings with an executive who worked for Menendez, James Paquette, the two agreed on the revenue recognition issue. But other groups in accounting were fighting them. Paquette was concerned what would happen even if they made a convincing case and still the other accountants and executives didn't budge. Menendez had replied that he hoped that wouldn't happen, but that there were "avenues for us to hold up our integrity."

On July 18, 2005, Menendez turned on a digital recorder, put it in the front pocket of his slacks. and walked into a meeting with McCollum. Even though McCollum had indicated that Menendez's position had merits, he told Menendez that the approach he was using and memo he had prepared on the matter was wrong. He was making his colleagues feel stupid and needed to be more collegial. He told Menendez that the Halliburton team, working with the external auditors from KPMG, had reached a different conclusion. He also offered that Menendez shouldn't put things in writing and had to be more "circumspect about the use of e-mail to communicate." He finished by telling Menendez that he wasn't asking him to compromise his ethics and compromise the position he felt so strongly about.

Menendez waited to see what would happen. Given that billions in equipment sales were involved, he knew this was no trivial matter. Finally, in the fall he realized nothing would happen. The company had justified its accounting treatment by indicating that the equipment sitting in Halliburton's warehouses was "customer-owned inventory." Menendez agonized and several days later filed a confidential complaint with the SEC in November 2005.

He spoke to the SEC about the matter and was told to go to the audit committee. Menendez assumed the SEC would take action, but nothing seemed to occur, until February 4, 2006, when he heard the SEC was poking around.

Unbeknownst to Menendez, his complaint went to the Halliburton legal department as well as the board committee, an apparent violation of company policy. The audit committee was supposed to keep such reports confidential. A few days later, the SEC notified the company that it had opened an investigation into the company's revenue recognition. Then, the e-mail from McCollum got distributed. Halliburton's general counsel said "the SEC is investigating Mr. Menendez's complaints" to the company's chief financial officer, KPMG, other top executives, and McCollum. McCollum had forwarded it to at least 15 of Menendez's colleagues in accounting. As far as Halliburton was concerned, they had a traitor in their ranks.

The ramifications were immediate. Menendez was stripped of his responsibilities and became a pariah at the firm. Halliburton contracted with an outside law firm to conduct an "investigation." Not surprisingly, it cleared the company. The SEC informed Halliburton it would not bring any enforcement action against it.

Menendez went back to the SEC to no avail. The commission wouldn't even accept the documents he had provided. Finally, he felt he had to leave Halliburton having been punished for blowing the whistle. He brought a claim under SOX in May 2006 based on retaliation, but the government would not take up his case. He brought separate lawsuits, but lost. He persisted even when others told him he had no chance of prevailing. No one would take his case. Finally, he decided to represent himself in the appeals process. It went on for three years. In September

(Continued)

2011, the administrative laws appeals panel had ruled. It overturned the original trial judge. After five years, Menendez had his first victory.

Halliburton appealed the reversal. Another two years went by and in April 2013, the appeals panel ruled that he had been retaliated against for blowing the whistle, just as he had argued all along.

Menendez acted on principle in his quest for the truth. He only wanted to be proven right so he had asked for a token sum. The panel, noting the importance of punishing retaliations against whistleblowers, awarded him $30,000.

Menendez ultimately got a job at General Motors based on a recommendation from the expert witness, Doug Carmichael. GM's chief accounting officer who hired Menendez was quoted as telling him it took a lot of courage to stand tall and the company needed people with high integrity who would work hard and were trustworthy.

Menendez still works at GM. Halliburton has thrived, never being penalized by the SEC. In 2014, the company generated $3.5 billion in profit on $33 billion in revenue.

Menendez's case was filed before Dodd-Frank became effective. It is interesting to contemplate what might have happened had he filed a whistleblower claim under the act. Would he have been rewarded for his efforts?

Obligation to Report Fraud

The foundation for making moral judgments in accounting is the public interest ideal. The provisions of Dodd-Frank allow for responsible behavior by describing a process for reporting unresolved differences between an auditor and the firm. The confidentiality obligation for CPAs not withstanding, whistleblowing in accounting is a duty when it is motivated by a desire to protect the public.

The reporting requirements for fraud are detailed in Section 10A of the Securities Exchange Act of 1934 and are based on the principles of integrity and acting in the public interest. The following steps are part of a prescribed process that should be followed in deciding whether to report fraud.

1. Determine whether the violations have a material effect, quantitatively or qualitatively, on the financial statements.
2. If yes, has management, or the board of directors, caused management to take remedial action, including reporting externally if necessary?
3. If no, then the auditor must make a formal report of its conclusions and provide the report to the board of directors. The board then has one business day to inform the SEC and provide a copy of the communication to the external auditor.

If the auditing firm does not receive a copy within one business day, then it has two choices:

a. Provide a copy of its own report to the SEC within one business day, or
b. Resign from the engagement and provide a copy of the report to the SEC within one business day of resigning.

Although external auditors might turn to whistleblowers against clients, in reality this is unlikely to occur until and unless the process prescribed under Section 10A has played out to first resolve the matter internally through the client's internal compliance system. However, if an internal resolution cannot be found, the auditor should consider any disclosure responsibilities to regulatory authorities. Furthermore, external auditors must follow the process described in Interpretation 102-4 when an auditor contemplates blowing the whistle on the client or audit firm.

Dodd-Frank Provisions

The Dodd-Frank Wall Street Reform and Consumer Protection Act (Dodd-Frank) was adopted by Congress on January 5, 2010, and became effective on August 12, 2011.[85] It changes the regulatory landscape for internal accountants and auditors, and external auditors and auditing firms, by protecting whistleblowers that "voluntarily" provide the SEC with "original information" about a violation of federal securities laws that leads to a successful enforcement proceeding. Under the United States Code (US Code), the enforcement action must result in monetary sanctions of more than $1 million.[86]

Dodd-Frank defines a whistleblower as any individual who provides information to the SEC relating to a violation of the securities laws that has occurred, is ongoing, or is about to occur. *Voluntarily* means the whistleblower has provided information prior to the government, a self-regulatory organization, or the PCAOB asking for it directly from the whistleblower. Original information must be based upon the whistleblower's independent knowledge or independent analysis, not already known to the SEC and not derived exclusively from an allegation made in a judicial or administrative hearing or a governmental report, hearing, audit, or investigation (HR 4173).[87]

Section 922 of Dodd-Frank provides an award for whistleblowers (who meet certain criteria) of "not less than 10 percent and not more than 30 percent, in total, of what has been collected of the monetary sanctions imposed in the section." Kastiel believes the award incentivizes whistleblowing and provides a payment for disclosing the relevant information to the SEC.[88]

The "incentivization" provision of Dodd-Frank has been referred to as a "bounty hunter" program. Is it ethical to provide financial incentives to motivate employees to come forward and report financial wrongdoing? This is not an easy question to answer.

One major concern with this new provision is that it may cause would-be whistleblowers to go external with the information rather than internal using the organization's prescribed reporting mechanisms. Employees have a loyalty obligation to their employers that include maintaining confidentiality and not doing anything to harm their employers. However, as discussed in Chapter 1, the loyalty obligation should never be used to mask one's ethical obligation to maintain integrity and protect the public interest. Assuming the internal reporting process has played out and nothing has been done to correct for the wrongdoing, we believe from an ethical perspective external whistleblowing is the proper course of action especially if it is the *only* way for the public to know. An employee should not fall victim to the bystander effect and assume others will report it. Along with knowledge comes the responsibility to correct wrongdoings, which is in the best long-term interests of the organization.

Internal Accountants' Eligibility

Under Dodd-Frank, internal accountants are excluded from receiving whistleblower awards because of their pre-existing legal duty to report securities violations.[89] This includes individuals with internal compliance or audit responsibilities at an entity who receive information about potential violations since it is part of their job responsibilities to report suspicion of illegal acts and fraud to management.

Under certain circumstances, internal accountants are eligible to become Dodd-Frank whistleblowers in three situations: (1) Disclosure to the SEC is needed to prevent "substantial injury" to the financial interest of an entity or its investors; (2) the whistleblower "reasonably believes" the entity is impeding investigation of the misconduct (e.g., destroying documents or improperly influencing witnesses); or (3) the whistleblower has first reported the violation internally and at least 120 days have passed with no action.

The substantial injury provision does not require the whistleblower to reasonably believe that the entity might commit a "material violation"; rather, the whistleblower will generally only need to demonstrate that responsible management or governance personnel at the entity were aware of an "imminent violation" and were not taking steps to prevent it. The 120-day "look-back" period begins after the internal accountant or auditor either provided information of a possible violation to the relevant entity's management (i.e., audit committee, chief legal officer, or chief compliance officer), or at least 120 days have elapsed since the whistleblower received the information, if the whistleblower received it under circumstances indicating that these people were already aware of the information. The internal accountant cannot become eligible for a whistleblower award by learning of possible misconduct, realizing that those responsible for the entity's compliance are not aware of the possible misconduct, failing to provide the information to them, waiting for the 120-day period to run, and then reporting the information to the SEC (SEC 2010).[90]

External Auditor Eligibility

External auditors are generally prohibited from blowing the whistle on their clients because the information gained during a mandated audit would not be considered to derive from an individual's independent knowledge or analysis. The Dodd-Frank Act prohibits an external auditor who is already obligated to report information to the SEC from personally profiting from reporting that same information as a whistleblower. However, for auditors and their firms the whistleblower rules allow the auditor or an employee associated with the auditor to make a whistleblower submission alleging that the firm failed to assess, investigate, or report wrongdoing in accordance with Section 10A, or that the firm failed to follow other professional standards. If the whistleblower makes such a submission, the whistleblower will be able to obtain an award not only from a successful enforcement action against the auditing firm, but also from any successful action against the firm's engagement client. In allowing such claims, the goal of the SEC is to "help insure that wrongdoing by the [accounting] firm (or its employees) is reported on a timely fashion." According to the SEC, this goal is paramount "because of the important gatekeeper role that auditors play in the securities markets."[91]

The disclosure of confidential information about clients raises questions about a possible violation of Rule 301 of the AICPA Code (AICPA 2013, ET Section 301) and of state privilege laws.[92] The external disclosure of confidential information can, under certain circumstances, be treated as an exception to the rule if disclosure is linked to compliance with applicable laws and government regulations, which include the Dodd-Frank. The act defines the circumstances under which the disclosure of confidential information by external auditors will not violate confidentiality and entails a good faith effort to get the company or client to alter the accounting that triggers the concern.

Rosenthal and Smith point out that several members of the public accounting profession, including KPMG, Ernst & Young, PricewaterhouseCoopers and the Center for Audit Quality, believe that permitting CPAs to obtain monetary rewards for blowing the whistle on their own firms' performance of services for clients could create several significant problems including: (1) undermining the ethical obligations of CPAs not to divulge confidential client information by providing a financial reward for whistleblowing; (2) harming the quality of external audits because client management might restrict access to client information for fear the financial incentive for whistleblowing could lead to reporting client-specific information to the SEC; (3) overriding the firms' internal reporting mechanisms for audit-related disagreements; and (4) incentivizing an individual to bypass existing programs to report disagreements including hotlines.[93]

Integrity Considerations

Rule 102 of the AICPA Code requires that "In the performance of any professional service, a member shall maintain objectivity and integrity, shall be free of conflicts of interest, and shall not knowingly misrepresent facts or subordinate his or her judgment to others."[94] Interpretation 102-4 was revised effective August 31, 2013, to provide additional guidelines as to the scope and application of Rule 102 with respect to extending the subordination of judgment provision to include not only differences of opinion between an internal accountant and his or her supervisor but differences between an external auditor and the audit firm.

Assume that an auditor does not believe the audit firm has done everything that it can to resolve differences with the client over proper accounting and the firm has decided to accept the client's position on the matter. The auditor knows the audit firm's decision violates the rights of the investors and creditors who expect auditors to act in their best interests. It is the integrity standard that establishes the basis for moral action and to avoid subordinating judgment. Integrity is a critical component of choosing the means necessary to report wrongdoing even if it leads to blowing the whistle on an employer and in the face of possible retaliation for one's action. Interpretation 102-4 forms the basis of the ethical obligations of external auditors to meet the requirements of Dodd-Frank prior to blowing the whistle and becoming eligible for a whistleblower award. The process to follow is depicted in Exhibit 3.13.

EXHIBIT 3.13   Ethical Responsibilities of CPAs to Avoid Subordination of Judgment*

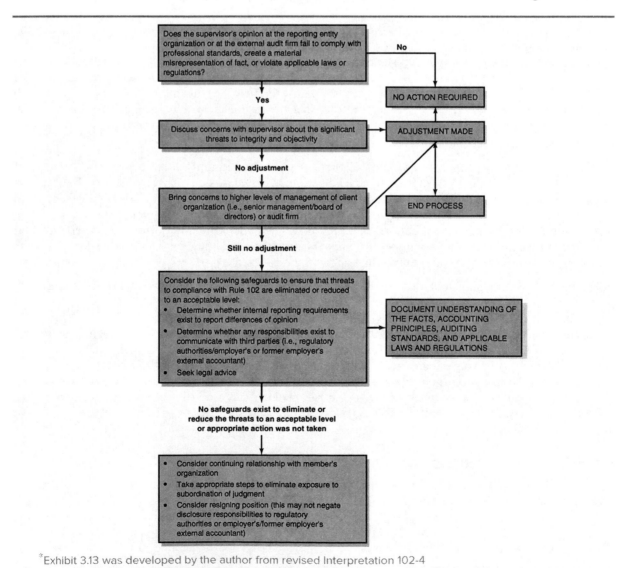

*Exhibit 3.13 was developed by the author from revised Interpretation 102-4

Under Interpretation 102-4, when differences of opinion exist on how best to handle disagreements with the client and the firm refuses to make the required adjustments, then the external auditor should consider whether safeguards exist to ensure that threats to compliance with Rule 102 are eliminated or reduced to an acceptable level. In doing so, the external auditor should determine whether internal reporting requirements exist within the firm to report differences of opinion and any responsibilities that may exist to communicate with third parties, such as regulatory authorities. In that regard, the CPA is advised to seek legal advice on the matter.

If the external auditor concludes that safeguards cannot eliminate or reduce the threats to integrity and objectivity to an acceptable level or other appropriate action was not taken, then the auditor should consider whether the relationship with the organization should be terminated including possibly resigning one's position. These steps are necessary to prevent subordination of judgment.

Nothing in Interpretation 102-4 precludes an external auditor from resigning from the audit firm; however, resignation does not negate the auditor's disclosure responsibilities to the SEC. As previously discussed, the confidentiality requirement of Rule 301 does not prohibit an auditor from complying with applicable laws and government regulations such as Dodd-Frank. As Taylor and Thomas (2013) point out, there are times when CPAs might choose to report internal disputes over accounting issues to an external party in order to maintain professional integrity.[95]

The Morality of Whistleblowing

Whistleblowing always involves an actual or at least declared intention to prevent something bad that would otherwise occur. It always involves information that would not ordinarily be revealed. Most ethicists agree whistleblowing is an ethical action. According to the "standard theory" on whistleblowing of Michael Davis, whistleblowing is morally required when it is required at all; people have a moral obligation to prevent serious harm to others if they can do so with little costs to themselves. Thus, a utilitarian analysis might be used to evaluate the ethics of whistleblowing, keeping in mind that the application of a rule-utilitarian perspective could lead to the conclusion that a categorical imperative exists to do whatever it takes to stop fraudulent behavior regardless of whether a particular action might bring more harm than good to the stakeholders.[96]

DeGeorge analyzes when whistleblowing is a moral act. His starting position is based on the universal ethical principle that "corporations have a moral obligation not to harm." DeGeorge identifies five criteria when whistleblowing is morally permitted. Briefly, (1) the firm's actions will do serious and considerable harm to others; (2) the whistleblowing act is justifiable once the employee reports it to her immediate supervisor and makes her moral concerns known; (3) absent any action by the supervisor, the employee should take the matter all the way up to the board, if necessary; (4) documented evidence must exist that would convince a reasonable and impartial observer that one's views of the situation is correct and that serious harm may occur; and (5) the employee must reasonably believe that going public will create the necessary change to protect the public and is worth the risk to oneself.[97]

DeGeorge's criteria establish the foundation for moral behavior to occur when contemplating whistleblowing. He rejects the position that external whistleblowing is *always* morally justifiable, and also rejects the position that external whistleblowing is *never* morally justifiable. Basically his position is that the whistleblower should have a moral motivation to engage in the act (i.e., to expose unnecessary harm, and illegal or immoral actions). In this way DeGeorge's propositions meet Rest's conditions for ethical decision making and have a virtues-based dimension to them.

Whistleblowing Experiences

Since its inception in 2011, the SEC's whistleblower program has paid more than $50 million to 16 whistleblowers who provided the SEC with unique and useful information that contributed to a successful enforcement action.

On August 29, 2014, the SEC announced a whistleblower award of more than $300,000, 20 percent of the $1.5 million settlement, to a company employee who performed audit and compliance functions and reported wrongdoing (insider trading and numerous securities violations) to the SEC after the company failed to take action within 120 days after the employee reported it internally. It was the first award for a whistleblower with an audit or compliance function at a company. The SEC mistakenly released the reference number of the case for which the whistleblower received the award, resulting in the indirect release of that individual's name. The SEC quickly redacted the reference number but it still violated the confidentiality requirement to protect the identity of the whistleblower.

On April 22, 2015, the SEC announced its second award of more than a million dollars to a compliance professional. The award involves a compliance officer who had a reasonable basis to believe that disclosure to the SEC was necessary to prevent imminent misconduct from causing substantial financial harm to the company or investors.

While we believe the whistleblowing program is the right thing to do to protect the public interest, we are concerned about two things:

1. A self-interested and opportunistic person may be induced to reveal company information to the SEC after following the prescribed internal compliance process, that led to no action by the company, with inadequate safeguards as to the quality of the information provided, and
2. Permitting compliance officers to become whistleblowers merely because of the passage of time (i.e., 120 days), rather than on a case-specific consideration of whether the company adequately addressed the underlying compliance issues in good faith, can erode corporate culture and trust in compliance officials; the result may be to subvert the overarching objectives of preventing, detecting, and remediating corporate misconduct on an enterprise-wide basis.[98]

We agree with others who have pointed out that, by reporting through the internal compliance process, others in the organization become informed of the facts and become potential whistleblowers.[99] As a practical matter, there may be no way around widening the circle of those in the know, but organizations should, at a minimum, take steps to protect the identity of the whistleblower.

Concluding Thoughts

Our journey in this chapter leads us to conclude that organizations should take reasonable steps to ensure that they develop an ethical culture, including instilling ethical values within the firm's policies, procedures, and practices; develop a code of ethics that is enhanced through training; establish a hotline for the anonymous reporting of alleged wrongdoing; develop whistleblowing guidelines; appoint a chief ethics and compliance officer; monitor ethical behavior and compliance with applicable regulations; and create an ethical tone at the top, all of which should occur with ethical leadership at the helm and strong internal controls. Research supports the proposition that "strong ethical cultures" diminish organizational misconduct and thereby the need for employees to blow the whistle internally or externally.[100]

Creating an ethical culture is a necessary but insufficient condition to ensure that ethical behavior occurs. Individuals within the organization may attempt to subvert the systems and pressure others to look the other way or go along with wrongdoing under the guise of being a team player or accepting a one-time fix to a perceived problem. In these situations, outlets should exist for employees to voice their values when they believe unethical or fraudulent behavior has occurred. Just imagine how Anthony Menendez's experiences would have changed had Halliburton created such a supportive environment.

Discussion Questions

1. In her book *The Seven Signs of Ethical Collapse,* Jennings explains: "When an organization collapses ethically, it means that those in the organization have drifted into rationalizations and legalisms, and all for the purpose of getting the results they want and need at almost any cost." Discuss what you think Jennings meant by this statement in the context of the giving voice to values discussions in Chapter 2.

2. Have you ever been faced with a personal dilemma whether to blow the whistle on wrongdoing? What did you do and why? How did elements of the giving voice to values framework influence your decision?

3. Identify a company that you believe has an ethical culture. Explain why you selected that company.

4. One way of analyzing whether National Security Agency (NSA) whistleblower Edward Snowden's actions were justified in leaking classified materials exposing the breadth of the U.S. government's surveillance activities is by weighing personal morality against the morality that comes with one's adopted professional role. Using this perspective, do you believe Snowden's act was ethical?

5. How does employee perceptions of commitment, integrity, and transparency in the workplace contribute toward creating an ethical corporate culture?

6. It has been said that recent graduates from a business school majoring in accounting and just entering the profession are especially vulnerable to ethical missteps because they are often naive and may not see the ethical aspects of situations they confront. Explain the various dimensions of such alleged ethical challenges in the workplace.

7. Explain how "groupthink" might lead a person to ignore moral and ethical duty in an organization.

8. Do you believe that employees who observe more occupational fraud in their organizations are more likely to engage in occupational fraud themselves?

9. The following questions are about corporate governance and executive compensation:

   (a) How does agency theory address the issue of executive compensation?

   (b) How might stakeholder theory argue against the current model of executive compensation in the United States?

   (c) What is meant by the statement, "Compensation systems always become in part *end* and not simply *means*"?

10. The issue of the size of executive compensation packages is explored in the text. The highest paid CEO in 2014 was David Zaslav, the CEO of Discovery Communications, whose total executive compensation package was $156.1 million, the vast majority of which was from stock awards. Critics claim that CEOs receive excessive executive compensation packages when compared with the average worker. Consider that NBA basketball star LeBron James took in $64.8 million in 2014, the majority of which was from endorsements, while radio and TV entertainer Howard Stern earned $95 million? Are the top paid corporate executives overpaid when compared to top entertainers? Why or why not?

11. Five months before the new 2002 Lexus ES hit showroom floors, the company's U.S. engineers sent a test report to Toyota City in Japan: The luxury sedan shifted gears so roughly that it was "not acceptable for production." Days later, another Japanese executive sent an e-mail to top managers saying that despite misgivings among U.S. officials, the 2002 Lexus was "marginally acceptable for production." The new ES went on sale across the nation on October 1, 2001.

In years to come, thousands of Lexus owners discovered that some of the vehicles had transmission problems, which caused it to hesitate when motorists hit the gas or lurch forward unintentionally. The 2002–2006 ES models would become the target of lawsuits, federal safety investigations, and hundreds of consumer complaints, including claims of 49 injuries.

In an August 15, 2005, memo explaining the company's position, a staff attorney wrote, "The objective will be to limit the number of vehicles to be serviced to those owners who complain and to limit the per-vehicle cost."

In 2010, Toyota was fined a record $16.4 million for delays in notifying U.S. federal safety officials about defects that could lead to sudden acceleration.

Do you believe national culture might have played a role in how Toyota handled the matter? What about corporate culture? What are the similarities between the Toyota case and the Ford and GM situations discussed in the chapter?

12. The 2011 National Business Ethics Survey defines "active social networkers" as people who spend more than 30 percent of the workday participating on social networking sites. According to the results of the survey, active social networkers air company linen in public. Sixty percent would comment on their personal sites about their company if it was in the news, 53% say they share information about work projects once a week or more, and more than a third say they often comment, on their personal sites, about managers, coworkers, and even clients. What are the dangers of such behavior for the employee and employer?

13. Brief and Motowidlo define prosocial behavior within the organizational setting as "behavior which is (a) performed by a member of an organization, (b) directed toward an individual, group, or organization with whom she interacts while carrying out her organizational role, and (c) performed with the intention of promoting the welfare of the individual, group, or organization toward which it is directed."[101]

The researchers on whistleblowing using this model have generally argued that stages 5 and 6 represent cognitive moral development consistent with prosocial behavior. Discuss why stages 5 and 6 of Kohlberg's model are more likely to be associated with prosocial behavior than lower stages of moral development.

14. What is the link between the internal control environment and accountability?

15. The Committee of Sponsoring Organizations (COSO) explains the importance of the control environment to internal controls by stating that it sets the tone of an organization, influencing the control consciousness of its people. It is the foundation for all aspects of internal control, providing discipline and structure. Explain what is meant by this statement.

16. It has been argued that an organization that does not support those that whistle-blow because of violation of professional standards is indicative of a failure of organizational ethics. Explain what you think this statement means from the perspective of corporate culture.

17. Evaluate the ethics of the practice of whistleblowing from the perspectives of virtue, rights theory, and utilitarianism.

18. Just because a person has a right to blow the whistle, does that mean she has a duty to blow the whistle? How might we make that determination?

19. How do the concepts of cognitive dissonance and organizational/ethical dissonance relate to whether an accountant might choose to blow the whistle on corporate wrongdoing?

20. Explain how we might evaluate auditors' whistleblowing intentions? Why would this be important to do?

21. Explain how internal auditors' sensitivity to ethical dilemmas might be influenced by corporate governance mechanisms.

22. On October 24, 2013, the Second Circuit Court of Appeals ruled that a tipster who provided information to the SEC about illegal payments to foreign government officials by Stryker Corporation under the Foreign Corrupt Practices Act (FCPA) was not eligible to receive a Dodd-Frank award because his information was provided before the act went into effect in 2010. Stryker had made those payments between August 2003 and February 2008. The commission ruled the company had incorrectly described the unlawful payments in its books and records and failed to devise and maintain an adequate system of internal accounting controls, as required under the FCPA. Stryker was fined $13.3 million: $7.5 million in disgorgement; $2.3 million in prejudgment interest; and a $3.5 million civil penalty. Do you believe the court's opinion was ethical from a fairness perspective? From a rights perspective? Explain.

23. The following relates to the Menendez–Halliburton situation described in the text.

    (a) How would you characterize Halliburton's accounting for revenue from ethical and professional perspectives?

    (b) Once KPMG learned that Menendez had provided a complaint to Halliburton's audit committee highlighting questionable accounting and auditing practices, the KPMG audit partner instructed the audit team members to avoid communications with Menendez. How would you characterize those actions ethically and professionally?

24. "Give me the 'McFacts,' ma'am, nothing but the McFacts!" So argued the defense attorney for McDonald's Corporation as she questioned Stella Liebeck, an 81-year-old retired sales clerk, two years after her initial lawsuit against McDonald's claiming that it served dangerously hot coffee. Liebeck had bought a 49-cent cup of coffee at the drive-in window of an Albuquerque McDonald's, and while removing the lid to add cream and sugar, she spilled the coffee and suffered third-degree burns of the groin, inner thighs, and buttocks. Her suit claimed that the coffee was "defective." During the trial, it was determined that testing of coffee at other local restaurants found that none came closer than 20° to the temperature at which McDonald's coffee is poured (about 180°F). The jury decided in favor of Liebeck and awarded her compensatory damages of $200,000, which they reduced to $160,000 after determining that 20 percent of the fault belonged with Liebeck for spilling the coffee. The jury then found that McDonald's had engaged in willful, reckless, malicious, or wanton conduct, the basis for punitive damages. It awarded $2.7 million in punitive damages. That amount was ultimately reduced by the presiding judge to $480,000. The parties then settled out of court for an unspecified amount reported to be less than the $480,000.

    For its part, McDonald's had suggested that Liebeck may have contributed to her injuries by holding the cup between her legs and not removing her clothing immediately. The company also argued that Liebeck's age may have made the injuries worse than they might have been in a younger individual, "since older skin is thinner and more vulnerable to injury."

    Who is to blame for the McSpill? Be sure to support your answer with a discussion of personal responsibility, corporate accountability, and ethical reasoning.

25. Is business ethics an oxymoron?

Endnotes

1. Craig E. Johnson, *Meeting the Ethical Challenges of Leadership: Casting Light or Shadow* (New York: Sage Publications, 2015).

2. Johnson, pp. 321–323.

3. O.C. Ferrell, John Fraedich, and Linda Ferrell, *Business Ethics: Ethical Decision Making and Cases*, 9th ed. (Mason, OH: South-Western, 2011).

4. O.C. Ferrell, John Fraedrich, and Linda Ferrell, *Business Ethics: Ethical Decision Making and Cases* (Stamford, CT: Cengage Learning, 2015), pp. 128–146.

5. O.C. Ferrell and Linda Ferrell, "Role of Ethical Leadership in Organizational Performance," *Journal of Management Systems* 13, (2001), pp. 64–78.

6. Ferrell et al.

7. H. R. Smith and Archie B. Carroll, "Organizational Ethics: A Stacked Deck," *Journal of Business Ethics*, Vol. 3, No. 2 (May 1984), pp. 95–100.

8. Thomas M. Jones, "Ethical Decision Making by Individuals in Organizations: An Issue-Contingent Model," *Academy of Management Review*, Vol. 16, No. 2 (1991), pp. 366–395.

9. Susan E. Fiske and Shelley E. Taylor, *Social Cognition* (NY: McGraw-Hill, 1991).

10. MaryJo Burchard, "Ethical Dissonance and Response to Destructive Leadership: A Proposed Model," *Emerging Leadership Journeys*, 4, no. 1, pp. 154–176.

11. Scott K. Jones and Kenneth M. Hiltebeitel, "Organizational Influence in a Model of the Moral Decision Process of Accountants," *Journal of Business Ethics* 14, no. 6 (1995), pp. 417–431.

12. Jones.

13. Burchard.

14. Burchard, pp. 158–159.

15. Lawrence A. Pervin, "Performance and Satisfaction as a Function of Individual-Environment Fit," *Psychological Bulletin* 69, no. 1 (January 1968), pp. 56–68.

16. Burchard, pp. 162–163.

17. Hian Chye Koh and El'fred H. Y. Boo, "Organizational Ethics and Job Satisfaction and Commitment," *Management Decision* 4, nos. 5 and 6 (2004), pp. 677–693.

18. Burchard, pp. 163–164.

19. Art Padilla, Robert Hogan, and Robert B. Kaiser, "The Toxic Triangle: Destructive Leaders, Susceptible Followers, and Conducive Environments," *Leadership Quarterly* 18 (3), (2007), pp. 176–194.

20. Burchard, pp. 164–165.

21. V. Lee Hamilton and Herbert Kelman, *Crimes of Obedience: Toward a Social Psychology of Authority and Responsibility* (New Haven, CT: Yale University Press, 1989).

22. Burchard, pp. 163–164.

23. Koh and Boo.

24. Randi L. Sims and Thomas L. Keon, "The Influence of Ethical Fit on Employee Satisfaction, Commitment, and Turnover," *Journal of Business Ethics* 13, no. 12 (1994), pp. 939–948.

25. Marianne M. Jennings, *The Seven Signs of Ethical Collapse: How to Spot Moral Meltdowns in Companies Before It's Too Late* (New York: St. Martin's Press, 2006).

26. Jennings.

27. Jennings.

28. Jennings, pp. 138–139.

29. Archie B. Carroll and Ann K. Buchholtz, *Business & Society: Ethics and Stakeholder Management* (Mason, OH: Cengage Learning, 2009).

30. Ferrell et al, p. 35.

31. Isabelle Maignan and O. C. Ferrell, "Corporate Social Responsibility: Toward a Marketing Conceptualization," *Journal of the Academy of Marketing Science* 32 (2004), pp. 3–19.

32. *United States v. Carroll Towing,* 159 F.2d 169 (2d Cir. 1947).

33. Douglas Birsch and John H. Fiedler, *The Ford Pinto Case: A Study in Applied Ethics, Business, and Technology* (Albany: State University of New York, 1994).

34. *Grimshaw v. Ford Motor Co.,* 1 19 Cal.App.3d 757, 174 Cal. Rptr. 348 (1981).

35. David De Cremer and Ann E. Tenbrunsel, *Behavioral Business Ethics: Shaping an Emerging Field* (New York: Routledge, 2012).

36. *General Motors v. Moseley,* 213 Ga. App. 875 (1984).

37. Jay W. Lorsch, "Managing Culture: The Invisible Barrier to Strategic Change," *California Management Review* 28 (1986), pp. 95–109.

38. Cam Caldwell, Linda A. Hayes, and Do Tien Long, "Leadership, Trustworthiness, and Ethical Stewardship," *Journal of Business Ethics* 96 (2010), pp. 497–512.

39. Tamara Kaplan, "The Tylenol Crisis: How Effective Public Relations Saved Johnson & Johnson," Pennsylvania State University. Available here: http://www.aerobiologicalengineering.com/wxk116/TylenolMurders/crisis.html.

40. Katie Thomas, "J. & J. to Pay $2.2 Billion in Risperdal Settlement," November 4, 2013, Available at: http://www.nytimes.com/2013/11/05/business/johnson-johnson-to-settle-risperdal-improper-marketing-case.html.

41. Ed Silverman, "Johnson & Johnson Loses Trial Over Risperdal And Male Breasts," February 24, 2015, Available at: http://blogs.wsj.com/pharmalot/2015/02/24/johnson-johnson-loses-trial-over-risperdal-and-male-breasts/tab/print/.

42. *KPMG Integrity Survey 2013.*

43. Ethics Resource Center (ERC), *2013 National Business Ethics Survey (NBES) of the U.S. Workforce.*

44. Association of Certified Fraud Examiners, *2012 Global Fraud Study: Report to the Nations on Occupational Fraud and Abuse,* www.acfe.com/uploadedFiles/ACFE_Website/Content/rttn/2012-report-to-nations.pdf.

45. ACFE, p. 6.

46. ACFE, p. 57.

47. Center for Audit Quality, *Guide to Internal Control over Financial Reporting,* 2013.

48. Ernst & Young, *Detecting Financial Statement Fraud: What Every Manager Needs to Know,* October 2010, Center for Audit Quality.

168   Chapter 3   Organizational Ethics and Corporate Governance

49. AICPA Professional Standards, *Consideration of Fraud in a Financial Statement Audit* (AU-C Section 240), (NY: AICPA, 2014).

50. Ferrell et al., p. 42.

51. Andrei Shleifer and Robert Vishny, "A Survey of Corporate Governance," *Journal of Finance* (1997).

52. J. E. Parkinson, *Corporate Power and Responsibility* (Oxford, UK: Oxford University Press, 1994).

53. Bob Tricker, *Corporate Governance: Principles, Policies, and Practices,* 3rd ed., (Oxford, UK: Oxford University Press, 2015).

54. Tricker.

55. O.C. Ferrell, John Fraedrich, and Linda Ferrell, *Business Ethics: Ethical Decision Making and Cases* (Stamford, CT: Cengage Learning, 2015, p. 44).

56. W. Steve Albrecht, Conan C. Albrecht, and Chad O. Albrecht, "Fraud and Corporate Executives: Agency, Stewardship, and Broken Trust," *Journal of Forensic Accounting* 5 (2004), pp. 109–130.

57. Lex Donaldson and James H. Davis, "Stewardship Theory," *Australian Journal of Management* 16, no. 1 (June 1991).

58. Michael Jensen and William H. Meckling, "Theory of the Firm: Managerial Behavior, Agency Costs, and Ownership Structure," *Journal of Financial Economics* (1976), pp. 305–360.

59. Chamu Sundaramurthy and Marianne Lewis, "Control and Collaboration: Paradoxes and Government," *Academy of Management Review* 28, Issue 3 (July 2003), pp. 397–416.

60. Tricker, pp. 65–71.

61. Michael Murphy, "Restatements Affect Bottom Line Less Often," *The CFO Journal*, April 21, 2015.

62. John A. Byrne with Louis Lavelle, Nanette Byrnes, Marcia Vickers, and Amy Borrus, "How to Fix Corporate Governance," *BusinessWeek,* May 6, 2002, pp. 69–78.

63. "Current Controversies in Executive Compensation: 'Issues of Justice and Fairness,'" Knowledge@Wharton, May 2, 2007, Available at: http://knowledge.wharton.upenn.edu/article/current-controversies-in-executive-compensation-issues-of-justice-and-fairness/.

64. Dodd-Frank Wall Street Reform and Consumer Protection Act (H.R. 4173), www.sec.gov/about/laws/wallstreetreform-cpa.pdf.

65. Robert E. Scully, Jr. "Executive Compensation, the Business Judgment Rule, and the Dodd-Frank Act: Back to the Future for Private Litigation?" *The Federal Lawyer,* January 2011.

66. Zabihollah Rezaee, *Corporate Governance and Ethics* (New York: Wiley, 2009).

67. Leo L. Strine, Jr., "Derivative Impact? Some Early Reflections on the Corporation Law Implications of the Enron Debacle," *57 Business Lawyer,* 1371, 1373 (2002).

68. *Skilling v. United States,* 561 U.S. 358, 130 S. Ct. 2896, 177 L. Ed. 2d 619, 8 EXC 59 (2010).

69. Committee of Sponsoring Organizations of the Treadway Commission (COSO), 2013 *Internal Control—Integrated Framework,* Report Available at: http://www.coso.org/documents/Internal%20Control-Integrated%20Framework.pdf.

70. Available at: http://www.bloomberg.com/news/articles/2012-04-02/groupon-revisions-highlight-new-model-s-risks.

71. Securities and Exchange Commission, "SEC Charges Company CEO and Former CFO With Hiding Internal Controls Deficiencies and Violating Sarbanes-Oxley Requirements," July 30, 2014.

72. Ethics and Compliance Officer Association (ECOA), www.theecoa.org.

73. Alison Frankel, "Sarbanes-Oxley's Lost Promise: Why CEOs Haven't been Prosecuted," *Reuters.com On the Case* blog, July 27, 2012, Available at: www.blogs.reuters.com/alison-frankel/2012/07/27/sarbanes-oxleys-lost-promise-why-ceos-havent-been-prosecuted/.

74. Janet P. Near and Marcia P. Miceli, "Organizational Dissidence: The Case of Whistle-blowing," *Journal of Business Ethics* 4 (1985), pp. 1–16.

75. Eva Tsahuridu and Wim Vandekerchove, "Organizational Whistleblowing Policies: Making Employees Responsible or Liable?" *Journal of Business Ethics* 82 (2008), pp. 107-118.

76. Alan Wolfe, *Whose Keeper? Social Science and Moral Obligation*(Berkeley, CA: University of California Press, 1991).

77. Immanuel Kant, *Foundations of Metaphysics of Morals*, trans. Lewis White Beck (New York: Liberal Arts Press, 1959), p. 39.

78. Tsahuridu & Vandekerchove, 2008.

79. Marion Mogielnicki, "Hunting for 'Bounty' and Finding 'Moral Autonomy': The Dodd-Frank Act Expansion of Whistle Blower Protections,"*Academy of Business Research*, Vol. 2, (2011), pp. 74-84.

80. Tsahuridu & Vandekerchove, 2008.

81. Miceli and Near, pp. 698-699.

82. Ethics Resource Center (ERC), 2013 National Business Ethics Survey (NBES) of the U.S. Workforce.

83. Tsahuridu & Vandekerchove, 2008.

84. Jesse Eisinger, "The Whistleblower's Tale: How an Accountant took on Halliburton and Won," *Pro Publica,* April 21, 2015.

85. Dodd-Frank Wall Street Reform and Consumer Protection Act (H.R. 4173), www.sec.gov/about/laws/wallstreetreform-cpa.pdf.

86. SEC, "Implementation of the Whistleblower Provisions of Section 21F of the Securities Exchange Act of 1934," Available at: https://www.sec.gov/rules/final/2011/34-64545.pdf.

87. Dodd-Frank Wall Street Reform and Consumer Protection Act (H.R. 4173), www.sec.gov/about/laws/wallstreetreform-cpa.pdf.

88. Kobi Kastiel, "Elements of an Effective Whistleblower Hotline," *Harvard Law School Forum on Corporate Governance and Financial Regulation*, October 25, 2014. Available at: http://corpgov.law.harvard.edu/2014/10/25/elements-of-an-effective-whistleblower-hotline/.

89. SEC, "Implementation of the Whistleblower Provisions of Section 21F of the Securities Exchange Act of 1934," Available at: https://www.sec.gov/rules/final/2011/34-64545.pdf.

90. SEC, "Implementation of the Whistleblower Provisions of Section 21F of the Securities Exchange Act of 1934," Available at: https://www.sec.gov/rules/final/2011/34-64545.pdf.

91. SEC, "Implementation of the Whistleblower Provisions of Section 21F of the Securities Exchange Act of 1934," Available at: https://www.sec.gov/rules/final/2011/34-64545.pdf.

92. AICPA, *Code of Professional Conduct and Bylaws*, June 1, 2011, Available at: https://www.aicpa.org/research/standards/codeofconduct/downloadabledocuments/2011june1codeofprofessionalconduct.pdf

93. Jason Rosenthal, Esq. and Lesley Smith, Esq, "Should CPAs be Financially Rewarded As Whistleblowers?" *CPA Insider*, 2011, Available at: https://www.cpa2biz.com/Content/media/PRODUCER_CONTENT/Newsletters/Articles_2011/CPA/Jul/Whistleblowers.jsp.

94. AICPA, *Code of Professional Conduct and Bylaws*, June 1, 2011, Available at: https://www.aicpa.org/research/standards/codeofconduct/downloadabledocuments/2011june1codeofprofessionalconduct.pdf

95. Eileen Z. Taylor and Jordan A. Thomas, "Enhanced Protections for Whistleblowers under the Dodd-Frank Act," *The CPA Journal* (2013) pp. 66-71.

96. Michael Davis, "Some Paradoxes of Whistleblowing," *Business & Professional Ethics Journal*, Vol. 15, No. 1 (1996), pp.147-155.

97. Richard T. De George, *Business Ethics,* 7th ed. (NY: Prentice-Hall, 2010).

98. Philip Stamatakos and Ted Chung, "Dodd-Frank's Whistleblower Provisions and the SEC's Rule: Compliance and Ethical Considerations," *Corporate Governance Advisor*, September/October 2011.

99. Daniel Hurson, "United States: Ten 'Rules' For Becoming A Successful SEC Whistleblower," September 11, 2013, Available at: http://www.mondaq.com/unitedstates/x/261844/Corporate+Commercial+Law/The+New+Rules+For+Becoming+A+Successful+SEC+Whistleblower.

100. Mark S. Schwartz, "Developing and Sustaining an Ethical Corporate Culture: The Core Elements," *Business Horizons* 56 (2013), pp. 39–50.

101. Arthur P. Brief and Stephan J. Motowidlo, "Prosocial Organizational Behaviors," *The Academy of Management Review*, Vol. 11, No. 4 (Oct., 1986), pp. 710-725.

Chapter 3 Cases

Case 3-1 The Parable of the Sadhu

Bowen H. McCoy

Reprinted with permission from "The Parable of the Sadhu," by Bowen H. McCoy, *Harvard Business Review*. Copyright © Harvard Business Publishing.

Last year, as the first participant in the new six-month sabbatical program that Morgan Stanley has adopted, I enjoyed a rare opportunity to collect my thoughts as well as do some traveling. I spent the first three months in Nepal, walking 600 miles through 200 villages in the Himalayas and climbing some 120,000 vertical feet. My sole Western companion on the trip was an anthropologist who shed light on the cultural patterns of the villages that we passed through.

During the Nepal hike, something occurred that has had a powerful impact on my thinking about corporate ethics. Although some might argue that the experience has no relevance to business, it was a situation in which a basic ethical dilemma suddenly intruded into the lives of a group of individuals. How the group responded holds a lesson for all organizations, no matter how defined.

The Sadhu

The Nepal experience was more rugged than I had anticipated. Most commercial treks last two or three weeks and cover a quarter of the distance we traveled.

My friend Stephen, the anthropologist, and I were halfway through the 60-day Himalayan part of the trip when we reached the high point, an 18,000-foot pass over a crest that we'd have to traverse to reach the village of Muklinath, an ancient holy place for pilgrims.

Six years earlier, I had suffered pulmonary edema, an acute form of altitude sickness, at 16,500 feet in the vicinity of Everest base camp—so we were understandably concerned about what would happen at 18,000 feet. Moreover, the Himalayas were having their wettest spring in 20 years; hip-deep powder and ice had already driven us off one ridge. If we failed to cross the pass, I feared that the last half of our once-in-a-lifetime trip would be ruined.

The night before we would try the pass, we camped in a hut at 14,500 feet. In the photos taken at that camp, my face appears wan. The last village we'd passed through was a sturdy two-day walk below us, and I was tired.

During the late afternoon, four backpackers from New Zealand joined us, and we spent most of the night awake, anticipating the climb. Below, we could see the fires of two other parties, which turned out to be two Swiss couples and a Japanese hiking club.

To get over the steep part of the climb before the sun melted the steps cut in the ice, we departed at 3.30 a.m. The New Zealanders left first, followed by Stephen and myself, our porters and Sherpas, and then the Swiss. The Japanese lingered in their camp. The sky was clear, and we were confident that no spring storm would erupt that day to close the pass.

At 15,500 feet, it looked to me as if Stephen was shuffling and staggering a bit, which are symptoms of altitude sickness. (The initial stage of altitude sickness brings a headache and nausea. As the condition worsens, a climber may encounter difficult breathing, disorientation, aphasia, and paralysis.) I felt strong—my adrenaline was flowing—but I was very concerned about my ultimate ability to get across. A couple of our porters were also suffering from the height, and Pasang, our Sherpa sirdar (leader), was worried.

Just after daybreak, while we rested at 15,500 feet, one of the New Zealanders, who had gone ahead, came staggering down toward us with a body slung across his shoulders. He dumped the almost naked, barefoot body of an Indian holy man—a sadhu—at my feet. He had found the pilgrim lying on the ice, shivering and suffering from hypothermia. I cradled the sadhu's head and laid him out on the rocks. The New Zealander was angry. He wanted to get across the pass before the bright sun melted the snow. He said, "Look, I've done what I can. You have porters and Sherpa guides. You care for him. We're going on!" He turned and went back up the mountain to join his friends.

I took a carotid pulse and found that the sadhu was still alive. We figured he had probably visited the holy shrines at Muklinath and was on his way home. It was fruitless to question why he had chosen this desperately high route instead of the safe, heavily traveled caravan route through the Kali Gandaki gorge. Or why he was shoeless and almost naked, or how long he had been lying in the pass. The answers weren't going to solve our problem.

Stephen and the four Swiss began stripping off their outer clothing and opening their packs. The sadhu was soon clothed from head to foot. He was not able to walk, but he was very much alive. I looked down the mountain and spotted the Japanese climbers, marching up with a horse.

Without a great deal of thought, I told Stephen and Pasang that I was concerned about withstanding the heights to come and wanted to get over the pass. I took off after several of our porters who had gone ahead.

On the steep part of the ascent where, if the ice steps had given way, I would have slid down about 3,000 feet, I felt vertigo. I stopped for a breather, allowing the Swiss to catch up with me. I inquired about the sadhu and Stephen. They said that the sadhu was fine and that Stephen was just behind them. I set off again for the summit.

Stephen arrived at the summit an hour after I did. Still exhilarated by victory, I ran down the slope to congratulate him. He was suffering from altitude sickness—walking 15 steps, then stopping, walking 15 steps, then stopping. Pasang accompanied him all the way up. When I reached them, Stephen glared at me and said, "How do you feel about contributing to the death of a fellow man?"

I did not completely comprehend what he meant. "Is the sadhu dead?" I inquired.

"No," replied Stephen, "but he surely will be!"

After I had gone, followed not long after by the Swiss, Stephen had remained with the sadhu. When the Japanese had arrived, Stephen had asked to use their horse to transport the sadhu down to the hut. They had refused. He had then asked Pasang to have a group of our porters carry the sadhu. Pasang had resisted the idea, saying that the porters would have to exert all their energy to get themselves over the pass. He believed they could not carry a man down 1,000 feet to the hut, reclimb the slope, and get across safely before the snow melted. Pasang had pressed Stephen not to delay any longer.

The Sherpas had carried the sadhu down to a rock in the sun at about 15,000 feet and pointed out the hut another 500 feet below. The Japanese had given him food and drink. When they had last seen him, he was listlessly throwing rocks at the Japanese party's dog, which had frightened him.

We do not know if the sadhu lived or died.

For many of the following days and evenings, Stephen and I discussed and debated our behavior toward the sadhu. Stephen is a committed Quaker with deep moral vision. He said, "I feel that what happened with the sadhu is a good example of the breakdown between the individual ethic and the corporate ethic. No one person was willing to assume ultimate responsibility for the sadhu. Each was willing to do his bit just so long as it was not too inconvenient. When it got to be a bother, everyone just passed the buck to someone else and took off. Jesus was relevant to a more individualistic stage of society, but how do we interpret his teaching today in a world filled with large, impersonal organizations and groups?"

I defended the larger group, saying, "Look, we all cared. We all gave aid and comfort. Everyone did his bit. The New Zealander carried him down below the snow line. I took his pulse and suggested we treat him for hypothermia. You and the Swiss gave him clothing and got him warmed up. The Japanese gave him food and water. The Sherpas carried him down to the sun and pointed out the easy trail toward the hut. He was well enough to throw rocks at a dog. What more could we do?"

"You have just described the typical affluent Westerner's response to a problem. Throwing money—in this case, food and sweaters—at it, but not solving the fundamentals!" Stephen retorted.

"What would satisfy you?" I said. "Here we are, a group of New Zealanders, Swiss, Americans, and Japanese who have never met before and who are at the apex of one of the most powerful experiences of our lives. Some years the pass is so bad no one gets over it. What right does an almost naked pilgrim who chooses the wrong trail have to disrupt our lives? Even the Sherpas had no interest in risking the trip to help him beyond a certain point."

Stephen calmly rebutted, "I wonder what the Sherpas would have done if the sadhu had been a well-dressed Nepali, or what the Japanese would have done if the sadhu had been a well-dressed Asian, or what you would have done, Buzz, if the sadhu had been a well-dressed Western woman?"

"Where, in your opinion," I asked, "is the limit of our responsibility in a situation like this? We had our own well-being to worry about. Our Sherpa guides were unwilling to jeopardize us or the porters for the sadhu. No one else on the mountain was willing to commit himself beyond certain self-imposed limits."

Stephen said, "As individual Christians or people with a Western ethical tradition, we can fulfill our obligations in such a situation only if one, the sadhu dies in our care; two, the sadhu demonstrates to us that he can undertake the two-day walk down to the village; or three, we carry the sadhu for two days down to the village and persuade someone there to care for him."

"Leaving the sadhu in the sun with food and clothing—where he demonstrated hand-eye coordination by throwing a rock at a dog—comes close to fulfilling items one and two," I answered. "And it wouldn't have made sense to take him to the village where the people appeared to be far less caring than the Sherpas, so the third condition is impractical. Are you really saying that, no matter what the implications, we should, at the drop of a hat, have changed our entire plan?"

The Individual versus the Group Ethic

Despite my arguments, I felt and continue to feel guilt about the sadhu. I had literally walked through a classic moral dilemma without fully thinking through the consequences. My excuses for my actions include a high adrenaline flow, a superordinate goal, and a once-in-a-lifetime opportunity—common factors in corporate situations, especially stressful ones.

Real moral dilemmas are ambiguous, and many of us hike right through them, unaware that they exist. When, usually after the fact, someone makes an issue of one, we tend to resent his or her bringing it up. Often, when the full import of what we have done (or not done) hits us, we dig into a defensive position from which it is very difficult to emerge. In rare circumstances, we may contemplate what we have done from inside a prison.

Had we mountaineers been free of stress caused by the effort and the high altitude, we might have treated the sadhu differently. Yet isn't stress the real test of personal and corporate values? The instant decisions that executives make under pressure reveal the most about personal and corporate character.

Among the many questions that occur to me when I ponder my experience with the sadhu are: What are the practical limits of moral imagination and vision? Is there a collective or institutional ethic that differs from the ethics of the individual? At what level of effort or commitment can one discharge one's ethical responsibilities?

Not every ethical dilemma has a right solution. Reasonable people often disagree; otherwise there would be no dilemma. In a business context, however, it is essential that managers agree on a process for dealing with dilemmas.

Our experience with the sadhu offers an interesting parallel to business situations. An immediate response was mandatory. Failure to act was a decision in itself. Up on the mountain, we could not resign and submit our résumés to a headhunter. In contrast to philosophy, business involves action and implementation—getting things done. Managers must come up with answers based on what they see and what they allow to influence their decision-making processes. On the mountain, none of us but Stephen realized the true dimensions of the situation we were facing.

One of our problems was that, as a group, we had no process for developing a consensus. We had no sense of purpose or plan. The difficulties of dealing with the sadhu were so complex that no one person could handle them. Because the group did not have a set of preconditions that could guide its action to an acceptable resolution, we reacted instinctively as individuals. The cross-cultural nature of the group added a further layer of complexity. We had no leader with whom we could all identify and in whose purpose we believed. Only Stephen was willing to take charge, but he could not gain adequate support from the group to care for the sadhu.

Some organizations do have values that transcend the personal values of their managers. Such values, which go beyond profitability, are usually revealed when the organization is under stress. People throughout the organization generally accept its values, which, because they are not presented as a rigid list of commandments, may be somewhat ambiguous. The stories people tell, rather than printed materials, transmit the organization's conceptions of what is proper behavior.

For 20 years, I have been exposed at senior levels to a variety of corporations and organizations. It is amazing how quickly an outsider can sense the tone and style of an organization and, with that, the degree of tolerated openness and freedom to challenge management.

Organizations that do not have a heritage of mutually accepted, shared values tend to become unhinged during stress, with each individual bailing out for himself or herself. In the great takeover battles we have witnessed during past years, companies that had strong cultures drew the wagons around them and fought it out, while other companies saw executives—supported by golden parachutes—bail out of the struggles.

Because corporations and their members are interdependent, for the corporation to be strong, the members need to share a preconceived notion of correct behavior, a "business ethic," and think of it as a positive force, not a constraint.

As an investment banker, I am continually warned by well-meaning lawyers, clients, and associates to be wary of conflicts of interest. Yet if I were to run away from every difficult situation, I wouldn't be an effective investment banker. I have to feel my way through conflicts. An effective manager can't run from risk either; he or she has to confront risk. To feel "safe" in doing that, managers need the guidelines of an agreed-upon process and set of values within the organization.

After my three months in Nepal, I spent three months as an executive-in-residence at both the Stanford Business School and the University of California at Berkeley's Center for Ethics and Social Policy of the Graduate Theological Union. Those six months away from my job gave me time to assimilate 20 years of business experience. My thoughts turned often to the meaning of the leadership role in any large organization. Students at the seminary thought of themselves as antibusiness. But when I questioned them, they agreed that they distrusted all large organizations, including the church. They perceived all large organizations as impersonal and opposed to individual values and needs. Yet we all know of organizations in which people's values and beliefs are respected and their expressions encouraged. What makes the difference? Can we identify the difference and, as a result, manage more effectively?

The word *ethics* turns off many and confuses more. Yet the notions of shared values and an agreed-upon process for dealing with adversity and change—what many people mean when they talk about corporate culture—seem to be at the heart of the ethical issue. People who are in touch with their own core beliefs and the beliefs of others and who are sustained by them can be more comfortable living on the cutting edge. At times, taking a tough line or a decisive stand in a muddle of ambiguity is the only ethical thing to do. If a manager is indecisive about a problem and spends time trying to figure out the "good" thing to do, the enterprise may be lost.

Business ethics, then, has to do with the authenticity and integrity of the enterprise. To be ethical is to follow the business as well as the cultural goals of the corporation, its owners, its employees, and its customers. Those who cannot serve the corporate vision are not authentic businesspeople and, therefore, are not ethical in the business sense.

At this stage of my own business experience, I have a strong interest in organizational behavior. Sociologists are keenly studying what they call corporate stories, legends, and heroes as a way organizations have of transmitting value systems. Corporations such as Arco have even hired consultants to perform an audit of their corporate culture. In a company, a leader is a person who understands, interprets, and manages the corporate value system. Effective managers, therefore, are action-oriented people who resolve conflict, are tolerant of ambiguity, stress, and change, and have a strong sense of purpose for themselves and their organizations.

If all this is true, I wonder about the role of the professional manager who moves from company to company. How can he or she quickly absorb the values and culture of different organizations? Or is there, indeed, an art of management that is totally transportable? Assuming that such fungible managers do exist, is it proper for them to manipulate the values of others?

What would have happened had Stephen and I carried the sadhu for two days back to the village and become involved with the villagers in his care? In four trips to Nepal, my most interesting experience occurred in 1975, when I lived in a Sherpa home in the Khumbu for five days while recovering from altitude sickness. The high point of Stephen's trip was an invitation to participate in a family funeral ceremony in Manang. Neither experience had to do with climbing the high passes of the Himalayas. Why were we so reluctant to try the lower path, the ambiguous trail? Perhaps because we did not have a leader who could reveal the greater purpose of the trip to us.

Why didn't Stephen, with his moral vision, opt to take the sadhu under his personal care? The answer is partly because Stephen was hard-stressed physically himself and partly because, without some support system that encompassed our involuntary and episodic community on the mountain, it was beyond his individual capacity to do so.

I see the current interest in corporate culture and corporate value systems as a positive response to pessimism such as Stephen's about the decline of the role of the individual in large organizations. Individuals who operate from a thoughtful set of personal values provide the foundation for a corporate culture. A corporate tradition that encourages freedom of inquiry, supports personal values, and reinforces a focused sense of direction can fulfill the need to combine individuality with the prosperity and success of the group. Without such corporate support, the individual is lost.

That is the lesson of the sadhu. In a complex corporate situation, the individual requires and deserves the support of the group. When people cannot find such support in their organizations, they don't know how to act. If such support is forthcoming, a person has a stake in the success of the group and can add much to the process of establishing and maintaining a corporate culture. Management's challenge is to be sensitive to individual needs, to shape them, and to direct and focus them for the benefit of the group as a whole.

For each of us, the sadhu lives. Should we stop what we are doing and comfort him, or should we keep trudging up toward the high pass? Should I pause to help the derelict I pass on the street each night as I walk by the Yale Club en route to Grand Central Station? Am I his brother? What is the nature of our responsibility if we consider ourselves to be ethical persons? Perhaps it is to change the values of the group so that it can, with all its resources, take the other road.

Questions

1. Throughout *The Parable of the Sadhu,* Bowen McCoy refers to the breakdown between the individual and corporate ethic. Explain what he meant by that and how, if we view the hikers on the trek up the mountain in Nepal as an organization, the ethical person-organization fit applied to the decisions made on the climb.

2. Using the various ethical discussions in the first three chapters as your guide, evaluate the actions of McCoy, Stephen, and the rest of the group from an ethical perspective.

3. What role did leadership and culture play in this case?

4. What is the moral of the story of the sadhu from your perspective?

Case 3-2 Rite Aid Inventory Surplus Fraud

Occupational fraud comes in many shapes and sizes. The fraud at Rite Aid is one such case. On February 10, 2015, the U.S. Attorney's Office for the Middle District of Pennsylvania announced that a former Rite Aid vice president, Jay Findling, pleaded guilty to charges in connection with a $29.1 million dollar surplus inventory sales/kickback scheme. Another former vice president, Timothy P. Foster, pleaded guilty to the same charges and making false statements to the authorities. Both charges are punishable by up to five years' imprisonment and a $250,000 fine.

The charges relate to a nine-year conspiracy to defraud Rite Aid by lying to the company about the sale of surplus inventory to a company owned by Findling when it was sold to third parties for greater amounts. Findling would then kick back a portion of his profits to Foster.

Findling admitted he established a bank account under the name "Rite Aid Salvage Liquidation" and used it to collect the payments from the real buyers of the surplus Rite Aid inventory. After the payments were received,

Findling would send lesser amounts dictated by Foster to Rite Aid for the goods, thus inducing Rite Aid to believe the inventory had been purchased by J. Finn Industries, not the real buyers. The government alleged Findling received at least $127.7 million from the real buyers of the surplus inventory but, with Foster's help, only provided $98.6 million of that amount to Rite Aid, leaving Findling approximately $29.1 million in profits from the scheme. The government also alleged that Findling kicked back approximately $5.7 million of the $29.1 million to Foster.

Foster admitted his role during the guilty plea stage of the trial. He voluntarily surrendered $2.9 million in cash he had received from Findling over the life of the conspiracy. Foster had stored the cash in three 5-gallon paint containers in his Phoenix, Arizona, garage.

Assume you are the director of internal auditing at Rite Aid and discover the surplus inventory scheme. You know that Rite Aid has a comprehensive corporate governance system that complies with the requirements of Sarbanes-Oxley and the company has a strong ethics foundation. Moreover, the internal controls are consistent with the COSO framework. Explain the steps you would take to determine whether you would blow the whistle on the scheme applying the requirements of AICPA Interpretation 102-4 that are depicted in Exhibit 3.13. In that regard, answer the following questions.

Questions

1. What steps must you take to be eligible to blow the whistle to the SEC under the Dodd-Frank Financial Reform Act?

2. Would you inform the external auditors about the fraud? Explain.

3. Assume you met all the requirements to blow the whistle under Dodd-Frank. Would you do so? Why or why not?

Case 3-3 United Thermostatic Controls (a GVV case)

United Thermostatic Controls is a publicly owned company that engages in the manufacturing and marketing of residential and commercial thermostats. The thermostats are used to regulate temperature in furnaces and refrigerators. United sells its product primarily to retailers in the domestic market, with the company headquartered in Detroit. Its operations are decentralized according to geographic region. As a publicly owned company, United's common stock is listed and traded on the NYSE. The organization chart for United is presented in Exhibit 1.

EXHIBIT 1   United Thermostatic Controls Organization Chart

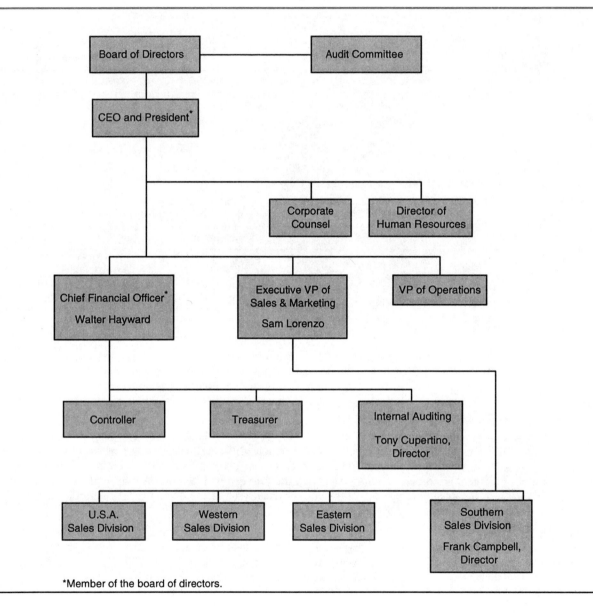

*Member of the board of directors.

Frank Campbell is the director of the Southern sales division. Worsening regional economic conditions and a reduced rate of demand for United's products have created pressures to achieve sales revenue targets set by United management nonetheless. Also, significant pressures exist within the organization for sales divisions to maximize their revenues and earnings for 2015 in anticipation of a public offering of stock early in 2016. Budgeted and actual sales revenue amounts, by division, for the first three quarters in 2015 are presented in Exhibit 2.

EXHIBIT 2   United Thermostatic Controls—Sales Revenue, 2015 (1st 3Qs)

Budgeted and Actual Sales Revenue
First Three Quarters in 2015

	U.S.A. Sales Division			Western Sales Division		
Quarter Ended	Budget	Actual	% Var.	Budget	Actual	% Var.
March 31	$ 632,000	$ 638,000	.009%	$ 886,000	$ 898,000	.014%
June 30	640,000	642,000	.003	908,000	918,000	.011
September 30	648,000	656,000	.012	930,000	936,000	.006
Through September 30	$1,920,000	$1,936,000	.008%	$2,724,000	$2,752,000	.010%

	Eastern Sales Division			Southern Sales Division		
Quarter Ended	Budget	Actual	% Var.	Budget	Actual	% Var.
March 31	$ 743,000	$ 750,000	.009%	$ 688,000	$ 680,000	(.012)%
June 30	752,000	760,000	.011	696,000	674,000	(.032)
September 30	761,000	769,000	.011	704,000	668,000	(.051)
Through September 30	$2,256,000	$2,279,000	.010%	$2,088,000	$2,022,000	(.032)%

Campbell knows that actual sales lagged even further behind budgeted sales during the first two months of the fourth quarter. He also knows that each of the other three sales divisions exceeded their budgeted sales amounts during the first three quarters in 2015. He is very concerned that the Southern division has been unable to meet or exceed budgeted sales amounts. He is particularly worried about the effect this might have on his and the division managers' bonuses and share of corporate profits.

In an attempt to improve the sales revenue of the Southern division for the fourth quarter and for the year ended December 31, 2015, Campbell reviewed purchase orders received during the latter half of November and early December to determine whether shipments could be made to customers prior to December 31. Campbell knows that sometimes orders that are received before the end of the year can be filled by December 31, thereby enabling the division to record the sales revenue during the current fiscal year. It could simply be a matter of accelerating production and shipping to increase sales revenue for the year.

Reported sales revenue of the Southern division for the fourth quarter of 2015 was $792,000. This represented an 18.6 percent increase over the actual sales revenue for the third quarter of the year. As a result of this increase, reported sales revenue for the fourth quarter exceeded the budgeted amount by $80,000, or 11.2 percent. Actual sales revenue for the year exceeded the budgeted amount for the Southern division by $14,000, or 0.5 percent. Budgeted and actual sales revenue amounts, by division, for the year ended December 31, 2015, are presented in Exhibit 3.

During the course of their test of controls, the internal audit staff questioned the appropriateness of recording revenue of $150,000 on two shipments made by the Southern division in the fourth quarter of the year. These shipments are described as follows:

1. United shipped thermostats to Allen Corporation on December 31, 2015, and billed Allen $85,000, even though Allen had specified a delivery date of no earlier than February 1, 2016, to take control of the product. Allen intended to use the thermostats in the heating system of a new building that would not be ready for occupancy until March 1, 2016.

2. United shipped thermostats to Bilco Corporation on December 30, 2015, in partial (one-half) fulfillment of an order. United recorded $65,000 revenue on that date. Bilco had previously specified that partial shipments would not be accepted. Delivery of the full shipment had been scheduled for February 1, 2016.

EXHIBIT 3   United Thermostatic Controls—Sales Revenue, 2015 (4 Qs)

| | Budgeted and Actual Sales Revenue in 2015 | | | | | |
| | U.S.A. Sales Division | | | Western Sales Division | | |
Quarter Ended	Budget	Actual	% Var.	Budget	Actual	% Var.
March 31	$ 632,000	$ 638,000	.009%	$ 886,000	$ 898,000	.014%
June 30	640,000	642,000	.003	908,000	918,000	.011
September 30	648,000	656,000	.012	930,000	936,000	.006
December 31	656,000	662,000	.009	952,000	958,000	.006
2015 Totals	$2,576,000	$2,598,000	.009%	$3,676,000	$3,710,000	.009%

| | Eastern Sales Division | | | Southern Sales Division | | |
Quarter Ended	Budget	Actual	% Var.	Budget	Actual	% Var.
March 31	$ 743,000	$ 750,000	.009%	$ 688,000	$ 680,000	(.012)%
June 30	752,000	760,000	.011	696,000	674,000	(.032)
September 30	761,000	769,000	.011	704,000	668,000	(.051)
December 31	770,000	778,000	.010	712,000	792,000	.112
2015 Totals	$3,026,000	$3,057,000	.010%	$2,800,000	$2,814,000	.005%

During their investigation, the internal auditors learned that Campbell had pressured United's accounting department to record these two shipments early to enable the Southern division to achieve its goals with respect to the company's revenue targets. The auditors were concerned about the appropriateness of recording the $150,000 revenue in 2015 in the absence of an expressed or implied agreement with the customers to accept and pay for the prematurely shipped merchandise. The auditors noted that, had the revenue from these two shipments not been recorded, the Southern division's actual sales for the fourth quarter would have been below the budgeted amount by $70,000, or 9.8 percent. Actual sales revenue for the year ended December 31, 2015, would have been below the budgeted amount by $136,000, or 4.9 percent. The revenue effect of the two shipments in question created a 5.4 percent shift in the variance between actual and budgeted sales for the year. The auditors felt that this effect was significant with respect to the division's revenue and earnings for the fourth quarter and for the year ended December 31, 2015. The auditors decided to take their concerns to Tony Cupertino, director of the internal auditing department. Cupertino is a licensed CPA.

Cupertino discussed the situation with Campbell. Campbell informed Cupertino that he had received assurances from Sam Lorenzo, executive vice president of sales and marketing, that top management would support the recording of the $150,000 revenue because of its strong desire to meet or exceed budgeted revenue and earnings amounts. Moreover, top management is very sensitive to the need to meet financial analysts' consensus earnings estimates. According to Campbell, the company is concerned that earnings must be high enough to meet analysts' expectations because any other effect might cause the stock price to go down. In fact, Lorenzo has already told Campbell that he did not see anything wrong with recording the revenue in 2015 because the merchandise had been shipped to the customers before the end of the year and the terms of shipment were FOB shipping point.

At this point, Cupertino is uncertain whether he should take his concerns to Walter Hayward, the CFO, who is also a member of the board of directors, or take them directly to the audit committee. Cupertino knows that the majority of the members of the board, including those on the audit committee, have ties to the company and members of top management. Cupertino is not even certain that he should pursue the matter any further because of the financial performance pressures that exist within the organization. However, he is very concerned about his responsibilities as a CPA and obligations to work with the external auditors who will begin their audit in a few weeks. It is at this point that Cupertino learns from Campbell that the CFO of Bilco agreed to accept full shipment when the goods arrive in return for a 20 percent discount on the total price that would be paid on February 1, 2016. Cupertino asked Campbell how he had found out. It seems Campbell took the initiative to help solve the revenue problem by going directly to the Bilco CFO.

Questions

1. Identify the stakeholders in this case and their interests.
2. Describe the ethical and professional responsibilities of Tony Cupertino.
3. Assume you are in Cupertino's position and know you have to do something about the improper accounting in the Southern sales division. Consider the following in crafting a plan how best to voice your values and take appropriate action:

   - How can you get it done effectively and efficiently?
   - What do you need to say, to whom, and in what sequence?
   - What will the objections or pushback be, and then,
   - What would you say next? What data and other information do you need to make your point and counteract the reasons and rationalizations you will likely have to address?

Case 3-4 Franklin Industries' Whistleblowing (a GVV Case)

Natalie got the call she had been waiting for over six long months. Her complaint to the human resources department of Franklin Industries had been dismissed. It was HR's conclusion that she was not retaliated against for reporting an alleged embezzlement by the Accounting Department manager. In fact, HR ruled there was no embezzlement at all. Natalie had been demoted from assistant manager of the department to staff supervisor seven months ago after informing Stuart Masters, the controller, earlier in 2015, about the embezzlement. Her blood started to boil as she thought about all the pain and agony she'd experienced these past six months without any level of satisfaction for her troubles.

Natalie Garson is a CPA who works for Franklin Industries, a publicly owned company and manufacturer of trusses and other structural components for home builders throughout the United States. Six months ago she filed a complaint with HR after discussing a sensitive matter with her best friend and coworker, Roger Harris. Natalie trusted Harris, who had six years of experience at Franklin. The essence of the discussion was that Natalie was informed by the accounting staff of what appeared to be unusual transactions between Denny King, the department manager, and an outside company no one had never heard of before. The staff had uncovered over $5 million in payments, authorized by King, to Vic Construction. No one could find any documentation about Vic, so the staff dug deeper and discovered that the owner of Vic Construction was Victoria King. Further examination determined that Victoria King and Denny King were siblings.

Once Natalie was convinced there was more to the situation than meets the eye, she informed the internal auditors, who investigated and found that Vic Construction made a $5 million electronic transfer to a separate business owned by Denny King. One thing lead to another, and it was determined by the internal auditors that King had funneled $5 million to Vic Construction, which, at a later date, transferred the money back to King. It was a $5 million embezzlement from Franklin Industries.

Natalie met with Roger Harris that night and told him about the HR decision that went against her. She was concerned whether the internal auditors would act now in light of that decision She knew the culture at Franklin was "don't rock the boat." That didn't matter to her. She was always true to her values and not afraid to act when a wrongdoing had occurred. She felt particularly motivated in this case—it was personal. She felt the need to be vindicated. She hoped Roger would be supportive.

As it turned out, Roger cautioned Natalie about taking the matter any further. He had worked for Franklin a lot longer than Natalie and knew the board of directors consisted mostly of insider directors. The CEO of Franklin was also the chair of the board. It was well known in the company that whatever the CEO wanted to do, the board rubber-stamped it.

Natalie left the meeting with Roger realizing she was on her own. She knew she had to act but didn't know the best way to go about it. Even though Roger cautioned against going to the CEO or board, Natalie didn't dismiss that option.

Questions

Assume you are in Natalie's position. Answer the following questions.

1. Consider the following assuming you have decided to act on your values:

   - What are the main arguments you are trying to counter? That is, what are the reasons and rationalizations you need to address?
   - What is at stake for the key parties, including those who disagree with you?
   - What levers can you use to influence those who disagree with you?
   - What is your most powerful and persuasive response to the reasons and rationalizations you need to address? To whom should the argument be made? When and in what context?

2. Assume you decide not to follow the script outlined in question 1 to bring the matter to the attention of others in the organization for fear of being fired. Do you think you have sufficient standing to file a whistleblower claim with the SEC under the Dodd-Frank Act? Explain.

Case 3-5 Walmart Inventory Shrinkage (a GVV Case)

The facts of this case are from the Walmart shrinkage fraud discussed in an article in *The Nation* on June 11, 2014. "Literary license" has been exercised for the purpose of emphasizing important issues related to organizational ethics at Walmart. Any resemblance to actual people and events is coincidental.[1]

Shane O'Hara always tried to do the right thing. He was in touch with his values and always tried to act in accordance with them, even when the going got tough. But, nothing prepared him for the ordeal he would face as a Walmart veteran and the new store manager in Atomic City, Idaho.

In 2013, Shane was contacted by Jeffrey Cook, the regional manager, and told he was being transferred to the Atomic City store in order to reduce the troubled store's high rate of "shrinkage"—defined as the value of goods that are stolen or otherwise lost—to levels deemed acceptable by the company's senior managers for the region. As a result of fierce competition, profit margins in retail can be razor thin, making shrinkage a potent—sometimes critical—factor in profitability. Historically, Walmart had a relatively low rate of about 0.8 percent of sales. The industry average was 1 percent.

Prior to his arrival at the Atomic City store, Shane had heard the store had shrinkage losses as high as $2 million or more—a sizable hit to its bottom line. There had even been talk of closing the store altogether. He knew the pressure was on to keep the store open, save the jobs of 40 people, and cut losses so that the regional manager could earn a bonus. It didn't hurt that he would qualify for a bonus as well, so long as the shrinkage rate was cut by more than two-thirds.

Shane did what he could to tighten systems and controls. He managed to convince Cook to hire an "asset-protection manager" for the store. The asset-protection program handles shrink, safety, and security at each of its stores. The program worked. Not only did shrinkage decline but other forms of loss, including changing price tags on items of clothing, were significantly reduced.

However, it didn't seem to be enough to satisfy Cook and top management. During the last days of August 2013, Shane's annual inventory audit showed a massive reduction in the store's shrinkage rate that surprised even him:

[1]Spencer Woodman, "Former Managers Allege Pervasive Inventory Fraud at Walmart: How Deep Does the Rot Go?" *The Nation*, June 11, 2014.

down to less than $80,000 from roughly $800,000 the previous year. He had no explanation for it, but was sure the numbers had been doctored in some way.

During the remainder of 2013, a number of high-level managers departed from the company. Cindy Rondel, the head of Walmart's Idaho operations, retired; so did her superior, Larry Brooks. Walmart's regional asset-protection manager for Idaho, who was intimately involved with inventory tracking in the state, was fired as well. Shane wondered if he was next.

Shane decided to contact Cook to discuss his concerns. Cook explained why the shrinkage rate had shrunk so much by passing it off as improper accounting at the Atomic City store that had been corrected. He told Shane that an investigation would begin immediately and he was suspended with pay until it was completed. Shane was in shock. He knew the allegations weren't true. He sensed he might become the fall guy for the fraud.

Shane managed to discretely talk about his situation with another store manager in the Atomic City area. That manager said she had been the target of a similar investigation the year before. In her case, she had discovered how the fraud was carried out and the numbers were doctored, but she had told no one—until now.

She explained to Shane that the fraud involved simply declaring that missing items were not in fact missing. She went on to say you could count clothing items in the store and if the on-hand count was off—as in, you were supposed to have 12 but you only had 10—you could explain that the other 2 were in a bin where clothing had been tried on by customers, not bought, and left in the dressing room often with creases that had to be cleaned before re-tagging the clothing for sale. So, even though some items may have been stolen, they were still counted as part of inventory. There was little or no shrinkage to account for.

At this point Shane did not know what his next step should be. He needed to protect his good name and reputation. But what steps should he take? That was the question.

Questions

Assume you are in Shane O'Hara's position. Answer the following questions.

1. Who are the stakeholders in this case and what are the ethical issues?
2. What would you do next and why? Consider the following in crafting your response.

  - How should the organizational culture at Walmart influence your actions?
  - What do you need to say, to whom, and in what sequence?
  - What are the reasons and rationalizations you are likely to hear from those who would try to detract you from your goal?
  - How can you counteract those pressures? What is your most powerful and persuasive response to these arguments? To whom should you make them? When and in what context?

Case 3-6 Bennie and the Jets (a GVV Case)

Bennie Gordon graduated with a master's in accounting two years ago and now works as an accounting manager at the division level at Jet Energy Company, a company headquartered in Winston-Salem, North Carolina. Jet Energy is a utility company regulated by the state and provides electricity to 7 million customers in southern states. Jet Energy is allowed a maximum rate of return on operating income of 12.5 percent on electricity it sells. If the company is earning more than that, regulators can cut the rate that it charges its customers.

Gordon reports to Sarah Higgins, the controller of the division. Higgins reports to Sam Thornton, the chief financial officer. Thornton reports to Vanessa Jones, the CEO of the company. Joan Franks is the chief compliance officer. The company has an audit committee of three members, all of whom sit on the board of directors.

Gordon has identified irregular accounting entries dealing with the reclassification of some accounting items to make the company's returns lower so state regulators would not cut rates. One example is that Jet Energy often gets rebates from insurers of its nuclear plants, based on safety records. Although the cost of the premiums is expensed to the electricity business, the rebates—approximately $26 million to $30.5 million each—were not booked back to the same accounts. On a number of occasions, they were booked below operating income in a non-operating account. The moves kept Jet Energy from exceeding its allowable returns and kept the states from reducing electricity rates.

After two years of being silent, Gordon decided it was time to address the issue. He knows his options include to report the matter to top management and/or the North Carolina Utilities Commission.

Questions

1. What process would you recommend Bennie Gordon follow in bringing his concerns out in the open? Do these include whistleblowing?

2. Assume you are Bennie's best friend and he asks you for advice. Consider the following in putting together a plan of action for Bennie to follow.

   - What are the ethical values that should be front and center in deciding how best to advise Bennie on what to do?
   - What reasons and rationalizations do you anticipate may be lodged by stakeholders based on the advice you might give? How would you counter them?
   - What levers can Bennie use to influence those that might disagree with him?
   - What is your final advice to Bennie and why?

Case 3-7 Olympus

Summary of the Case *

On September 25, 2012, Japanese camera and medical equipment maker Olympus Corporation and three of its former executives pleaded guilty to charges related to an accounting scheme and cover-up in one of Japan's biggest corporate scandals. Olympus admitted that it tried to conceal investment losses by using improper accounting under a scheme that began in the 1990s.

The scandal was exposed in 2011 by Olympus's then-CEO, Michael C. Woodford. As the new president of Olympus, he felt obliged to investigate the matter and uncovered accounting irregularities and suspicious deals involving the acquisition of U.K. medical equipment manufacturer Gyrus. He called the company's auditors, PwC, to report it. The firm examined payments of £1.1 billion (US$687) related to financial advice on the acquisition paid to a non-existent Cayman Islands firm. A fraud of $1.7 billion emerged, including an accounting scandal to hide the losses. Along the way, the Japanese way of doing business came under attack by Woodford.

Olympus initially said that it fired Woodford, one of a handful of foreign executives at top Japanese companies, over what it called his aggressive Western management style. Woodford disclosed internal documents to show he was dismissed after he raised questions about irregular payouts related to mergers and acquisitions. Without any serious attempt by management to investigate, he went behind the board's back and commissioned a report by PwC into the Gyrus deal, including the unusually high advisory fee and apparent lack of due diligence. On October 11, 2011, he circulated the report to the board and called on the chair of the board, Tsuyoshi Kikukawa, and executive vice president Hisashi Mori to resign. Three days later, the board fired Woodford.

Ultimately, the accounting fraud was investigated by the Japanese authorities. "The full responsibility lies with me, and I feel deeply sorry for causing trouble to our business partners, shareholders, and the wider public," Kikukawa told the Tokyo district court. "I take full responsibility for what happened."

---

* The facts of this case are drawn from: Michael Woodford, *Exposure: Inside the Olympus Scandal: How I Went from CEO to Whistleblower* (NY: Penguin Books, 2012).

Prosecutors charged Kikukawa, Mori, and a former internal auditor, Hideo Yamada, with inflating the company's net worth in financial statements for five fiscal years up to March 2011 due to accounting for risky investments made in the late-1980s bubble economy. The three former executives had been identified by an investigative panel, commissioned by Olympus, as the main suspects in the fraud. In December 2011, Olympus filed five years' worth of corrected financial statements plus overdue first-half results, revealing a $1.1 billion hole in its balance sheet.

An Olympus spokesman said the company would cooperate fully with the investigative authorities. It is under investigation by law enforcement agencies in Japan, Britain, and the United States. On April 2, 2015, Olympus reached an ¥11 billion ($92 million) out-of-court settlement in Japan with institutional investors over allegations of accounting fraud.

Olympus Spent Huge Sums on Inflated Acquisitions, Advisory Fees to Conceal Investment Losses

Olympus's cover-up of massive losses has shed light on several murky methods that some companies employed to clean up the mess left after Japan's economic bubble burst. Many companies turned to speculative investments as they suffered sluggish sales and stagnant operating profits. The company used "loss-deferring practices" to make losses look smaller on the books by selling bad assets to related companies.

To take investment losses off its books, Olympus spent large sums of money to purchase British medical equipment maker Gyrus Group PLC and three Japanese companies and paid huge consulting fees. Olympus is suspected of having deliberately acquired Gyrus at an inflated price, and in the year following the purchase, it booked impairment losses as a result of decreases in the company's value.

To avert a rapid deterioration of its financial standing, Olympus continued corporate acquisitions and other measures for many years, booking impairment losses to improve its balance sheet. Losses on the purchases of the three Japanese companies amounted to $34.5 billion. With money paid on the Gyrus deal included, Olympus may have used more than $62.5 billion in funds for past acquisitions to conceal losses on securities investments.

The previous method that recorded stocks and other financial products by book value—the price when they were purchased—was abolished. The new method listed them by market value (mark-to-market accounting). Under this change, Olympus had to report all the losses in its March 2001 report. However, Olympus anticipated this change a year in advance and posted only about $10.6 billion of the nearly $62.5 billion as an extraordinary loss for the March 2000 settlement term. The company did not post the remainder as a deficit; rather, it deferred it using questionable measures.

Olympus's Tobashi Scheme

At the heart of Olympus's action was a once-common technique to hide losses called *tobashi*, which Japanese financial regulators tolerated before clamping down on the practice in the late 1990s. *Tobashi*, translated loosely as "to blow away," enables companies to hide losses on bad assets by selling those assets to other companies, only to buy them back later through payments, often disguised as advisory fees or other transactions, when market conditions or earnings improve.

Tobashi allows a company with the bad assets to mask losses temporarily, a practice banned in the early 2000s. The idea is that you pay off the losses later, when company finances are better.

Olympus appears to have pushed to settle its *tobashi* amounts from 2006 to 2008, when the local economy was picking up and corporate profits were rebounding, in an effort to "clean up its act." Business was finally strong enough to be able to withstand a write-down. It was during those years that the company engineered the payouts that came under scrutiny: $687 million in fees to an obscure financial adviser over Olympus's acquisition of Gyrus in 2008, a fee that was roughly a third of the $2 billion acquisition price, more than 30 times the norm. Olympus also acquired three small Japanese companies from 2006 to 2008 with little in common with its core business for a total of $773 million, only to write down most of their value within the same fiscal year.

Olympus Scandal Raises Questions about the "Japan Way" of Doing Business

The scandal rocked corporate Japan, not least because of the company's succession of firings, denials, admissions, and whistleblowing. It also exposed weaknesses in Japan's financial regulatory system and corporate governance.

"This is a case where Japan's outmoded practice of corporate governance remained and reared its ugly head," according to Shuhei Abe, president of Tokyo-based Sparx Group Company. "With Olympus's case, it will no longer be justifiable for Japan Inc. to continue practicing under the excuse of the 'Japan way of doing things.'"

On the surface, Olympus seemed to have checks on its management. For example, it hired directors and auditors from outside the company, as well as a British president who was not tied to corporate insiders. In reality, however, the company's management was ruled by former chairman Kikukawa and a few other executives who came from its financial sections.

The company's management is believed to have been effectively controlled by several executives who had a background in financial affairs, including Kikukawa and Mori, both of whom were involved in the cover-up of past losses. Olympus's board of auditors, which is supposed to supervise the board of directors, included full-time auditor Hideo Yamada, who also had financial expertise.

After Woodford made his allegations, he was confronted by a hostile board of directors that acted based on the premise that whistleblowing offended their corporate culture. Subsequently, the board fired him saying that he had left because of "differences in management styles." Employees were warned not to speak to him or jeopardize their careers.

One problem with corporate governance in Japan is truly independent non-executive directors are unusual. Many Japanese do not see the need for such outside intervention. They question how outsiders can know enough about the company to make a valuable contribution. Moreover, how could they be sensitive to the corporate culture? They could even damage the credibility of the group.

Accounting Explanations

Olympus hid a $1.7 billion loss through an intricate array of transactions.

A one-paragraph summary of what it did appears in the investigation report:

> The lost disposition scheme is featured in that Olympus sold the assets that incurred loss to the funds set up by Olympus itself, and later provided the finance needed to settle the loss under the cover of the company acquisitions. More specifically, Olympus circulated money either by flowing money into the funds by acquiring the entrepreneurial ventures owned by the funds at the substantially higher price than the real values, or by paying a substantially high fee to the third party who acted as the intermediate in the acquisition, resulting in recognition of a large amount of goodwill, and subsequently amortized goodwill recognized impairment loss, which created substantial loss.

Here is a more understandable version of the event:

> Olympus indirectly loaned money to an off-the-books subsidiary and then sold the investments that had the huge losses to the subsidiary at historical cost, eventually paying a huge premium to buy some other small companies and writing off the underwater investments as if they were goodwill impairments.

A more detailed bookkeeping analysis of the complicated transactions appears in Exhibit 1.

Auditor Responsibilities

Arthur Andersen was the external auditor through March 31, 2002, after which Andersen closed its doors for good in the post-Enron era. Then KPMG AZSA LLC was the auditor through March 31, 2009. The 2010 and 2011 fiscal years were audited by Ernst & Young ShinNihon LLC.

The investigative report noted that the fraud was hidden quite well. Three banks were involved in hiding information from the auditors. The summary report said that all three of them agreed not to tell auditors the information that would normally be provided on an audit confirmation.

KPMG did come across one of the *tobashi* schemes carried out through one of the three different routes that had been set up. According to the investigative report:

Not everything was going smoothly. The report said that in 1999, Olympus's then-auditor, KPMG AZSA LLC, came across information that indicated the company was engaged in *tobashi*, which recently had become illegal in

Japan. Mori and Yamada initially denied KPMG's assertion, but the auditor pushed them that same year to admit to the presence of one fund and unwind it, booking a loss of $10.5 billion. The executives assured KPMG that that was the only such deal, the report said. However, the schemes expanded, without detection, for another six years or so and was in place, without detection, until the last component was unwound at the end of fiscal year 2010.

Olympus Finally Had Enough of the Deception

The last part of the bad investments was finally written off in March 2011. That was the last month of the fiscal year, when Ernst & Young took over the audit from KPMG. Mori and Yamada had finally decided to unwind and write off the underwater financial assets and repay the loans that Olympus had made through its unconsolidated subsidiary. Of course, by then, the financial press had gotten wind of what was going on at Olympus.

EXHIBIT 1   Detailed Bookkeeping Analysis of Olympus's Accounting Fraud*

PHASE 1

Transaction 1:

This is a summary of a complex move—it involved purchasing a certificate of deposit (CD) at several banks that were asked to loan the money back to an unrelated entity, with the CD as collateral, so the subsidiary can buy investments from Olympus.

Note: According to the investigative committee's report, three banks were involved through the course of the whole project: Commerzbank, LGT, and Société Générale. The committee's report indicates that all three banks agreed to Olympus's request not to tell the auditors about the CDs being collateral for a loan.

(Olympus books)

DR Certificate of deposit
CR Cash
    (CD purchase at banks; banks loan it to unconsolidated subsidiary)

(Unconsolidated subsidiary books)

DR Cash
CR Note payable to banks
    (Cash from banks; collateralized by Olympus)

Transaction 2:

(Olympus books)

DR Cash
CR Financial assets (Investments)
    (Proceeds from selling underwater investments to unconsolidated subsidiary; may have triggered gain on sale)

(Unconsolidated subsidiary books)

DR Financial assets (Investments)
CR Cash
    (To buy underwater investments from Olympus)

PHASE 2

Eventually the CDs would have to be rolled over and brought back. In addition, the unrealized losses would have to be written down eventually, so the second phase was launched.

*"Olympus Scandal: $1.5 billion in Losses Hidden in Dodgy Acquisitions," Available at http://factsanddetails.com/japan.php?itemid=2305&catid=24&subcatid=157.

(Continued)

Transaction 3:

Olympus bought some tiny (startup) companies. It paid significantly more than they were worth and paid large amounts for consultants for their service as finders and intermediaries.

(Olympus books)
DR Investments (startup subsidiary)
DR Goodwill—(cash paid less fair market value of subsidiary net assets)
CR Cash
   (Investments in new subsidiaries)

Note: The investment in the consolidated subsidiary shows a large amount of goodwill, which could then be written down.

(Entries by the newly formed consolidated subsidiary)
DR Cash
CR Common stock
   (Cash investment from Olympus)

Transaction 4:

The effect of these transactions was to transfer money into the newest consolidated subsidiary, which used the money to buy the bad investments from the older, unconsolidated subsidiary. The unconsolidated subsidiary then repaid the note payable to the bank and Olympus liquidated its CD.

(Entries by the newly formed consolidated subsidiary)
DR Financial assets (Investments)
CR Cash
   (Buy underwater investments from unconsolidated subsidiary at book value)

(Unconsolidated subsidiary books)

DR Cash (from consolidated subsidiary)
CR Financial assets (Investments)
   (Proceeds received from consolidated subsidiary from sale of underwater investments)
DR Note payable to banks
CR Cash
   (Repay loan to banks)

Entries by Olympus
DR Cash
CR Certificate of deposit
   (CD liquidated)

Questions

1. Does it seem reasonable that Olympus engaged in an accounting fraud for so long and the auditors did not detect it? Were the transactions in question and accounting for them something that should have been detected earlier through proper auditing procedures? What caused the failure of the auditors to act on the fraud? Explain.

2. Evaluate the corporate culture at Olympus including corporate governance. What were the shortcomings and what do you think caused them?

3. Do you believe Michael Woodford did the right thing by blowing the whistle on accounting irregularities? Were there other options open to him? Once he was fired, could he have made a whistleblower's claim with the SEC under Dodd-Frank? Why or why not?

Case 3-8 Accountant takes on Halliburton and Wins!

The whistleblowing aspects of this case were first discussed in the text. What follows is a more comprehensive discussion of accounting and auditing issues.

In 2005, Tony Menendez, a former Ernst & Young LLP auditor and director of technical accounting and research training for Halliburton, blew the whistle on Halliburton's accounting practices. The fight cost him nine years of his life. Just a few months later in 2005, Menendez received an e-mail from Mark McCollum, Halliburton's chief accounting officer, and a top-ranking executive at Halliburton, that also went to much of the accounting department. "The SEC has opened an inquiry into the allegations of Mr. Menendez," it read. Everyone was to retain their documents until further notice.

What happened next changed the life of Menendez and brought into question how such a large and influential company could have such a failed corporate governance system. Further, the role of the auditors, KPMG, with respect to its handling of accounting and auditing matters, seemed off, and independence was an issue. Exhibit 1 summarizes some of the relevant accounting and auditing issues in the case.

EXHIBIT 1   Issues Related to the Sarbanes-Oxley Act, SEC, and KPMG

Tony Menendez contacted Halliburton's audit committee because he believed it was in the best interest of the employees and shareholders if he made himself available to the committee in its efforts to investigate the questionable accounting and auditing practices and properly respond to the SEC. It was discovered that Halliburton did not have in place, as required by Section 301 of the Sarbanes-Oxley Act (SOX), a process for "(1) the receipt and treatment of complaints received by the issuer regarding accounting, internal controls, or auditing matters; and (2) the confidential, anonymous submission of employees of the issuer of concerns regarding questionable accounting or auditing matters."

After waiting for the company to take action to no avail, Menendez felt there was no alternative to blowing the whistle and on November 4, 2005, he contacted the SEC and PCAOB stating in part:

"As a CPA and the Director of Technical Accounting Research and Training for Halliburton, I feel it is my duty and obligation to report information that I believe constitutes both a potential failure by a registered public accounting firm, KPMG, to properly perform an audit and the potential filing of materially misleading financial information with the SEC by Halliburton."

Two weeks later, at the agencies' request, he met with SEC enforcement staff at their Fort Worth office. On November 30, 2005, he approached members of top management of Halliburton. On February 4, 2006, Menendez provided what he believed would be a confidential report to Halliburton's audit committee, giving the company yet another opportunity for self-examination. However, on the morning of February 6, 2006, Menendez's identity was disclosed to Mark McCollum, Halliburton's chief accounting officer, and less than an hour after finding out that Menendez had reported the questionable accounting and auditing practices to the SEC, McCollum distributed information about Menendez's investigation and identity.

The disclosure was followed by a series of retaliatory actions. Halliburton management stripped Menendez of teaching and researching responsibilities, ordered subordinates to monitor and report on his activity, excluded him from meetings and accounting decisions, and ordered financial and accounting personnel to pre-clear any conversations about accounting issues before discussing them with Menendez.

In May 2005, Menendez filed a civil whistleblower complaint under SOX. In July 2006, Halliburton told the Department of Labor committee handling the case that KPMG had insisted that Menendez be excluded from a meeting concerning accounting for a potential joint venture arrangement called "RTA." Halliburton indicated it acceded to KPMG's demand and excluded Menendez from the meeting. SOX prohibits an employer from discriminating against an employee, contractor, or agent and from prohibiting such party from engaging in activity protected under the Act, and the SEC

(Continued)

stated that the assertion by the company that KPMG's presence was mandatory was misleading. In fact, the SEC opined that KPMG's presence was not even advisable since KPMG was supposed to be an independent auditor in both appearance and in fact.

The RTA meeting was scheduled to determine whether or not Halliburton would be required to consolidate the proposed joint venture. Senior management explicitly stated that the division management would not receive approval to proceed unless Halliburton could both avoid consolidation and maintain control over the joint venture activities. Earlier in the development of the accounting position regarding this joint venture, KPMG told management that it would allow the company to avoid consolidation and FIN 46R's Anti-Abuse criteria on the basis that the determination required professional judgment, and indicated that KPMG would be willing to support a conclusion that Halliburton was not significantly involved in the joint venture activities, when clearly the facts and circumstances did not support such a conclusion. Menendez had vehemently objected to KPMG and management's proposed conclusion on the basis that such a position was absurd.

According to the SEC, given KPMG's previous guidance to the company regarding RTA, and its willingness to accommodate unsupportable conclusions, continued input by KPMG on RTA was inappropriate and, once again, put KPMG in the position of auditing its own recommendations and advice. In the end, the concerted failures of management and the external auditor underscored the lack of independence between company and KPMG, which was a root cause of the accounting violations Menendez fought to correct and, at last, had to report.

Nature of Halliburton's Revenue Transactions in Question

During the months following the "leaked" e-mail, Menendez waited and watched to see if Halliburton would act on his claims that the company was cooking the books. The issue was revenue recognition as discussed following.

Halliburton enters into long-term contracts with energy giants like Royal Dutch Shell or BP to find and exploit huge oil and gas fields. It sells services—the expertise of its geologists and engineers. Halliburton also builds massive and expensive machinery that its professionals use to provide those services. Then, the company charges its customers for that equipment, which has particularly high profit margins. At the crux of the matter, the company's accountants had been allowing the company to count the full value of the equipment right away as revenue, sometimes even before it had assembled the equipment. But the customers could walk away in the middle of the contracts. Menendez realized that if the equipment were damaged, Halliburton, not the customer, was on the hook.

Menendez accused Halliburton of using so-called bill-and-hold techniques that distort the timing of billions of dollars in revenue and allowed Halliburton to book product sales before they occurred.

Menendez explained Halliburton's accounting this way:

> For example, the company recognizes revenue when the goods are parked in company warehouses, rather than delivered to the customer. Typically, these goods are not even assembled and ready for the customer. Furthermore, it is unknown as to when the goods will be ultimately assembled, tested, delivered to the customer, and, finally, used by the company to perform the required oilfield services for the customer.

Based on Menendez's claims, Halliburton's accounting procedures violated generally accepted accounting principles. For companies to recognize revenue before delivery, "the risks of ownership must have passed to the buyer," the SEC's staff wrote in a 2003 accounting bulletin. There also "must be a fixed schedule for delivery of the goods" and the product "must be complete and ready for shipment" among other things.

Shortly after joining Halliburton in March 2005, Menendez said he discovered a "terribly flawed" flow chart on the company's in-house Web site, called the Bill and Hold Decision Tree. The flow chart, a copy of which Menendez included in his complaint, walks through what to do in a situation where a "customer has been billed for completed inventory which is being stored at a Halliburton facility."

First, it asks: Based on the contract terms, "has title passed to customer?" If the answer is no—and here's where it gets strange—the employee is asked: "Does the transaction meet all of the 'bill-and-hold' criteria for revenue recognition?" If the answer to that question is yes, the decision tree says to do this: "Recognize revenue." The decision tree didn't specify what the other criteria were.

In other words, Halliburton told employees to recognize revenue even though the company still owned the product. Ironically, the accelerated revenue for financial statement purposes led to higher income taxes paid to the IRS.

"The policy in the chart is clearly at odds with generally accepted accounting principles," said Charles Mulford, a Georgia Institute of Technology accounting professor, who reviewed the court records. "It's very clear cut. It's not gray."

According to the accounting rules, it is possible to use bill-and-hold and comply with the rules. But it's hard. The customer, not the seller, must request such treatment. The customer also must have a compelling reason for doing so. Customers rarely do.

Top Halliburton accounting executives had agreed with Menendez's analysis, including McCollum, the company's chief accounting officer. But according to Menendez, they dragged their feet on implementing a change that was certain to slow revenue growth. In an e-mail response to detailed questions, a Halliburton spokeswoman wrote, "The accounting allegations were made by Mr. Menendez almost nine years ago and were promptly reviewed by the company and the Securities and Exchange Commission. The company's accounting was appropriate and the SEC closed its investigation." This seems curious when we examine the SEC's own rules for recognition.

Hocus Pocus Accounting: Bill-and-Hold Schemes

The proper accounting for Halliburton's bill-and-hold transactions was not lost on its external auditors, KPMG. In fact, in early 2005, KPMG published an article entitled: *Bill and Hold Transactions in the Oilfield Services Industry,* which made it clear that oilfield services companies had to comply with all four criteria of SEC Staff Accounting Bulletin (SAB 101) to recognize revenue early. These include:

- Persuasive evidence of an arrangement exists;
- Delivery has occurred or services have been rendered;
- The seller's price to the buyer is fixed or determinable; and
- Collectibility is reasonably assured.

KPMG went on to recognize that it would be rare for an oilfield services company to actually meet the necessary criteria. The impact to Halliburton was highlighted by KPMG's recognition that bill-and-hold transactions for oilfield services companies were "common" and "involve very large and complex products and equipment that carry significant amounts of economic value." KPMG went on to state that "perhaps no area of revenue recognition has received as much scrutiny as bill-and-hold."

Menendez's Complaint to the DOL

Menendez's allegations are part of a 54-page complaint he filed against Halliburton with a Department of Labor (DOL) administrative-law judge in Covington, Louisiana, who released the records to Menendez in response to a Freedom of Information Act request. Menendez claimed Halliburton retaliated against him in violation of the Sarbanes-Oxley Act's whistleblower provisions after he reported his concerns to the SEC and the company's audit committee.

According to a company spokesperson, Halliburton's audit committee "directed an independent investigation" and "concluded that the allegations were without merit." She declined to comment on bill-and-hold issues, and Halliburton's court filings in the case don't provide any details about its accounting practices.

Menendez filed his complaint shortly after a DOL investigator in Dallas rejected his retaliation claim. His initial claim was rejected by the court and subsequently appealed after many years, and the decision was ultimately overturned, but not until after he and his family had endured a nine-year ordeal during which time he was an outcast at Halliburton.

The Final Verdict Is In: Accountant Takes on Halliburton and Wins!

The appeals process went on for three years. In September 2011, the administrative-law appeals panel ruled. It overturned the original trial judge. After five years, Menendez had his first victory.

But it wasn't over. Halliburton appealed to the Fifth Circuit Court of Appeals. There were more legal filings, more hours of work, more money spent.

Finally, in November 2014, almost nine years after Menendez received "The E-mail," he prevailed. The appeals panel ruled that he indeed had been retaliated against for blowing the whistle, just as he had argued all along.

Because he had wanted only to be proven right, he'd asked for a token sum. The administrative-law panel, noting the importance of punishing retaliations against whistleblowers, pushed for an increase and Menendez was awarded $30,000.

To say that the outcome stunned experts is something of an understatement. "Accountant beats Halliburton!" said Thomas, the attorney and expert on whistleblower law. "The government tries to beat Halliburton and loses."

Post-Decision Interview about Whistleblowing

In an interview with a reporter, Menendez offered that Halliburton had a whistleblower policy prior to this incident as required under Sarbanes-Oxley. It was required to be confidential, and although Halliburton's policy promised confidentiality, at the same time it discouraged anonymous complaints on the basis that if you didn't provide your identity, the company might not be able to properly investigate your concern. Menendez added that confidentiality was absolutely central to his case and he relied on this policy but it was Halliburton that blatantly ignored its own policy and betrayed his trust.

He was asked how the whistleblowing policy of the SEC might be improved. He said that all too often it is almost impossible for a whistleblower to prevail and that there needs to be more protections and a more balanced playing field. "It shouldn't take nine years and hundreds of thousands of dollars to even have a remote chance of prevailing," he said.

The Human Aspect of the Case

Menendez felt he had to leave Halliburton because of the retaliation and how everyone treated him differently after the e-mail. During the appeals process, as Menendez and his wife waited for vindication and money got tight, he finally caught a break. Through the accounting experts he had met during his legal odyssey, he heard that General Motors was looking for a senior executive.

He agonized over whether to tell interviewers about his showdown with Halliburton. Ultimately, he figured they would probably find out anyway. When he flew up to Detroit and met with Nick Cypress, GM's chief accounting officer and comptroller, he came clean. Cypress had heard good things about Menendez from Doug Carmichael, the accounting expert who had been Menendez's expert witness at trial.

After telling him, Menendez asked Cypress, "Does this bother you?"

"Hell no!" the GM executive replied.

This was not the typical reaction top corporate officers have to whistleblowers. The interviewer asked Cypress about it: "I was moved by it," he explained. "It takes a lot of courage to stand tall like that, and I needed that in the work we were doing. I needed people with high integrity who would work hard who I could trust" to bring problems directly to senior management.

Today, Menendez still works at GM. His job is overseeing how GM recognizes about $100 billion worth of revenue, the very issue underlying his struggle with Halliburton. In the meantime, Halliburton has thrived. The SEC never levied any penalty for the accounting issue raised by Menendez. In 2014, the company generated $3.5 billion in profit on $33 billion in revenue. It's not possible to tell if the company maintains the same revenue recognition policy from its public filings, says GT professor Mulford. But since the SEC passed on an enforcement action on the issue, the company likely feels it is in accordance with accounting rules. (Mulford believes that Menendez was right back then and that the SEC should have looked harder at the issue initially.)

Many of the Halliburton and KPMG officials involved in the accounting issue or the retaliation have continued to prosper in the corporate ranks. One is now Halliburton's chief accounting officer. McCollum is now the company's executive vice president overseeing the integration of a major merger. The KPMG executive who disagreed with Menendez is now a partner at the accounting firm.

Menendez did not tell his friends and family of his legal victory. He's more cautious than he used to be. "I changed a lot. It was almost 10 years where everything was in question. Wondering what would people think of you."

He and his wife still worry that disaster could arrive in the next e-mail. "It can really weaken a soul and tear apart a family or a marriage, if you aren't careful. Because of the enormous powers of a company," said his wife. If people asked her advice, she said, "I'd probably say don't do it."

Recently, Menendez finally explained the story to his son, Cameron, who is now 13 and old enough to understand. Cameron's response: "You should have asked for more money, Dad," the teenager said. "We could use it."

Years ago, Menendez and his wife bought a bottle of champagne to celebrate his eventual victory. They still haven't opened it.

Questions

1. Describe the inadequacies in the corporate governance system at Halliburton.
2. Consider the role of KPMG in the case with respect to the accounting and auditing issues. How did the firm's actions relate to the ethical and professional expectations for CPAs by the accounting profession?
3. Some critics claim that while Menendez's actions may have been courageous, he harmed others along the way. His family was in limbo for many years and had to deal with the agony of being labeled a whistleblower and disloyal to Halliburton. The company's overall revenue did not change; a small amount was merely shifted to an earlier period. Halliburton didn't steal any money, cheat the IRS, or cheat their customers or their employees. In fact, it lessened its cash flows by paying out taxes earlier than it should have under the rules.

   How do you respond to these criticisms?

Case 3-9 Bhopal, India: A Tragedy of Massive Proportions

> We are citizens of the world. The tragedy of our times is that we do not know this.
> *Woodrow T. Wilson (1856–1924), 28th president of the United States*

At five past midnight on December 3, 1984, 40 tons of the chemical methyl isocynate (MIC), a toxic gas, started to leak out of a pesticide tank at the Union Carbide plant in Bhopal, India. The leak was first detected by workers about 11:30 p.m. on December 2, 1984, when their eyes began to tear and burn. According to AcuSafe,[1] "in 1991 the official Indian government panel charged with tabulating deaths and injuries counted more than 3,800 dead and approximately 11,000 with disabilities." However, estimates now range as high as 8,000 killed in the first three days and over 120,000 injured.[2] There were 4,000 deaths officially recorded by the government, although 13,000 death claims were filed with the government, according to a United Nations report, and hundreds of thousands more claim injury as a result of the disaster.[3] On June 7, 2010, an Indian court convicted eight former senior employees of Union Carbide's Indian subsidiary to two years in jail each for causing "death by negligence" over their part in the Bhopal gas tragedy in which an estimated 15,000 people died more than 25 years ago. While the actual numbers may be debatable, there can be no doubt that the Bhopal incident raises a variety of interesting ethical questions, including:

---

[1] AcuSafe is an Internet resource for safety and risk management information that is a publication of AcuTech, a global leader in process safety and security risk management located in Houston, Texas; see www.acusafe.com/Incidents/Bhopal1984/incidentbhopal1984.htm.

[2] According to CorpWatch, www.corpwatch.org/.

[3] United Nations, *United Nations University Report (UNU Report) on Toxic Gas Leak*, Available at: www.unu.edu/unupress/unupbooks/uu21le/uu21le0c.htm.

- What were the values that motivated the response of Union Carbide to the Bhopal disaster?
- Did the company wittingly or unwittingly do a utilitarian analysis of the potential harms and costs of fixing the problems at the Bhopal plant and benefits of doing so?
- Do the actions of management at Union Carbide reflect failed leadership?

You make up your own mind as you read about the tragedy that is Bhopal.

In the Beginning

On May 4, 1980, the first factory exported from the West to make pesticides using MIC began production in Bhopal, India. The company planned to export the chemicals from the United States to make the pesticide Sevin. The new CEO of Union Carbide came over from the United States especially for the occasion.[4]

As you might expect, the company seemed very concerned about safety issues. "Carbide's manifesto set down certain truths, the first being that 'all accidents are avoidable provided the measures necessary to avoid them are defined and implemented.'" The company's slogan was "Good safety and good accident prevention practices are good business."

Safety Measures

The Union Carbide plant in Bhopal was equipped with an alarm system with a siren that was supposed to be set off whenever the "duty supervisor in the control room" sensed even the slightest indication that a possible fire might be developing "or the smallest emission of toxic gas." The "alarm system was intended to warn the crews working on the factory site." Even though thousands of people lived in the nearby *bustees* (shantytowns), "none of the loudspeakers pointed outward" in their direction. Still, they could hear the sirens coming from the plant. The siren went off so frequently that it seemed as though the population became used to it and wasn't completely aware that one death and several accidental poisonings had occurred before the night of December 2, and there was a "mysterious fire in the alpha-naphtol unit."

In May 1982, three engineers from Union Carbide came to Bhopal to evaluate the plant and confirm that everything was operating according to company standards. However, the investigators identified more than 60 violations of operational and safety regulations. An Indian reporter managed to obtain a copy of the report that noted "shoddy workmanship," warped equipment, corroded circuitry, "the absence of automatic sprinklers in the MIC and phosgene production zones," a lack of pressure gauges, and numerous other violations. The severest criticism was in the area of personnel. There was "an alarming turnover of inadequately trained staff, unsatisfactory instruction methods, and a lack of rigor in maintenance reports."

The reporter wrote three articles proclaiming the unsafe plant. The third article was titled "If You Refuse to Understand, You Will Be Reduced to Dust." Nothing seemed to matter in the end because the population was assured by Union Carbide and government representatives that no one need be concerned because the phosgene produced at the plant was not a toxic gas.

The Accident

The accident occurred when a large volume of water entered the MIC storage tanks and triggered a violent chain reaction. Normally, water and MIC were kept separate, but on the night of December 2, "metal barriers known as slip blinds were not inserted and the cleaning water passed directly into the MIC tanks." It is possible that additional water entered the tanks later on in the attempts to control the reaction. Shortly after the introduction of water, "temperatures and pressures in the tanks increased to the point of explosion."

The report of consultants that reviewed the facts surrounding the accident indicates that workers made a variety of attempts to save the plant, including:[5]

---

[4]Dominique LaPierre and Javier Moro, *Five Past Midnight in Bhopal* (New York: Warner Books, 2002).

[5]Ron Graham, "FAQ on Failures: Union Carbide Bhopal," Barrett Engineering Consulting, www.tcnj.edu/rgraham/failures/UCBhopal.html.

- They tried to turn on the plant refrigeration system to cool down the environment and slow the reaction, but the system had been drained of coolant weeks before and never refilled as a cost-saving measure.
- They tried to route expanding gases to a neighboring tank, but the tank's pressure gauge was broken, indicating that the tank was full when it was really empty.
- They tried other measures that didn't work due to inadequate or broken equipment.
- They tried to spray water on the gases and have them settle to the ground, but it was too late as the chemical reaction was nearly completed.

The Workers and Their Reaction

It was reported that the maintenance workers did not flush out the pipes after the factory's production of MIC stopped on December 2. This was important because the pipes carried the liquid MIC produced by the plant's reactors to the tanks. The highly corrosive MIC leaves chemical deposits on the lining of tanks that can eventually get into the storage tanks and contaminate the MIC. Was it laziness, as suggested by one worker?

Another worker pointed out that the production supervisor of the plant left strict instructions to flush the pipes, but it was late at night and neither worker really wanted to do it. Still, they followed the instructions for the washing operation, but the supervisor had omitted the crucial step to place solid metal discs at the end of each pipe to ensure hermetically sealed tanks.

The cleansing operation began when one worker connected a hosepipe to a drain cock on the pipework and turned on the tap. After a short time, it was clear to the worker that the injected water was not coming out of two of the four drain cocks. The worker called the supervisor, who walked over to the plant and instructed the worker to clean the filters in the two clogged drain cocks and turn the water back on. They did that, but the water did not flow out of one drain. After informing the supervisor, who said to just keep the water flowing, the worker left for the night. It would now be up to the night shift to turn off the tap.

The attitude of the workers as they started the night shift was not good as Union Carbide had started to cut back on production and lay off workers. They wondered if they might be next. The culture of safety that Union Carbide tried to build up was largely gone, as the workers typically handled toxic substances without protective gear. The temperature readings in the tanks were made less frequently, and it was rare that anyone checked the welding on the pipework in the middle of the night.

Even though the pressure gauge on one of the tanks increased beyond the "permitted maximum working pressure," the supervisor ignored warnings coming from the control room because he was under the impression that Union Carbide had built the tanks with special steel and walls thick enough to resist even greater pressures. Still, the duty head of the control room and another worker went to look directly at the pressure gauge attached to the three tanks. They confirmed the excessive pressure in one tank.

The duty head climbed to the top of that tank, examined the metal casing carefully, and sensed the stirring action. The pressure inside was increasing quickly, leading to a popping sound "like champagne corks." Some of the gas then escaped, and a brownish cloud appeared. The workers returned to where the pipes had been cleaned and turned off the water tap. They smelled the powerful gas emissions, and they heard the fizzing, which sounded as if someone was blowing into an empty bottle. One worker had a cool enough head to sound the general alarm, but it was too late for most of the workers and many of those living in the shantytowns below the plant.

The Political Response

Union Carbide sent a team to investigate the catastrophe, but the Indian government had seized all records and denied the investigators access to the plant and the eyewitnesses. The government of the state of Madhya Pradesh (where the plant was located) tried to place the blame squarely on the shoulders of Union Carbide. It sued the company for damages on behalf of the victims. The ruling Congress Party was facing national parliamentary elections three weeks after the accident, and it "stood to lose heavily if its partners in the state government were seen to be implicated, or did not deal firmly with Union Carbide."[6]

---

[6]United Nations, *United Nations University Report (UNU Report) on Toxic Gas Leak.*

The government thwarted early efforts by Union Carbide to provide relief to the victims to block the company's attempt to gain the goodwill of the public. The strategy worked: The Congress Party won both the state legislative assembly and the national parliament seats from Madhya Pradesh by large margins.

Economic Effects

The economic impact of a disaster like the one that happened in Bhopal is staggering. The $25 million Union Carbide plant in Bhopal was shut down immediately after the accident, and 650 permanent jobs were lost. The loss of human life meant a loss of future earning power and economic production. The thousands of accident victims had to be treated and in many cases rehabilitated. The closure of the plant had peripheral effects on local businesses and the population of Bhopal. It is estimated that "two mass evacuations disrupted commercial activities for several weeks, with resulting business losses of $8 to $65 million."

In the year after the accident, the government paid compensation of about $800 per fatality to relatives of the dead persons. About $100 apiece was awarded to 20,000 victims. Beginning in March 1991, new relief payments were made to all victims who lived in affected areas, and a total of $260 million was disbursed. Overall, Union Carbide agreed to pay $470 million to the residents of Bhopal. By the end of October 2003, according to the Bhopal Gas Tragedy Relief and Rehabilitation Department, compensation had been awarded to 554,895 people for injuries received and 15,310 survivors of those killed. The average amount that families of the dead received was $2,200.

Union Carbide's Response

Shortly after the gas release, Union Carbide launched what it called "an aggressive effort to identify the cause." According to the company, the results of an independent investigation conducted by the engineering consulting firm Arthur D. Little were that "the gas leak could only have been caused by deliberate sabotage. Someone purposely put water in the gas storage tank, causing a massive chemical reaction. Process safety systems had been put in place that would have kept the water from entering the tank by accident."[7]

A 1993 report prepared by Jackson B. Browning, the retired vice president of Health, Safety, and Environmental Programs at Union Carbide Corporation, stated that he didn't find out about the accident until 2:30 a.m. on December 3. He claims to have been told that "no plant employees had been injured, but there were fatalities—possibly eight or twelve—in the nearby community."

A meeting was called at the company's headquarters in Danbury, Connecticut, for 6 a.m. The chair of the board of directors of Union Carbide, Warren M. Anderson, had received the news while returning from a business trip to Washington, DC. He had a "bad cold and a fever," so Anderson stayed at home and designated Browning as his "media stand-in" until Anderson could return to the office.[8]

At the first press conference called for 1:00 p.m. on December 3, the company acknowledged that a disaster had occurred at its plant in Bhopal. The company reported that it was sending "medical and technical experts to aid the people of Bhopal, to help dispose of the remaining [MIC] at the plant and to investigate the cause of the tragedy." Notably, Union Carbide halted production at its only other MIC plant in West Virginia, and it stated its intention "to convert existing supplies into less volatile compounds."

Anderson traveled to India and offered aid of $1 million and the Indian subsidiary of Union Carbide pledged the Indian equivalent of $840,000. Within a few months, the company offered an additional $5 million in aid that was rejected by the Indian government. The money was then turned over to the Indian Red Cross and used for relief efforts.

The company continued to offer relief aid with "no strings attached." However, the Indian government rejected the overtures, and it didn't help the company to go through third parties. Union Carbide believed that the volatile

---

[7]After the leak, Union Carbide started a Web site, www.bhopal.com, to provide its side of the story and details about the tragedy. In 1998, the Indian state government of Madhya Pradesh took over the site.

[8]Jackson B. Browning, *The Browning Report*, Union Carbide Corporation, 1993. Available at: www.bhopal.com/pdfs/browning.pdf.

political situation in India—Prime Minister Indira Gandhi had just been assassinated in October—hindered its relief efforts, especially after the election of Rajiv Gandhi on a government reform platform shortly after the assassination. It appeared to the company that Union Carbide was to be made an example of as an exploiter of Indian natural resources, and it suspected that the Indian government may have wanted to "gain access to Union Carbide's financial resources."

Union Carbide had a contingency plan for emergencies, but it didn't cover the "unthinkable." The company felt compelled to show its "commitment to employee and community safety and, specifically, to reaffirm the safety measures in place at their operation." Anderson went to West Virginia to meet with the employees in early February 1985. At that meeting, as "a measure of the personal concern and compassion of Union Carbide employees," the workers established a "Carbide Employees Bhopal Relief Fund and collected more than $100,000 to aid the tragedy's victims."[9]

Analysis of Union Carbide's Bhopal Problems

Documents uncovered in litigation[10] and obtained by the Environmental Working Group of the Chemical Industry Archives, an organization that investigates chemical company claims of product safety, indicate that Union Carbide "cut corners and employed untested technologies when building the Bhopal Plant." The company went ahead with the unproven design even though it posed a "danger of polluting subsurface water supplies in the Bhopal area." The following excerpt is from a document numbered UCC 04206 and included in the Environmental Working Group Report on Bhopal, India.[11] It also reveals the indifferent attitude of the Indian government toward environmental safety:

> The systems described have received provisional endorsement by the Public Health Engineering Office of the State of Madhya Pradesh in Bhopal. At present, there are no state or central government laws and/or regulations for environmental protection, though enactment is expected in the near future. It is not expected that this will require any design modifications.

Technology Risks

> The comparative risk of poor performance and of consequent need for further investment to correct it is considerably higher in the [Union Carbide–India] operation than it would be had proven technology been followed throughout. . . . [T]he MIC-to-Sevin process, as developed by Union Carbide, has had only a limited trial run. Furthermore, while similar waste streams have been handled elsewhere, this particular combination of materials to be disposed of is new and, accordingly, affords further chance for difficulty. In short, it can be expected that there will be interruptions in operations and delays in reaching capacity or product quality that might have been avoided by adoption of proven technology.

> [Union Carbide–India] finds the business risk in the proposed mode of operation acceptable, however, in view of the desired long-term objectives of minimum capital and foreign exchange expenditures. So long as [Union Carbide–India] is diligent in pursuing solutions, it is their feeling that any shortfalls can be mitigated by imports. Union Carbide concurs.

As previously mentioned, there were one death and several accidental poisonings at the Bhopal plant before December 3, 1984. The International Environmental Law Research Center prepared a Bhopal Date Line showing that the death occurred on December 25, 1981, when a worker was exposed to phosgene gas. On January 9, 1982, 25 workers were hospitalized as a result of another leak. On October 5, 1982, another leak from the plant led to the hospitalization of hundreds of residents.[12]

---

[9] *The Browning Report*, p. 8.

[10] *Bano et al. v. Union Carbide Corp & Warren Anderson, 99cv11329 SDNY*, filed on 11/15/99.

[11] Environmental Working Group, *Chemical Industry Archives*, www.chemicalindustryarchives.org/dirtysecrets/bhopal/index.asp.

[12] S. Muralidhar, "The Bhopal Date Line," International Environmental Law Research Centre, Available at: www.ielrc.org/content/n0409.htm.

It is worth noting that the workers had protested unsafe conditions after the January 9, 1982, leak, but their warning went unheeded. In March 1982, a leak from one of the solar evaporation ponds took place, and the Indian plant expressed its concern to Union Carbide headquarters. In May 1982, the company sent its U.S. experts to the Bhopal plant to conduct the audit previously mentioned.

Union Carbide's reaction to newspaper allegations that Union Carbide–India was running an unsafe operation was for the plant's works manager to write a denial of the charges as baseless. The company's next step was, to say the least, bewildering. It rewrote the safety manuals to permit switching off of the refrigeration unit and a shutdown of the vent gas scrubber when the plant was not in operation. The staffing at the MIC unit was reduced from 12 workers to 6. On November 29, 1984, three days before the disaster, Union Carbide completed a feasibility report and the company had decided to dismantle the plant and ship it to Indonesia or Brazil.

India's Position

The Indian government has acknowledged that 521,262 persons, well over half the population of Bhopal at the time of the toxic leak, were "exposed" to the lethal gas. In the immediate aftermath of the accident, most attention was devoted to medical recovery. The victims of the MIC leak suffered damage to lung tissue and respiratory functions. The lack of medical documentation affected relief efforts. The absence of baseline data made it difficult to identify specific medical consequences of MIC exposure and to develop appropriate medical treatment. Another problem was that a lot medical expenses had to paid by Indians because funding was not sufficient.[13]

In his paper, Ungarala analyzed the *Browning Report* and characterized the company's response as one of public relations. He noted that the report identified the media and other interested parties such as customers, shareholders, suppliers, and other employees as the most important to pacify. Ungarala criticized this response for its lack of concern for the people of Bhopal and the Indian people in general. Instead, the corporation saw the urgency to assure the people of the United States that such an incident would not happen here.[14]

Browning's main strategy to restore Union Carbide's image was to distance the company from the site of the disaster. He points out early in the document that Union Carbide had owned only 50.9 percent of the affiliate, Union Carbide–India Ltd. He notes that all the employees in the company were Indians and that the last American employee had left two years before the leak.

The report contended that the company "did not have any hold over its Indian affiliate." This seems to be a contentious issue because while "many of the day-to-day details, such as staffing and maintenance, were left to Indian officials, the major decisions, such as the annual budget, had to be cleared with the American headquarters." In addition, according to both Indian and U.S. laws, a parent company (United Carbide in this case) holds full responsibility for any plants that it operates through subsidiaries and in which it has a majority stake. Ungarala concluded that Union Carbide was trying to avoid paying the $3 billion that India demanded as compensation and was looking to find a "scapegoat" to take the blame.[15]

After the government of Madhya Pradesh took over the information Web site from Union Carbide, it began to keep track of applications for compensation. Between 1985 and 1997, over 1 million claims were filed for personal injury. In more than half of those cases, the claimant was awarded a monetary settlement.[16]

The total amount disbursed as of March 31, 2003, was about $345 million. An additional $25 million was released through July 2004, at which time the Indian Supreme Court ordered the government to pay the victims and families of the dead the remaining $330 million in the compensation fund.

[13]Dr. Madabhushi Sridhar, "The Present And Continuous Disaster Of Bhopal: Environmental Dimensions," Available at: http://www.legalservicesindia.com/articles/bhopal.htm.

[14]Pratima Ungarala, *Bhopal Gas Tragedy: An Analysis*, Final Paper HU521/Dale Sullivan 5/19/98, Available at: www.hu.mtu.edu/hu_dept/tc@mtu/papers/bhopal.htm.

[15]Ungarala.

[16]Madhya Pradesh Government, Bhopal Gas Tragedy Relief and Rehabilitation Department, Available at: www.mp.nic.in/bgtrrdmp/facts.htm.

Lawsuits

The inevitable lawsuits began in December 1984 and March 1985, when the government of India filed against Union Carbide–India and the United States, respectively. Union Carbide asked for the case filed in the Federal District Court of New York to be moved to India because that was where the accident had occurred and most of the evidence existed. The case went to the Bhopal District Court—the lowest-level court that could hear such a case. During the next four years, the case made "its way through the maze of legal bureaucracy" from the state high court up to the Supreme Court of India.

The legal disputes were over the amount of compensation and the exoneration of Union Carbide from future liabilities. The disputes were complicated by a lack of reliable information about the causes of the event and its consequences. The government of India had adopted the "Bhopal Gas Leak Disaster Ordinance—a law that appointed the government as sole representative of the victims." It was challenged by victim activists, who pointed out that the victims were not consulted about legal matters or settlement possibilities. The result was, in effect, to dissolve "the victims' identity as a constituency separate and differing from the government."[17]

In 1989, India had another parliamentary election, and it seemed a politically opportune time to settle the case and win support from the voters. It had been five years since the accident and the victims were fed up with waiting. By that time, many of the victims had died and more had moved out of the gas-affected neighborhoods. Even though the Indian government had taken Union Carbide to court asking for $3 billion, the company reached a settlement with the government in January 1989 for $470 million; the agreement gave Union Carbide immunity from future prosecution.

In October 1991, India's Supreme Court upheld the compensation settlement but cancelled Union Carbide's immunity from criminal prosecution. The money had been held in a court-administered account until 1992 while claims were sorted out. By early 1993, there were 630,000 claims filed, of which 350,000 had been substantiated on the basis of medical records. The numbers are larger than previously mentioned because the extent of health problems grew continuously after the accident and hundreds of victims continued to die. Despite challenges by victims and activists to the settlement with Union Carbide, at the beginning of 1993, the government of India began to distribute the $470 million, which had increased to $700 million as a result of interest earned on the funds.[18]

What Happened to Union Carbide?

Not surprisingly, the lawsuits and bad publicity affected Union Carbide's stock price. Before the disaster, the company's stock traded between $50 and $58 a share. In the months immediately following the accident, it traded at $32 to $40. In the latter half of 1985, GAF Corporation of New York made a hostile bid to take over Union Carbide. The ensuing battle and speculative stock trading ran up the stock price to $96, and it forced the company into financial restructuring.

The company's response was to fight back. It sold off its consumer products division and received more than $3.3 billion for the assets. It took on additional debt and used the funds from the sale and borrowing to repurchase 38.8 million of its shares to protect the company from further threats of a takeover.

The debt burden had accounted for 80 percent of the company's capitalization by 1986. At the end of 1991, the debt levels were still high—50 percent of capitalization. The company sold its Linde Gas Division for $2.4 billion, "leaving the company at less than half its pre-Bhopal size."

The Bhopal disaster "slowly but steadily sapped the financial strength of Union Carbide and adversely affected" employee morale and productivity. The company's inability to prove its sabotage claim affected its reputation. In 1994, Union Carbide sold its Indian subsidiary, which had operated the Bhopal plant, to an Indian battery manufacturer. It used $90 million from the sale to fund a charitable trust that would build a hospital to treat victims in Bhopal.

---

[17]Michael R. Reich, *Toxic Politics: Responding to Chemical Disasters* (Ithaca, NY: Cornell University Press, 1991).

[18]*United Nations Report.*

Two significant events occurred in 2001. First, the Bhopal Memorial Hospital and Research Centre opened its doors. Second, Dow Chemical Company purchased Union Carbide for $10.3 billion in stock and debt, and Union Carbide became a subsidiary of Dow Chemical.

Subsequent to the initial settlement with Union Carbide, the Indian government took steps to right the wrong and its aftereffects caused by the failure of management and the systems at Union Carbide in Bhopal. On August 8, 2007, the Indian government announced that it would meet many of the demands of the survivors by taking legal action on the civil and criminal liabilities of Union Carbide and its new owner, Dow Chemical. The government established an "Empowered Commission" on Bhopal to address the health and welfare needs of the survivors, as well as environmental, social, economic, and medical rehabilitation.

On June 26, 2012, Dow Chemical Co. won dismissal of a lawsuit alleging polluted soil and water produced by its Union Carbide chemical plant in Bhopal, India, had injured area residents, one of at least two pending cases involving the facility known for the 1984 disaster that killed thousands.

U.S. District Judge John Keenan in Manhattan ruled that Union Carbide and its former chairman, Warren Anderson, weren't liable for environmental remediation or pollution-related claims made by residents near the plant, which had been owned and operated by a former Union Carbide unit in India.

Questions

1. Characterize the values illustrated by management at Union Carbide in the way it handled the Bhopal disaster.
2. Identify the ethical issues that arise from the facts of the case. How do you assess stakeholder responsibilities?
3. Compare the decision-making process used by Union Carbide to deal with its disaster with that of Ford Motor Co. in the Pinto case and Johnson & Johnson in the Tylenol incident as described in this chapter. Evaluate management decision making in these cases from an ethical reasoning perspective.
4. The document uncovered by the Environmental Working Group Report refers to the acceptable "business risk" in the Bhopal operation due to questions about the technology. Is it ethical for a company to use business risk as a measure of whether to go ahead with an operation that may have safety problems? How would you characterize such a thought process from the perspective of ethical reasoning?

Case 3-10 Accountability of Ex-HP CEO in Conflict of Interest Charges

How could a CEO and chairperson of the board of directors of a major company resign in disgrace over a personal relationship with a contractor that led to a sexual harassment charge and involved a conflict of interest, a violation of the code of ethics? It happened to Mark Hurd on August 6, 2010. Hurd was the former CEO for Hewlett-Packard (HP) for five years and also served as the chair of the board of directors for four years. On departure from HP, Hurd said he had not lived up to his own standards regarding trust, respect, and integrity.

The board of directors of HP began an investigation of Hurd in response to a sexual harassment complaint by Jodie Fisher, a former contractor, who retained lawyer Gloria Allred to represent her. While HP did not find that the facts supported the complaint, they did reveal behavior that the board would not tolerate. Subsequent to Hurd's resignation, a severance package was negotiated granting Hurd $12.2 million, COBRA benefits, and stock options, for a total package of somewhere between $40 and $50 million.

In a letter to employees of HP on August 6, interim CEO Cathie Lesjak outlined where Hurd violated the "Standards of Business Conduct" and the reasons for his departure.[1] Lesjak wrote that Hurd "failed to maintain accurate expense reports, and misused company assets." She indicated that each was a violation of the standards and "together they demonstrated a profound lack of judgment that significantly undermined Mark's credibility and his ability to effectively lead HP." The letter reminded employees that everyone was expected to adhere strictly to the standards in all business dealings and relationships and senior executives should set the highest standards for professional and personal conduct.

The woman who brought forward the sexual harassment complaint was a "marketing consultant" who was hired by HP for certain projects, but she was never an employee of HP. During the investigation, inaccurately documented expenses were found that were claimed to have been paid to the consultant for her services. Falsifying the use of company funds violated the HP Standards of Business Conduct.

As for the sexual harassment claim, Allred alleged in the letter that Hurd harassed Fisher at meetings and dinners over a several year period during which time Fisher experienced a number of unwelcome sexual advances from Hurd including kissing and grabbing. Fisher said that this continual sexual harassment made her uncertain about her employment status.

In August 2013, HP and former CEO, Mark Hurd, won dismissal of a lawsuit that challenged the computer maker's public commitment to ethics at a time when Hurd was allegedly engaging in sexual harassment.

HP did not violate securities laws despite making statements such as a commitment to be "open, honest, and direct in all our dealings" because such statements were too vague and general, U.S. District Judge Jon Tigar in San Francisco wrote.

As a result, shareholders led by a New York City union pension fund could not pursue fraud claims over Hurd's alleged violations of HP's standards of business conduct, the judge ruled.

"Adoption of the plaintiff's argument (would) render every code of ethics materially misleading whenever an executive commits an ethical violation following a scandal," Tigar wrote.

Shareholders led by the Cement & Concrete Workers District Council Pension Fund of Flushing, New York, claimed in their lawsuit that the share price had been fraudulently inflated because of Hurd's alleged activities.

They also claimed that HP's statements about its rules of conduct implied that Hurd was in compliance, and that Hurd ignored his duty to disclose violations.

At most, Tigar said, such statements "constitute puffery—if the market was even aware of them."

Tigar also said Hurd's alleged desire to keep his dealings with Fisher secret did not by itself give rise to a fraud claim.

"Nothing suggests that Hurd thought that he could mislead investors with the statements the court finds were immaterial," the judge wrote.

Questions

1. When he was CEO, Hurd wrote in the Standards of Business Conduct at HP that "We want to be a company known for its ethical leadership...." His message in the preface continued: "Let us commit together, as individuals and as a company, to build trust in everything we do by living our values and conducting business consistent with the high ethical standards embodied within our SBC."

   What is the role of trust in business? How does trust relate to stakeholder interests? How does trust engender ethical leadership? Evaluate Mark Hurd's actions in this case from an ethical and professional perspective.

2. Despite hundreds of pages of policies, codes of ethics, organizational values, and carefully defined work environments and company culture, lapses in workplace ethics occur every day. Explain why you think these lapses occur and what steps might be taken by an organization to ensure that its top executives live up to values it espouses.

3. Leo Apotheker, the former CEO of HP who succeeded Mark Hurd, resigned in September 2011, after just 11 months on the job—but he left with a $13.2 million severance package. Hurd left with a package between $40 million and $50 million. Do you think executives who resign from their positions or are fired because of unethical actions should be forced to give back some of those amounts to the shareholders to make them whole? Why or why not?